Happiness

Happiness

LESSONS FROM A NEW SCIENCE

Richard Layard

THE PENGUIN PRESS
New York
2005

THE PENGUIN PRESS
Published by the Penguin Group
Penguin Group (USA) Inc., 375 Hudson Street, New York, New York 10014, USA •
Penguin Group (Canada), 10 Alcorn Avenue, Toronto, Ontario, Canada M4V 3B2 (a division of
Pearson Penguin Canada Inc.) • Penguin Books Ltd, 80 Strand, London WC2R 0RL, England
• Penguin Ireland, 25 St Stephen's Green, Dublin 2, Ireland (a division of Penguin Books Ltd.) •
Penguin Books Australia Ltd, 250 Camberwell Road, Camberwell, Victoria 3124, Australia
(a division of Pearson Australia Group Pty Ltd) • Penguin Books India Pvt Ltd, 11 Community
Centre, Panchsheel Park, New Delhi–110-017, India • Penguin Group (NZ), Cnr Airborne and
Rosedale Roads, Albany, Auckland 1310, New Zealand (a division of Pearson New Zealand Ltd) •
Penguin Books (South Africa) (Pty) Ltd, 24 Sturdee Avenue, Rosebank,
Johannesburg 2196, South Africa

Penguin Books Ltd, Registered Offices: 80 Strand, London WC2R 0RL, England

First published in 2005 by The Penguin Press, a member of Penguin Group (USA) Inc.

Copyright © Richard Layard, 2005
All rights reserved

Page 310 constitutes an extension of this copyright page.

LIBRARY OF CONGRESS CATALOGING-IN-PUBLICATION DATA
Layard, P. R. G. (P. Richard G.)
Happiness : lessons from a new science / Richard Layard.
p. cm.
Includes bibliographical references and index.
ISBN 1-59420-039-4
1. Happiness.   I. Title.
BJ1481.L28 2005
170—dc22   2004060063

This book is printed on acid-free paper. ♾

Printed in the United States of America

1   3   5   7   9   10   8   6   4   2

DESIGNED BY LEE FUKUI

To Daniel Kahneman
fearless explorer

Contents

Preface

I am an economist—I love the subject and it has served me well. But economics equates changes in the happiness of a society with changes in its purchasing power—or roughly so. I have never accepted that view, and the history of the last fifty years has disproved it. Instead, the new psychology of happiness makes it possible to construct an alternative view, based on evidence rather than assertion. From this we can develop a new vision of what lifestyles and what policies are sensible, drawing on the new psychology, as well as on economics, brain science, sociology and philosophy.

The time has come to have a go—to rush in where angels fear to tread. So here is my effort at a new evidence-based vision of how we can live better. It will need massive refinement as our knowledge accumulates. But I hope it will hasten the shift to a new perspective, where people's feelings are treated as paramount. That shift is overdue.

So many people have helped in this book and helped so generously that I describe their role in a separate note at the end. I have been helped by psychologists, neuroscientists, sociologists, philosophers and of course economists—all sharing a desire for human betterment.

If the book does anything, I hope it creates a bit more happiness.

Richard Layard
LONDON, JULY 2004

PART

I

The

Problem

"Researchers say I'm not happier for being richer, but do you know how much researchers make?"

What's the problem?

There is a paradox at the heart of our lives. Most people want more income and strive for it. Yet as Western societies have got richer, their people have become no happier.

This is no old wives' tale. It is a fact proven by many pieces of scientific research. As I'll show, we have good ways to measure how happy people are, and all the evidence says that on average people are no happier today than people were fifty years ago. Yet at the same time average incomes have more than doubled. This paradox is equally true for the United States and Britain and Japan.[1]

But aren't our lives infinitely more comfortable? Indeed: we have more food, more clothes, more cars, bigger houses, more central heating, more foreign holidays, a shorter working week, nicer work and, above all, better health. Yet we are not happier. Despite all the efforts of governments, teachers, doctors and businessmen, human happiness has not improved.

This devastating fact should be the starting point for all discussion of how to improve our lot. It should cause each government to reappraise its objectives, and every one of us to rethink our goals.

One thing is clear: once subsistence income is guaranteed, making people happier is not easy. If we want people to be happier, we really have to know what conditions generate happiness and how to cultivate them. That is what this book is about—the causes of happiness and the means we have to affect it.

If we really wanted to be happier, what would we do differently? We do not yet know all the answers, or even half of them. But we have a lot of evidence, enough to rethink government policy and to reappraise our personal choices and philosophy of life.

The main evidence comes from the new psychology of happiness, but neuroscience, sociology, economics and philosophy all play their part. By bringing them together, we can produce a new vision of how we can live better, both as social beings and in terms of our inner spirit.

What Philosophy?

The philosophy is that of the eighteenth-century Enlightenment, as articulated by Jeremy Bentham. If you pass below the fine classical portico of University College London, you will find him there near the entrance hall—an elderly man dressed in eighteenth-century clothes, sitting in a glass case. The clothes are his and so is the body, except for the head, which is a wax replica. He is there because he inspired the founding of the college, and as he requested, he still attends the meetings of the College Council, being carried in for the purpose. A shy and kindly man, he never married, and he gave his money to good causes. He was also one of the first intellectuals to go jogging—or trotting as he called it—which he did until near his death. But despite his quirks, Bentham was one of the greatest thinkers of the Enlightenment.

The best society, he said, is one where the citizens are happiest. So the best public policy is that which produces the greatest happiness. And when it comes to private behaviour, the right moral action is that which produces the most happiness for the people it affects. This is the Greatest Happiness principle. It is fundamentally egalitarian, because everybody's happiness is to count equally. It is also fundamentally humane, because it says that what matters ultimately is what people feel. It is close in spirit to the opening passages of the American Declaration of Independence.

This noble ideal has driven much of the social progress that has occurred in the last two hundred years. But it was never easy to apply, because so little was known about the nature and causes of happiness. This left it vulnerable to philosophies that questioned the ideal itself. In the nineteenth century these alternative philosophies were often linked to religious conceptions of morality. But in the twentieth century religious belief diminished, and so eventually did belief in the secular religion of socialism. In consequence there remained no widely accepted system of ethical belief. Into the void stepped the non-philosophy of rampant individualism.

At its best this individualism offered an ideal of "self-realisation." But that gospel failed. It did not increase happiness, because it made each individual too anxious about what he could get for himself. If we really want to be happy, we need some concept of a common good, towards which we all contribute.

So now the tide is turning. People are calling out for a concept of the common good—and that is exactly what the Enlightenment ideal provides. It defines the common good as the greatest happiness of all, requiring us to care for others as well as for ourselves. And it advocates a kind of fellow-feeling for others that in itself increases our happiness and reduces our isolation.

What Psychology?

At the same time, the new psychology now gives us real insight into the nature of happiness and what brings it about. So the Enlightenment philosophy can now at last be applied using evidence instead of speculation.

Happiness is feeling good, and misery is feeling bad. At every moment we feel somewhere between wonderful and half-dead, and that feeling can now be measured by asking people or by monitoring their brains. Once that is done, we can go on to explain a person's underlying level of happiness—the quality of his life as he experiences it. Every life is complicated, but it is vital to separate out the factors that really count.

Some factors come from outside us, from our society: some societies really are happier. Other factors work from inside us, from our inner life. In part 1 of the book I sort out how these key factors affect us. Then, in part 2, I focus on what kind of society and what personal practices would help us lead happier lives. The last chapter summarises my conclusions.

What Social Message?

So how, as a society, can we influence whether people are happy? One approach is to proceed by theoretical reasoning, using elementary economics. This concludes that selfish behaviour is all right, provided markets are allowed to function: through the invisible hand, perfect markets will lead us to the greatest happiness that is possible, given our wants and our resources.[2] Since people's wants are taken as given, national income becomes a proxy for national happiness. Government's role is to correct market imperfections and to remove all barriers to labour mobility and flexible employment. This view of national happiness is the one that dominates the thinking and pronouncements of leaders of Western governments.

The alternative is to look at what actually makes people happy. People certainly hate absolute poverty, and they hated Communism. But there is more to life than prosperity and freedom. In this book we shall look at other key facts about human nature, and how we should respond to them.

- Our wants are not given, in the way that elementary economics assumes. In fact they depend heavily on what other people have, and on what we ourselves have got accustomed to. They are also affected by education, advertising and television. We are heavily driven by the desire to keep up with other people. This leads to a *status race,* which is self-defeating since if I do better, someone else must do worse. What can we do about this?

- People desperately want *security* — at work, in the family and in their neighbourhoods. They hate unemployment, family break-up and crime in the streets. But the individual cannot, entirely on his own, determine whether he loses his job, his spouse or his wallet. It depends in part on external forces beyond his control. So how can the community promote a way of life that is more secure?

- People want to *trust* other people. But in the United States and in Britain (though not in continental Europe), levels of trust have plummeted in recent decades. How is it possible to maintain trust when society is increasingly mobile and anonymous?

In the seventeenth century the individualist philosopher Thomas Hobbes proposed that we should think about human problems by considering men "as if but even now sprung out of the earth, and suddenly (like mushrooms) come to full maturity, without any kind of engagement with each other."[3] But people are not like mushrooms. We are inherently social, and our happiness depends above all on the quality of our relationships with other people. We have to develop public policies that take this "relationship factor" into account.

What Personal Message?

There is also an inner, personal factor. Happiness depends not only on our external situation and relationships; it depends on our attitudes as well. From his experiences in Auschwitz, Viktor Frankl concluded that in the last resort "everything can be taken from a man but one thing, the last of human freedoms—to choose one's attitude in any given set of circumstances."[4] *autonomy*

Our thoughts do affect our feelings. As we shall see, people are happier if they are compassionate; and they are happier if they are thankful for what they have. When life gets rough, these qualities become ever more important.

Throughout the centuries parents, teachers and priests have striven to instil these traits of compassion and acceptance. Today we know more than ever about how to develop them. Modern cognitive therapy was developed in the last thirty years as a forward-looking substitute for backward-looking psychoanalysis. Through systematic experimentation, it has found ways to promote positive thinking and to systematically dispel the negative thoughts that afflict us all. In recent years these insights have been generalised by "positive psychology," to offer a means by which all of us, depressed or otherwise, can find meaning and increase our enjoyment of life. What are these insights?

Many of the ideas are as old as Buddhism and have recurred throughout the ages in all the religious traditions that focus on the inner life. In every case techniques are offered for liberating the positive force in each of us, which religious people call divine. These techniques could well become the psychological basis of twenty-first-century culture.

Even so, our nature is recalcitrant, and for some people it seems impossible to be positive without some physical help. Until fifty years ago there was no effective treatment for mental illness. But in the 1950s drugs were found that, despite side effects, could provide relief to many who suffer from schizophrenia, depression or anxiety. This, followed by the development of cognitive and behavioural therapy, has given new life to millions of people who would otherwise have been half-dead. But how much further can this process go in the relief of misery?

Human beings have largely conquered nature, but they have still to conquer themselves. In the last fifty years we have eliminated absolute material scarcity in the West. With good policies and Western help, the same could happen throughout the world within a hundred years. But in the meantime we in the West are no happier. Changing this is the new challenge and the new frontier—and much more difficult than traditional wealth-creation. Fortunately, enough tools are already available to fill this small book.

"John Stuart Mill taught that the happiness of the individual is paramount. He didn't name names, but I suspect that you and I are the sort of individual he had in mind."

What is happiness?

If not actually disgruntled,
he was far from being gruntled.
P. G. WODEHOUSE[1]

I n the late nineteenth century doctors noticed something strange about people with brain injuries. If the damage was on the left side of the brain, they were more likely to become depressed than if it was on the right. As time passed, the evidence built up, and it was even found that damage on the right side of the brain could sometimes produce elation.[2] From these dim beginnings, a new science has emerged that measures what happens in the brain when people experience positive and negative feelings.

The broad picture is this.[3] Good feelings are experienced through activity in the brain's left-hand side behind the forehead; people feel depressed if that part of their brain goes dead. Bad feelings are connected with brain activity behind the right-hand side of the forehead; when that part of the brain is out of action, people can feel elated.

Such scientific breakthroughs have transformed the way we think about happiness. Until recently, if people said they were happy, sceptics would hold that this was just a subjective statement. There was no good way to show that it had any objective content at all. But now we know that what people say about how they feel corresponds closely to the actual levels of activity in different parts of the brain, which can be measured in standard scientific ways.

The Feeling of Happiness

So what is the feeling of happiness? Is there a state of "feeling good" or "feeling bad" that is a dimension of all our waking life? Can people say at any moment how they feel? Indeed, is your happiness something, a bit like your temperature, that is always there, fluctuating away whether you think about it or not? If so, can I compare my happiness with yours?

The answer to all these questions is essentially yes. This may surprise those of a sceptical disposition. But it would not surprise most people, past or present. They have always been aware of how they felt and have used their introspection to infer how others feel. Since they themselves smile when they are happy, they infer that when others smile, they are happy too. Likewise when they see others frown, or see them weep. It is through their feelings of imaginative sympathy that people have been able to respond to one another's joys and sorrows throughout history.

So by happiness I mean feeling good—enjoying life and wanting the feeling to be maintained. By unhappiness I mean feeling bad and wishing things were different. There are countless sources of happiness, and countless sources of pain and misery. But all our experience has in it a dimension that corresponds to how good or bad we feel. In fact most people find it easy to say how good they are feeling, and in social surveys such questions get very high response rates, much higher than the average survey question. The scarcity of "Don't knows" shows that people do know how they feel, and recognise the validity of the question.

When it comes to how we feel, most of us take a longish view. We accept the ups and downs and care mainly about our average happiness over a longish period of time. But that average is made up from a whole series of moments. At each moment of waking life we feel more or less happy, just as we experience more or less noise. There are many different sources of noise, from a trombone to a pneumatic drill, but we can feel how loud each noise is. In the same way there are many different sources of enjoyment, but we can compare the intensity of each. There are also many types of suffering, from toothache to a stomach ulcer to depression, but we can compare the pain of each. Moreover, as we shall see, happiness begins where unhappiness ends.[4]

So how can we find out how happy or unhappy people are — both in general and from moment to moment? Both psychology and brain science are beginning to give us the tools to arrive at precise answers.

Asking People

The most obvious way to find out whether people are happy in general is to survey individuals in a random sample of households and to ask them. A typical question is, "Taking all things together, would you say you are very happy, quite happy, or not very happy?" Here is how people reply in the United States and in Britain: very similarly, as the table on the next page shows. Interestingly, men and women reply very much the same.

How happy are we? (per cent)		
	United States	Britain
Very happy	38	36
Quite happy	53	57
Not very happy	9	7
	100	100

But is everyone who answers the question using the words in the same way? Fortunately, their replies can be independently verified. In many cases friends or colleagues of the individual have been asked separately to rate the person's happiness. These independent ratings turn out to be well related to the way the people rated themselves. The same is true of ratings made by an interviewer who has never met the person before.[5]

Feelings Fluctuate

Of course our feelings fluctuate from hour to hour, and from day to day. Psychologists have recently begun to study how people's mood varies from activity to activity. I will give only one example, from a study of around nine hundred working women in Texas.[6] They were asked to divide the previous working day into episodes, like a film: typically they identified about fourteen episodes. They then reported what they were doing in each episode and who they were doing it with. Finally, they were asked how they felt in each episode, along twelve dimensions that can be combined into a single index of good or bad feeling.

The table shows what they liked most (sex) and what they liked least (commuting). The table on the next page shows what company they most enjoyed. They are highly gregarious—preferring almost any company to being alone. Only the boss's company is worse than being alone.

Happiness in different activities		
Activity	Average happiness	Average hours a day
Sex	4.7	0.2
Socialising	4.0	2.3
Relaxing	3.9	2.2
Praying/worshipping/meditating	3.8	0.4
Eating	3.8	2.2
Exercising	3.8	0.2
Watching TV	3.6	2.2
Shopping	3.2	0.4
Preparing food	3.2	1.1
Talking on the phone	3.1	2.5
Taking care of my children	3.0	1.1
Computer/email/Internet	3.0	1.9
Housework	3.0	1.1
Working	2.7	6.9
Commuting	2.6	1.6

Note: More than one type of activity is possible at any one time.

We can also use these reports to measure how feelings change as the day goes on. As the bottom chart on page 16 shows, these people feel better as time passes, except for a blip up at lunchtime.

Happiness while interacting with different people

Interacting with	Average happiness	Average hours a day
Friends	3.7	2.6
Relatives	3.4	1.0
Spouse/partner	3.3	2.7
My children	3.3	2.3
Clients/customers	2.8	4.5
Co-workers	2.8	5.7
Alone	2.7	3.4
Boss	2.4	2.4

Note: More than one type of activity or type of company is possible at any one time.

Average happiness at different times of day

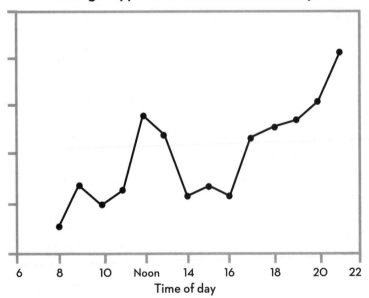

Time of day

I have showed these findings to stress the point that happiness is a feeling and that feelings occur continuously over time throughout our waking life. Feelings at any particular moment are of course influenced by memories of past experiences and anticipations of future ones. Memories and anticipations are very important parts of our mental life, but they pose no conceptual problems in measuring our happiness—be it instantaneous or averaged over a longer period of time.

It is the long-term *average* happiness of each individual that this book is about, rather than the fluctuations from moment to moment. Though our average happiness may be influenced by the pattern of our activities, it is mainly affected by our basic temperament and attitudes and by key features of our life situation—our relationships, our health, our worries about money.

Brainwaves

Sceptics may still question whether happiness is really an objective feeling that can be properly compared between people. To reassure doubters, we can turn to modern brain physiology with its sensational new insights into what is happening when a person feels happy or unhappy. This work is currently being led by Richard Davidson of the University of Wisconsin.[7]

In most of his studies Davidson measures activity in different parts of the brain by putting electrodes all over the scalp and reading the electrical activity. These EEG measurements are then related to the feelings people report. When people experience positive feelings, there is more electrical activity in the left front of the brain; when they experience negative feelings, there is more activity in the right front of the brain. For example, when someone is shown funny film clips, his left side becomes more active and his right side less so; he also smiles and gives positive reports on his mood. When frightening or distasteful film clips are shown, the opposite happens.

Similar findings come from direct scans of what is going on inside the brain. For instance, people can be put inside an MRI or PET scanner and then shown nice or unpleasant pictures. The chart gives an example. People are shown pictures, first of a happy baby and then of a baby that is deformed. The PET scanner picks up the corresponding changes in glucose usage in the brain and records it as light patches in the photographs. The nice picture activates the left side of the brain, and the horrendous picture activates the right side.[8]

So there is a direct connection between brain activity and mood. Both can be altered by an external experience like looking

The brain's response to two pictures

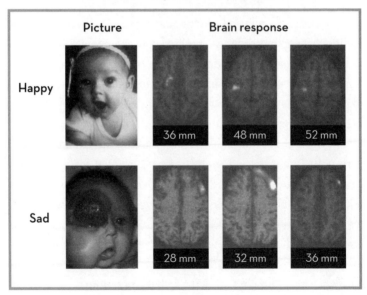

at pictures. Both can also be altered directly by physical means. By using very powerful magnets it is possible to stimulate activity in the left side of the forebrain, and this automatically produces a better mood. Indeed, this method has even been used to alleviate depression.[9] Even more remarkable, it has been found to improve the immune system, which is heavily influenced by a person's mood.[10]

So we have clear physical measures of how feelings vary over time. We can also use physical measures to compare the happiness of different people. People differ in the pattern of their EEGs, even when they are at rest. People whose left side is especially active ("left-siders") report more positive feelings and memories than "right-siders" do. Left-siders smile more, and their friends assess them as happier. By contrast, people who are especially active on the right side report more negative thoughts and memories, smile less and are assessed as less happy by their friends.

So a natural measure of happiness is the difference in activity between the left and right sides of the forebrain. This varies closely with many measures of self-reported mood. And one further finding is interesting. When different people are exposed to good experiences (like pleasant film clips), those who are naturally happy when at rest experience the greatest gain in happiness. And when they are exposed to nasty experiences, they experience the least increase in discomfort.

The EEG approach works even on newly born babies.[11] When they are given something nice to suck, their left forebrain starts humming, while a sour taste sets off activity in the right brain. At ten months old, a baby's brain activity at rest predicts how well it will respond if its mother disappears for a minute. Babies who are more active on the right side tend to howl, while the left-siders remain upbeat. At two and a half years old, left-sided youngsters are much more exploratory, while right-siders cling more to their mothers. However, up to their teens there are many changes in the differences between children, both by character traits and by brain-waves. Among adults the differences are more stable.

The frontal lobes are not the only part of the brain involved in emotion. For example, one seat of raw emotions is the amygdala, which is deeper in the brain. It triggers the command centre that mobilises the body to respond to a frightening stimulus—the fight-or-flight syndrome. But the amygdala in humans is not that different from the amygdala of the lowest mammals, and works unconsciously. Our conscious experience, however, is specially linked to the frontal lobes, which are highly developed in man.[12]

So brain science confirms the objective character of happiness. It also confirms the objective character of pain. Here is a fascinating experiment, performed on a number of people. A very hot pad is applied to each person's leg, the same temperature for all of them. The people then report the pain. They give widely varying reports, but these different reports are highly correlated with the different levels of brain activity in the relevant part of the cortex.[13] This confirms the link between what people report and objective brain activity. There is no difference between what people think they feel and what they "really" feel, as some social philosophers would have us believe.

A Single Dimension

But isn't this all a bit simplistic? Surely there are many types of happiness, and of pain? And in what sense is happiness the opposite of pain?

There are indeed many types of good and bad feeling. On the positive side there is loving and being loved, achievement, discovery, comfort, tranquillity, joy and many others. On the negative side there is fear, anger, sadness, guilt, boredom and many others again. But, as I have said, this is no different from the situation with pains and pleasures that are purely "physical": one pain can be compared with another, and one pleasure can be compared with another. Similarly, mental pain and physical pain can be compared,[14] and so can mental and physical enjoyment.

But is happiness really a *single* dimension of experience running from extreme misery to extreme joy? Or is it possible to be both happy and unhappy at the same time? The broad answer to this is no; it is not possible to be happy and unhappy at the same time. Positive feelings damp down negative feelings and vice versa.[15] So we have just one dimension—running from the extreme negative to the extreme positive.

Lest this seem very mechanical, we should immediately note that happiness can be excited or tranquil, and misery can be agitated or leaden. These are important distinctions, which correspond to different levels of "arousal." The range of possibilities is

Two dimensions of feeling

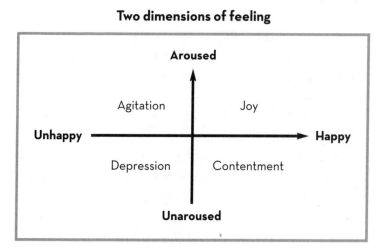

illustrated in the diagram, which dispels any impression that happiness can only be exciting or hedonistic.

(One of the most enjoyable forms of aroused experience is when you are so engrossed in something that you lose yourself in it. These experiences of "flow" can be wonderful, both at the time and in retrospect.[16])

Qualities of Happiness

The concept of happiness I have described is essentially the one developed by the eighteenth-century Enlightenment. It relates to how we feel as we live our lives. It famously inspired the authors of the American Declaration of Independence, and it has become central to our Western heritage.

It differs, for example, from the approach taken by Aristotle and his many followers. Aristotle believed that the object of life was *eudaimonia*, or a *type* of happiness associated with virtuous conduct and philosophic reflection. This idea of types of happiness, of higher and lower pleasures, was revived in the nineteenth century by John Stuart Mill and it survives to this day. Mill believed that the happiness of different experiences could vary both in quantity *and* quality. (He could not accept that a given amount of satisfaction derived from the game of "pushpin" was as valuable as the same amount of satisfaction derived from poetry.)

Mill's intuition was right but his formulation was wrong. People who achieve a sense of meaning in their lives *are* happier than those who live from one pleasure to another. Carol Ryff of the University of Wisconsin has provided ample evidence of this. She has compiled refined measures of such things as purpose in life, autonomy, positive relationships, personal growth and self-acceptance and used them to construct an index of psychological well-being. In a sample of U.S. adults this index is very highly correlated with standard self-reported measures of happiness and life satisfaction.[17]

Thus Mill was right in his intuition about the true *sources* of lasting happiness, but he was wrong to argue that some types of happiness are *intrinsically* better than others.[18] In fact to do so is essentially paternalistic. It is of course obvious that some enjoyments, like those provided by cocaine, cannot in their nature last long: they work against a person's long-term happiness, which means that we should avoid them. Similarly, some unhealthy enjoyments, like those of a sadist, should be avoided because they decrease the happiness of others. But no good feeling is bad in itself—it can only be bad because of its consequences.[19]

Happiness Improves Your Health

In September 1932 the mother superior of the American School Sisters of Notre Dame decided that all new nuns should be asked to write an autobiographical sketch. These sketches were kept, and they have recently been independently rated by psychologists to show the amount of positive feeling which they revealed. These ratings have then been compared with how long each nun lived. Remarkably, the amount of positive feeling that a nun revealed in her twenties was an excellent predictor of how long she would live.

Of the nuns who were still alive in 1991, only 21% of the most cheerful quarter died in the following nine years, compared with 55% of the least cheerful quarter of the nuns.[20] This shows how happiness can increase a person's length of life.

In fact most sustained forms of good feeling *are* good for you. However we measure happiness, it appears to be conducive to physical health (other things being equal).[21] Happy people tend to have more robust immune systems and lower levels of stress-causing cortisol. If artificially exposed to the flu virus, they are less likely to contract the disease. They are also more likely to recover from major surgery.

Equally, when a person has a happy experience, the body chemistry improves, and blood pressure and heart rate tend to fall.[22] Especially good experiences can have long-lasting effects on our health. If we take the 750 actors and actresses who were ever nominated for Oscars, we can assume that before the award-panel's decision the winners and losers were equally healthy on average. Yet those who got the Oscars went on to live four years longer, on average, than the losers.[23] Such was the gain in morale from winning.

The Function of Happiness

I hope I have now persuaded you that happiness exists and is generally good for your physical health. But that does not make it supremely important. It is supremely important because it is our overall motivational device. We seek to feel good and to avoid pain (not moment by moment but overall).[24]

Without this drive we humans would have perished long ago. For what makes us feel good (sex, food, love, friendship and so on) is also generally good for our survival. And what causes us pain is bad for our survival (fire, dehydration, poison, ostracism). So by seeking to feel good and to avoid pain, we seek what is good for us and avoid what is bad for us, and thus we have survived as a species. The search for good feeling is the mechanism that has preserved and multiplied the human race.

Some people question whether we have any overall system of motivation. They say we have separate drives for sex, feeding and so on, and that we respond to these drives independently of their effect on our general sense of well-being.[25] The evidence is otherwise. For we often have to choose between satisfying different drives, and our choices vary according to how easy it is to satisfy one drive compared with another. So there must be some overall evaluation going on that compares how different drives contribute to our overall satisfaction.

When one source of satisfaction becomes more costly relative to another, we choose less of it. This is the so-called law of demand, which has been confirmed throughout human life and among many species of animals.[26] It is not uniquely human and probably applies to most living things, all of which have a tendency to pursue their own good as best they can. In lower animals the process is unconscious, and even in humans it is mostly so, since consciousness could not possibly handle the whole of this huge task. However, we do have massive frontal lobes that other mammals lack, and that is probably where the conscious part of the balancing operation is performed.

Experiments show that at every moment we are evaluating our situation, often unconsciously.[27] We are attracted to those elements of our situation that we like and repelled by the elements we dislike. It is this pattern of "approach" and "avoidance" that is central to our behaviour.

Here are two ingenious experiments by the psychologist John Bargh that illustrate the workings of this approach-avoidance mechanism. His technique is to flash good or bad words on a screen and observe how people respond. In the first experiment he flashed the words subliminally and recorded the impact on the person's mood. The good words (like "music") improved mood, and the bad ones (like "worm") worsened mood. He next examined approach and avoidance behaviour by making the words on the screen legible, and asking the person to remove them with a lever. The human instinct is to pull towards you that which you like, and to push away that which you wish to avoid. So Bargh split his subjects into two groups. Group A was told to behave in the natural way—to pull the lever for the good words, and to push it for the bad ones. Group B was told to behave "unnaturally"—to pull for the bad words and to push for the good. Group A did the job much more quickly, confirming how basic are our mechanisms of approach and avoidance.

So there is an evaluative faculty in each of us that tells us how happy we are with our situation, and then directs us to approach what makes us happy and avoid what does not. From the various possibilities open to us, we choose whichever combination of activities will make us feel best. In doing this we are more than purely reactive: we plan for the future, which sometimes involves denying ourselves today for the sake of future gratification.

This overall psychological model is similar to what economists have used from Adam Smith onwards.[28] We want to be happy, and we act to promote our present and future happiness, given the opportunities open to us.

Of course we can make mistakes. Some things that people do are bad for survival, like cigarette smoking and the self-starvation of anorexia nervosa. Also, people are often short-sighted and bad at forecasting their future feelings. Natural selection has not produced perfect bodies, and neither has it produced perfect psyches. Yet we are clearly selected to be healthy, though we sometimes get sick. Similarly, we are selected to feel good, even if we sometimes make mistakes: it is impossible to explain human action and human survival except by the desire to achieve good feelings.

This raises the obvious issue of why, in that case, we are not happier than we are. Why is there so much anxiety and depression? Have anxiety and depression played any role in explaining our survival? Almost certainly, yes. Even today, it is a good idea to be anxious while driving a car—or while writing a book. A heavy dose of self-criticism will save you from some nasty mistakes. And it is often best to be sceptical about much of what you hear from other people, until it is independently confirmed.

It was even more important to be on guard when man first evolved on the African savannah. When you are in danger of being eaten by a lion, it is a good idea to be extremely cautious. (Better to have a smoke detector that goes off when you burn the toast than one that stays silent while the house burns down.) Even depression may have had some function. When confronted with an unbeatable opponent, dogs show signs of depression that turn off the opponent's will to attack. The same may have been true of humans.[29]

Nowadays these mechanisms of anxiety and depression are much less essential than they were in the African savannah. By using our brains, we have largely conquered nature. We have defeated most vertebrates and many insects and bacteria. In consequence we have increased our numbers from a few thousand to a few billion in a very short time—an astonishing achievement. Much of our anxiety and depression is no longer necessary. The great challenge now is to use our mastery over nature to master ourselves and to give us more of the happiness that we all want.

So how are we doing?

"I've got the bowl, the bone, the big yard. I know I <u>should</u> be happy."

Are we getting happier?

Money is better than poverty,
if only for financial reasons.
WOODY ALLEN

Some people have always believed that things are going downhill. But over the last fifty years we can check whether they are right. They are not. But neither are the shut-eyed optimists who tell us that life is better than ever before. Life may be better for some, but the evidence is that for most types of people in the West, happiness has not increased since 1950.[1]

In the United States people are no happier, although living standards have more than doubled. There has been no increase in the number of "very happy" people, nor any substantial fall in those who are "not very happy." The chart below highlights the situation in the starkest fashion. The story is similar in Britain, where happiness has been static since 1975 and (on flimsier evidence) is no

Income and happiness in the United States

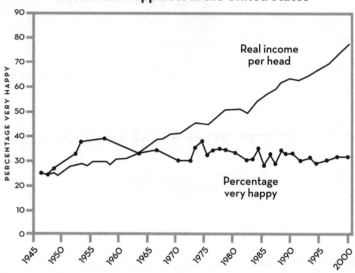

higher than in the 1950s.[2] This has happened despite massive increases in real income at every point of the income distribution. A similar story holds in Japan.[3]

In continental Europe, where regular data only begin in 1975, the position is slightly more encouraging. In many countries there is a slight upward trend in happiness, especially in Italy, but there is a sharp fall in Belgium. Overall, the change in happiness is small relative to the huge increase in incomes.

These findings are surprising since in any given society richer people are substantially happier than poorer people. As the table opposite shows, some 45% of the richest quarter of Americans are very happy, compared with only 33% of the poorest quarter. These figures have barely changed in the last thirty years. So the richest quarter have roughly doubled their living standards but they have

Happiness according to income position (percentage of each group of respondents)				
	United States		Britain	
	Top quarter	Bottom quarter	Top quarter	Bottom quarter
Very happy	45	33	40	29
Quite happy	51	53	54	59
Not too happy	4	14	6	12
	100	100	100	100

become no happier. The poor have also become richer, but no happier. In other countries the story is similar. The overall inequality in happiness has also been remarkably stable in most countries.

So here is the paradox. When people become richer compared with other people, they become happier. But when whole societies have become richer, they have not become happier—at least in the West. I shall try to explain this in the next chapter.

Testing the Facts

Wording

But first let us test out the facts. The sceptic's reaction is to say, "Because of rising expectations, people have increased the standard of happiness that they identify as 'very happy.' So people are in fact happier, but they just do not report it."[4]

We would of course like to have physical measurements on brain activity to help settle this argument, and eventually we shall have them year by year.[5] But we already have three further pieces of evidence that support the view that happiness has not risen in the West.

The first comes from looking at the same people over their life-times. One would not expect the same person to change his use of words—such as "very happy"—even if his children use the words differently from him. And when we look at the same people over their lifetimes, we find they got no happier, even though they got much richer.[6]

Comparing Countries

The second piece of evidence comes from comparing countries. If we compare the Western industrial countries, the richer ones are no happier than the poorer. This can be seen clearly in the follow-ing diagram, which again is based on population surveys in each country. If we look at the right-hand part of it, we can see that for

Income and happiness: Comparing countries

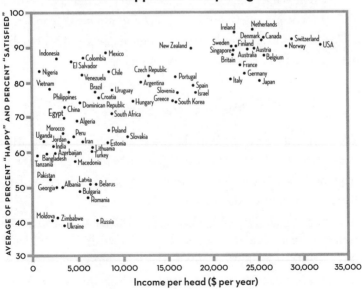

countries above $20,000 a head, additional income is not associated with extra happiness.[7]

For poorer countries things are different, because people are nearer to the breadline. So if we look at the left-hand part of the illustration, we do see a clear tendency for richer countries to be happier than poor ones.[8] Similarly, as poor countries like India, Mexico, the Philippines, Brazil and South Korea have experienced economic growth, there is some evidence that their average happiness has risen.[9] The reason is clear—extra income is really valuable when it lifts people away from sheer physical poverty.

This corresponds to one of the key beliefs of the nineteenth-century economists—that the extra happiness provided by extra income is greatest when you are poor, and declines steadily as you get richer. If we compare different people in any country, we can show empirically that this is true. And, as we would expect, the effect of income on happiness is greatest in the poorest countries, where people are nearest to the breadline.[10]

If the diagram tells us something about economics, it also tells us something about politics. The most striking finding is the misery of the former Communist countries, where oppression once degraded the human condition. At the height of Communism Russians were among the most miserable people on earth, as an earlier survey shows.[11] But the economic chaos that followed the collapse of Communism made things even worse, for the time being. All the former Communist countries are more unhappy than Algeria, and the suffering is greatest in the former Soviet Union.

Of course one could question whether the word for "happy" (or "satisfied") means the same thing in different languages. If it doesn't, we can learn nothing by comparing different countries. In fact it does. Countries can be rated separately on three different measures: how "happy" they are; how "satisfied" they are; and what score they give to their lives, using a scale running from "worst possible life" to the "best." The ranking of countries is broadly similar on all three measures.[12] This suggests that the words are not causing an insuperable problem.

Moreover, there is direct evidence that the words have a stable meaning across a number of different languages. For example, a group of Chinese students were asked to answer the happiness question, once in Chinese and once in English, with two weeks between the two events. The students reported almost exactly the same average level of happiness in both Chinese and English, and the answers in the different languages were highly correlated across the students.[13] This suggests that people who know both Chinese and English give very similar meanings to the word for "happy" in both languages. Since the English and Chinese languages are very dissimilar, this is reassuring.

In Switzerland most people speak French, German or Italian. But all these groups give similar replies to the question about happiness. Furthermore, the Swiss in all three groups are happier than the people speaking the same language next door—in France, Germany or Italy. So the way of life, not the language, seems to be what people's answers reflect.

No one would maintain that the figures in the diagram are perfectly accurate measures of happiness in each country. But, as we shall see in chapter 5, they are not meaningless. If they were, we should not be able to explain the main differences between countries by using a very few explanatory factors. Moreover, the concept of happiness seems equally familiar in all nations, bringing forth high response rates in every country. So comparing countries confirms what history also shows—that above $20,000 per head, higher average income is no guarantee of greater happiness.

The most likely story is this. Since the Second World War,

greater national income has indeed brought some increase in happiness, even in rich countries.[14] But this extra happiness has been cancelled out by greater misery coming from less harmonious social relationships, as I'll show in chapter 6.

Depression and Crime

This brings us to the third piece of evidence that overall happiness has not risen over the past half-century: the trends in depression, alcoholism and crime. All these concrete expressions of unhappiness have increased rapidly in the post-war period. The rest of this chapter should convince anyone, even those whose eyes have been glued to the gross national product, that the last fifty years have not been the era of life improvement that we would like them to have been.

Most evidence suggests that clinical depression has increased since the Second World War.[15] By clinical depression I do not mean the spells of misery that we all experience at some stage. I mean a well-defined psychiatric condition in which individuals cannot perform their normal social roles for at least some weeks.[16] To assess the prevalence of depression, we rely on interview surveys where people report their experiences, which are then classified by specialists in the survey organisation. By the age of thirty-five roughly 15% of people in the United States have experienced a major depression.[17] Many people suffer it more than once, so that in any one year about 6% of people in the United States experience a major depression.

It was not always thus. One piece of evidence comes from asking today's Americans about the symptoms which they can remember at different times in the past. If we take Americans aged thirty-five, roughly 15% remember symptoms that would be classified as major depression. But if we take Americans who were thirty-five in the 1960s, only 2% can remember such symptoms occurring before they were thirty-five. So if people's memories are right, there has been a huge increase in depression in the United States and other countries studied,[18] especially during the golden period of economic growth between the Second World War and the oil shocks of the 1970s.

However, there is always the problem that some people may have forgotten an earlier depression.[19] So it is good that we have in many countries studies of depression that have been repeated more than once over the years, using the same questions. Nearly all of these show that depression has increased.[20] A fair conclusion is that it has, even though we cannot be sure by how much.

One would not expect that economic growth would do much to prevent depression, since depression, though less common among the rich, is found at all income levels. What is worrying is that depression has actually increased as incomes have risen.

Alcohol abuse is another meaningful indicator of unhappiness. More people suffer from alcoholism than from drug addiction,[21] and the history of alcoholism is, if you will allow the phrase, very sobering. In the first quarter of the twentieth century alcohol consumption fell in many countries, despite higher spending power. So increased drinking is not an inevitable result of higher real incomes. In the second quarter of the century it stayed roughly constant. But since then it has soared in most countries except France and Italy, where it was already very high.

A part of this extra drinking is pathological. In the United States over a quarter of young white men say they have already experienced problems with alcohol. This compares with under 15% of older men (over sixty-five) who say they have ever experienced such problems. So, unless memories are very poor, alcoholism has risen in the United States. In Europe the main evidence comes from people dying of cirrhosis of the liver; the number is up since 1950 in every country except France.

Suicide data provide less relevant evidence on the scale of unhappiness, since in the typical country only about 1% of deaths are by suicide. Suicide reflects the very extreme of misery. But suicide has indeed increased in most advanced countries except the United States, Britain, Sweden and Switzerland, and youth suicide has increased in almost every advanced country.[22]

I shall not cite the growth of drug abuse, since this is partly propelled by easier access to the countries that supply drugs. In any case depression started rising long before drugs took hold.

More significant is crime. When social reformers looked forward in the 1930s to a future era of full employment and prosperity, they assumed it would bring greater satisfaction and therefore lower crime. Never did social forecasting go so far astray. Instead, in most countries between 1950 and 1980 recorded crime increased by at least 300%.[23] The striking exception is Japan, where crime, if anything, fell. Since 1980 there have been significant reductions in crime in the United States, Australia and Canada, and since 1995 in Britain. But crime is still way above its level of 1950.[24]

The extraordinary rise in crime during the golden era of post-war economic progress took almost everyone by surprise precisely because it contrasted so strongly with earlier experience. In the early nineteenth century there was high criminality in the newly grown industrial cities of Britain and the United States—Dickens' Fagin was anything but unique. But as prosperity grew, so did social order, and crime fell up to the First World War.[25] From then on it was fairly stable through the Great Depression, only to escalate in the period of post-war economic growth.

. . .

So we have in the First World a deep paradox—a society that seeks and delivers ever greater income, but is little if any happier than before. At the same time in the Third World, where extra income really does bring extra happiness, income levels are still very low. And the First World has more depression, more alcoholism and more crime than fifty years ago. What *is* going on?

"O.K., if you can't see your way to giving me a pay
raise, how about giving Parkerson a pay cut?"

If you're so rich, why aren't you happy?

A wealthy man is one who earns $100 a year
more than his wife's sister's husband.
H. L. MENCKEN[1]

uppose you were asked to choose between living in two imaginary worlds, in which prices were the same:

- In the first world you get $50 thousand a year, while other people get $25 thousand (average).

- In the second world you get $100 thousand a year, while other people get $250 thousand (average).

How would you vote? This question was put to a group of Harvard students and a majority preferred the *first* type of world.[2] They were happy to be poorer, provided their relative position improved. Many other studies have come to the same conclusion.[3] People care greatly about their relative income, and they would be willing to accept a significant fall in living standards if they could move up compared with other people.

People also compare their income with what they themselves have got used to. When they are asked how much income they need, richer people always say they need more than poorer people.[4]

So whether you are happy with your income depends on how it compares with some norm. And that norm depends on two things: what other people get, and what you yourself are used to getting. In the first case your feelings are governed by social comparison, and in the second by habituation.

Because these two forces are so strong in human nature, it is quite difficult for economic growth to improve our happiness.[5] For as actual incomes rise, the norm by which income is judged rises in step. You can see this from data collected by the Gallup Poll in the United States over many years. People were asked, "What is the smallest amount of money a family of four needs to get along in this community?" The chart opposite shows their "required real income" (adjusted for changes in the cost of living), and it also shows average "actual real income per head." As we can see, people's norms have adjusted rapidly to their actual living standards. No wonder people have got no happier.

Another survey provides further clues. Since 1972 Americans have been asked whether they are satisfied with their financial position. Although real income per head (corrected for price inflation) has nearly doubled, the proportion of people who say they are pretty well satisfied with their financial situation has actually fallen.[6]

Required real income and actual average real income
(as percentage of their 1952 levels)

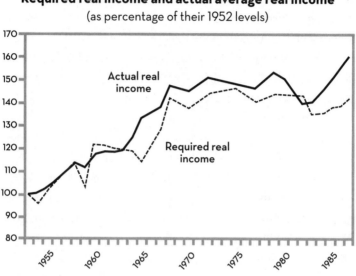

These facts are truly depressing. To understand them, we have to delve much more closely into the mechanisms of social comparison and habituation.

Social Comparison

We can begin with casual introspection. When we are at home, most of us like to live in roughly the same style as our friends or neighbours, or better. If our friends start giving more elaborate parties, we feel we should do the same. Likewise if they have bigger houses or bigger cars. When most people drove small Fords, you could feel fine about yours. But when some people have a BMW, others think that perhaps they should have one too. The first person to get a BMW feels really good. But when everybody has one, they may all feel much the same as when they all had Fords. This mechanism helps to explain the paradox in the previous chapter: in any society rich people are happier than poor people, but over time richer societies are no happier than poorer ones.

Similarly, at work, I compare my income with what my colleagues get, in so far as I hear about it. If they get a raise above inflation and I get inflation only, I get mad. This obvious piece of psychology is unknown to standard economics, which says that if one person's income rises and nobody's falls, things have improved because no one has suffered. But boy, have I suffered.

For income is much more than a means to buy things. We also use our income, compared to others', as a measure of how we are valued and (if we are not careful) a measure of how we value ourselves. We may compare our income with our colleagues', and also with others like us in different work-places. Even if we do not know their incomes precisely, we can see how they live. We clearly care about our income relative to theirs, as well as about its absolute level.

The only situation where we might willingly accept a pay cut is when others are doing the same.[7] That is why there was so little economic discontent during the Second World War. By contrast, in the great inflation of the 1970s there was great discontent, because in any one month most people's wages did not change, but some people had massive rises, leapfrogging those whose wages were unchanged.[8]

When people compare their wages, it is generally with people close to themselves, rather than with film stars or paupers. What matters is what happens to your "reference group," because what they get might have been feasible for you, while what Tom Cruise gets is not. That is why in Olympic races the bronze-medallists are happier about their result than the silver-medallists are about theirs—the bronze-medallists are comparing themselves with people who got no medal, while the silver-medallists believe they might have got the gold.[9] At the extreme we have the Russian peasant whose neighbour has a cow. When God asks how he can help, the peasant replies, "Kill the cow."

Because comparisons are made at such close quarters, some of the most intense rivalry is within organisations and within families. In organisations, calm can often be maintained only by keeping people's salaries secret. In families, it has been found that the more your spouse earns, the less satisfied you are with your own job.[10] And among women, if your sister's husband is earning more than your own husband earns, you are more likely to go out to work.[11] In other words people are concerned about their relative income and not simply about its absolute level. They want to keep up with the Joneses or if possible to outdo them.

If people change their reference group upwards, this can seriously affect their happiness. There are many clear cases where people became objectively better off but felt subjectively worse. One is East Germany, where the living standards of those employed soared after 1990, but their level of happiness fell: with the reunification of Germany the East Germans began to compare themselves with the West Germans, rather than with the other countries in the former Soviet bloc. Another case is women, whose pay and opportunities have improved considerably relative to men, but whose level of happiness has not. Indeed, in the United States women's happiness has fallen relative to men's. Perhaps women now compare themselves more directly with men than they used to and therefore focus more than before on the gaps that still exist.

There is, however, one certainty about reference groups. The rich are so near the top that their reference group is likely to include people who are poorer than they are, while the poor are so near the bottom that their reference group is likely to include people who are richer than they are. That helps to explain why the rich are on average happier than the poor.

For a society as a whole the implications of social comparisons are enormous. Imagine the most extreme case, where people cared only about their relative income and not at all about their income as such. Then economic growth could not make people better off. The only exception would be if people were to adopt reference groups that were lower in the pecking order than before. But if the reference groups remained stable and everyone's income changed at the same rate, everybody's happiness would remain the same. Each person would become happier because he was richer, but less happy because other people were richer. The two effects would cancel each other out, because relative income would be unchanged.

So how much in fact is a person's happiness affected by his own income, compared with the incomes of others? If we survey people and discover how happy they are, we can examine this question empirically. One study suggests that if everyone else earns another 1%, your happiness falls by one-third as much as it would rise if you yourself earned an extra 1%.[12] So if everybody's income rose in step, your happiness would rise, but only two-thirds as much as it would if only your income was rising. Another study probes the issue more deeply, by examining what really affects your happiness: is it your actual income that matters, or how you perceive it to compare with other people's? Your "perceived relative income" shows up as more important than your actual income.[13] These studies were done in the United States. A comparable study in Switzerland found that your happiness depends only on your income relative to your income aspirations—and your income aspirations in turn depend heavily on the average income of the people where you live.[14] These studies provide clear evidence that a rise in other people's income hurts your happiness.

This basic psychological mechanism reduces the power of economic growth to increase happiness. It also leads to distorted incentives. For if I work harder and raise my income, I make other people less happy. But when I decide how much to work, I do not take this "pollution" into account. So I will tend to work more than is socially efficient—and so will everyone else.

But wait a moment. If I work less and take more leisure, doesn't that extra leisure *also* make other people more miserable—because they also envy my *leisure*? Well, no. The Harvard researchers that I mentioned at the beginning of this chapter thought of this. So they also offered the students another pair of alternative worlds:

- You have 2 weeks' vacation, and others have 1 week.

- You have 4 weeks' vacation, and others have 8 weeks.

Only 20% of the students now chose the first of these. So most people are not rivalrous about their leisure. But they *are* rivalrous about income, and that rivalry is self-defeating. There is thus a tendency to sacrifice too much leisure in order to increase income.

What can be done about it? I leave this to the second part of the book. But here is one additional fact. Social comparisons affect some people more than others. In one experiment people were given a task which they did sitting next to an associate who was doing the same thing.[15] (The associates were agents for the experimenter.) The aim was to see how far a person's mood was affected by whether the associate did better or worse at the task. Not surprisingly, everybody's mood improved if they did better than the associate. But only unhappy people's moods deteriorated if they did worse than the associate. So one secret of happiness is to ignore comparisons with people who are more successful than you are: always compare downwards, not upwards.

Clearly, social comparisons are an important reason why hap-

piness has not risen with economic growth. Another reason is habituation.

The Hedonic Treadmill

We can start again with introspection. When I get a new home or a
new car, I am excited at first. But then I get used to it, and my mood
tends to revert to where it was before. Now I feel I *need* the bigger
house and the better car. If I went back to the old house and car, I
would be much less happy than I was before I had experienced
something better. *"I've seen how the other half lives"* *"getting spoiled."*

Personally, I grew up without central heating. It was fine. Sometimes I had to huddle over the fire or put my feet in a bowl of hot
water, but my mood was good. When I was forty, I got central heating. Now I would feel really miserable if I had to fight the cold as I
once did. In fact I have become addicted to central heating.

So living standards are to some extent like alcohol or drugs.
Once you have a certain new experience, you need to keep on having more of it if you want to sustain your happiness. You are in fact
on a kind of treadmill, a "hedonic" treadmill, where you have to
keep running in order that your happiness stand still.

In psychology this process is known as adaptation. If adaptation is "complete," only continual new stimuli can raise your well-
being. Once your situation becomes stable again, you will revert to
your "set-point" level of happiness. You will do this whether the initial change is for better or for worse.

Such adaptation is common in the natural world. When
things go badly, it can be a wonderful insurance policy. But when
things go well, it eventually dampens our joy.

People certainly adapt to some things pretty completely. But
there are some things that people never fully adjust to. People

never fully adjust to miseries like widowhood, loud and unpredictable noise, or caring for a person with Alzheimer's. And there are some good things that never pall—like sex, friends and even to some extent marriage.[16] Clearly the secret of happiness is to seek out those good things that you can never fully adapt to.

So how far do we adapt to higher income? The simplest approach is to find out how people's actual income affects the income which they feel they need.[17] We can ask people, "What after-tax income for your family would you consider to be: very bad, bad, insufficient, sufficient, good, very good?" From these answers we can pick out for each individual the income level that is midway between sufficient and insufficient. We find that this "required income" varies strongly with the actual income that an individual currently experiences. A dollar rise in experienced income causes a rise of at least forty cents in "required income."[18] So when I earn an extra dollar this year, it makes me happier, but next year I shall measure my income from a benchmark that is forty cents higher. In this sense at least 40% of this year's gain is "wiped out" next year.

That is the measure of our addiction to income.[19] The things that we get used to most easily and most take for granted are our material possessions—our car, our house. Advertisers understand this and invite us to "feed our addiction" with more and more spending. However, other experiences do not pale in the same way—the time we spend with our family and friends, and the quality and security of our job.[20]

If we do not foresee that we get used to our material possessions, we shall overinvest in acquiring them, at the expense of our leisure. People do underestimate this process of habituation:[21] As a result, our life can get distorted towards working and making money, and away from other pursuits.[22]

Work-Life Balance

Among rich countries, people in the United States work the longest hours.[23] As the chart below shows, they work much longer than in Europe. This difference is quite surprising because productivity per hour worked is the same in the United States as it is in France and Germany, and it is growing at a similar rate.[24]

In most countries and at most times in history, as people have become richer they have chosen to work less. In other words they have decided to "spend" a part of their extra potential income on a fuller private life. Over the last fifty years Europeans have continued this pattern, and hours of work have fallen sharply. But not in the United States. We do not fully know why this is. One reason may be significantly lower taxes in America, which increase the rewards to work.[25] Another may be more satisfying work, or less satisfying private lives.

Longer hours do of course increase the gross domestic product

Hours worked in the year
(full-time workers, 2002)

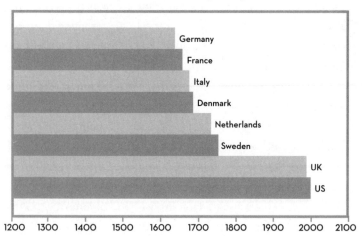

(GDP). So the United States has higher output per worker than, say, France.[26] The United States also has more of its people at work, while in France many more mothers and older workers have decided to stay at home (and unemployment is 3 percentage points higher). The overall result is that American GDP per head is 40% higher than in France, even though productivity per hour worked is the same.

It is not obvious which of the two situations is better. As we have seen, work has to be compared with other values like family life, which often get sacrificed in its interest. It is too early to explain systematically the different trends in happiness over time in different countries. But it is a provoking idea that in the United States happiness has stagnated since 1975, while it has risen in Europe. Could this have anything to do with trends in the work-life balance?

Inequality

I have concentrated so far on the self-defeating aspects of the search for income. But for billions of people more income is genuinely needed to provide an intrinsically better life for the family. This is most obviously the case in the Third World, where nearly 3 billion people are living on under $2 a day.[27] But it is also true in the First World, with which this book is concerned: how many of our fellow citizens would live much better if they had an extra $1000 a year? The answer is some, but not all.

Over a period of fourteen months Joyti De-Laurey, a secretary at Goldman Sachs in London, siphoned off some £4.5 million from the accounts of two people she worked for and spent the money on herself. For over a year neither of the two bosses even noticed.[28]

This story illustrates what nineteenth-century economists believed in their bones: that extra dollars make less difference if you are rich than if you're poor. Modern survey research confirms this belief.[29] We can examine how far extra income increases happiness for people at different points in the income scale, and we find that the benefit from extra income is indeed less and less the richer the person. For the same reason, extra income makes more difference to happiness in poor countries than in rich ones.

From this psychological reality it follows that if money is transferred from a richer person to a poorer person, the poor person gains more happiness than the rich person loses. So average happiness increases. Thus a country will have a higher level of average happiness the more equally its income is distributed—all else being equal.[30]

In this approach we are thinking of income as the relevant determinant of happiness: inequality is bad because extra income brings less benefit to the rich than the poor. However, there is a quite different tradition that focuses on income inequality as a thing in itself—a feature of your environment.[31] This holds that people have a view about inequality as such. The assumption used to be that people dislike inequality. But increasing evidence finds that some groups (those who are mobile or feel they are mobile) actually like it.[32] This is a complicated issue, and little is known about the balance of such preferences. Inequality may also of course affect the quality of social relationships. However, there is as yet no clear evidence to show that inequality as such affects the happiness of individuals in a community.[33] But we *do* know that the benefit from extra income is indeed less if people are rich, and this provides the main link between inequality and average happiness.

There is one siren argument that is raised against policies to reduce income inequality. It comes from those who believe taxation is a device to prevent social mobility—to stop an ambitious youngster from moving up from rags to riches (because riches can no longer be attained in one generation). I have even heard it said that high taxation in Britain perpetuates the class system. This is nonsense. The most classless societies in the world are those in Scandinavia, where taxes are high, basic education is good and there is a culture of mutual respect.

So where are we? We have a good idea why happiness has risen less than was expected: our norms have risen, as other people's incomes have risen and likewise our own experience of comfort. The central mechanism at work here is our habit of comparison.

This is deeply rooted in our psychology. If you look at the following illustration, a natural question to ask is which of the two vertical lines is longer. Most people would say the one on the right. Why? Because it is longer when compared with the gap between the two sloping lines above and below it. Yet in fact both vertical lines are the same height.

We constantly distort our perception of reality by unhelpful comparisons. So one "secret of happiness" is to enjoy things as they are, without comparing them with anything better. Another is to find out which things really make us happy. ⤷ "no one has greener grass"

Habits of comparison

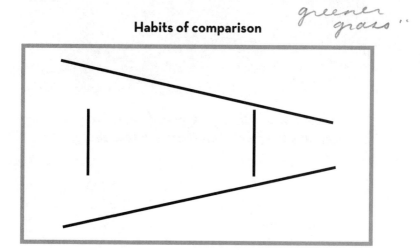

"*I could cry when I think of the years I wasted accumulating money, only to learn that my cheerful disposition is genetic.*"

So what does make us happy?

Is it so small a thing,
To have enjoyed the sun,
To have lived light in the spring,
To have loved, to have thought, to have done?
MATTHEW ARNOLD[1]

Happiness comes from without and within. It depends on our circumstances but also on our inner selves. As La Rochefoucauld put it, "Happiness and misery depend as much on temperament as on fortune." Temperament in turn depends on our genes and our upbringing.

Our Genes

Some people think we should not talk about genes, because it might give the impression that a person is foredoomed to happiness or misery when he is born, and nothing more can be done about it. That conclusion would be absurd. Even the most heritable traits can be radically altered by experience. You have only to think of height—so closely related to the height of one's parents. Yet the average height of British men has risen by two inches in the last hundred years, mainly because of better diet.[2]

Thus height is the joint product of genes and environment, as is almost everything else that is interesting about us. Genes are not a template that specifies how we shall inevitably be. Genes provide operating instructions about how we shall develop in response to our environment. The mouse has genes that tell it how to make a seeing eye, if circumstances are favourable. But if a baby mouse's eye is bandaged over for six months and then uncovered, the mouse will never gain its sight.

So why talk about genes at all? Because we are interested in the truth. We want to know what makes us how we are, and we shan't know it if we ignore any of the key factors. As every parent knows, children come into the world different, and they will not be happy unless the world responds appropriately to who they are.

So how do we know that genes affect our happiness? The key evidence comes from studies of twins. Twins that are identical have identical genes, while twins that aren't identical have only half their genes in common, just like ordinary siblings.[3] As a result identical twins are much more similar in happiness than twins that are not identical. The findings from the Minnesota Twins Registry are striking. Identical twins are remarkably close to each other in happiness, while non-identical twins are barely similar at all.[4] The happiness levels of the identical twins are much more similar because they have the same genes.

But wait a moment, you may say, aren't their experiences also more similar? The researchers have thought of that and made a special study of identical twins who were adopted apart as young babies. It turns out that among these identical twins raised apart from each other, the levels of happiness are as similar as among identical twins who grew up together.[5] So if identical twins are more similar than non-identical twins, it is not mainly because their experiences have been more similar. It is because their genes are more similar.

Comparable findings apply to many other human traits besides happiness—to schizophrenia, depression, alcoholism and criminal behaviour, as shown in the following table. For each such case the table asks, "If one twin has the problem, does the other twin have it also?" The table shows the percentage of twins for which the answer is yes. In every instance the identical twins are much more similar than twins who have different genes. But we would never say that a person's genes have determined that he be an alcoholic. All that the genes do is to provide or not provide some predisposition. Most of our traits come from a mixture of genes and experience; the genes affect how we respond to our experience.

If one twin has the problem, does the other twin have it also? (per cent)		
	Identical twins	Non-identical twins
Schizophrenia	48	17
Manic-Depression	65	14
Alcoholism (men)	41	22
Criminal conviction (adults)	52	23
Juvenile delinquency	91	73

In fact the table itself makes clear that genes are not everything. They do not totally determine anything. But they do affect its likelihood—the risk that it will occur. Thus if one twin is schizophrenic, the other twin is much more likely to become schizophrenic if he has the identical genes than if he has only half the same genes. But, even so, the likelihood for identical twins is less than 50%. So experience plays an important role as well as the genes.

Since we vary in happiness, it would be good to be able to say how much of the variation came from differences in genes and how much from differences in experience. Unfortunately, this cannot be done in any neat way, for two reasons. First, people with good genes also tend to get good experiences. Their parents are good at parenting. Their own niceness elicits good treatment from other people. And, as time passes, they themselves are good at seeking out good experiences. These effects are in truth effects of experience, but they are also correlated with a person's genes. There is no clear way of parcelling them out between the two influences. Then there is the second reason: that many genetic effects are only triggered by bad situations and vice versa. Thus in many cases bad genes only hurt if you also have bad experiences.

Despite these problems you will still hear that some trait is $x\%$ "heritable," meaning that $x\%$ of the variation is due to the genes. In most cases the figure given is an overestimate, because it includes as a genetic effect any effect of experience when this is positively correlated with the effect of the genes.[6] Even so, all psychological studies of heritability still leave a major role for experience.

Our chief interest has to be the effect of the experience, since this is something we can affect. But equally we shall only find out how our environment affects us if we have properly controlled for the effect of our genes. This is quite obvious when we look at the effects of our childhood experience.

Our Family Upbringing

Under the influence of Sigmund Freud, many people used to think that the first six years of life were critical for our happiness in life, and little else mattered. After all, children are so like their parents that their parents must have influenced them. But then came the reaction. What if the parents' influence had come through their sperm and egg, and not through their love or coldness as parents?[7]

The most obvious way to study this problem is to look at children who were adopted at birth and brought up by new parents with quite different genes. The upshot is broadly this: Upbringing still matters, though less than was once thought. The influence of the genes is also strong, even when the biological parent never sees the child. In addition, the combination of poor upbringing and bad genes produces bigger effects than the simple sum of their separate effects—their interaction can be particularly destructive.

We can do nothing about our genes except to live with them. But we can do something about how we bring up children. The adoption studies show clearly that this matters.

Adopted children who grow up in a disturbed home are indeed more likely to become mentally ill than if their adoptive parents are less disturbed. (They are also more likely to have problems if their biological mother was schizophrenic.[8]) Again, people who grow up in a criminal home are more likely to become criminals, especially if their biological parents were also criminals.[9] And if they grow up with antisocial adoptive parents, they are more likely to become antisocial, especially if their biological parents were also antisocial.[10]

As adoptees progress through life, the effect of their adoptive parents fades and the effect of their genes increases.[11] Cumulatively, life provides you with increasing opportunity to express your deepest nature. But your start is still important.

One way to examine the pure effect of upbringing is to focus solely on identical twins. For many reasons mothers treat one twin differently from another, and even by the age of seven we can see that the favoured twin behaves much better.[12]

These findings are striking, but we can now go further as a result of the Human Genome Project and its aftermath. We can begin to study directly the effects of the particular physical genes that we have. The pioneers here are an international group analysing a follow-up survey in Dunedin, New Zealand, which collected from people their actual DNA—the stuff in which their genes are written. To help explain depression, the group has isolated a certain gene that affects the supply of serotonin to the brain.[13] If a person has inferior versions of that gene, he is in danger of becoming depressed, but only if he is also maltreated as a child. Similarly, if a person is maltreated, he is in danger of becoming depressed, but only if he has inferior versions of the gene. This finding shows beautifully how genes and experience can interact to determine our make-up.[14]

Studies of animals confirm the importance of child-rearing. If rats whose mothers are bad at licking are fostered by other mothers who are good at licking, they grow up to be less stressed than they would have been if left with their biological mothers.[15] Similarly, monkeys that have overactive mothers can become quite calm if fostered by calmer mothers.[16] Among humans, controlled experiments to improve parenting behaviours have been shown to have lasting effects on the children.[17]

Family break-up

What about the effects of family break-up? Unfortunately, research that controls for genetic effects is still quite rare.[18] So researchers often try to control for genetic effects by measuring a child's personality when he is, say, seven and then looking at how he changes after that as a result of his parents' behaviour.

One study followed children aged seven whose parents were still living together. If the parents then split up, a child was roughly twice as likely to become a depressed adult as compared with children whose parents stayed together. It did not matter how old the child was when the separation happened.[19] But the main problem is the conflict between the parents — if the conflict is bad enough it may be better for parents to split up than to stay together.[20]

Other studies confirm the damage that can result from growing up with a single parent. If by sixteen you are living with only one of your biological parents, you are more likely to suffer from multiple disadvantages, compared with other children. You are 70% more likely to have a criminal conviction by the age of fifteen; you are twice as likely to leave high school with no diploma; you are twice as likely to have a child in your teens; and you are 50% more likely to be doing nothing at the age of twenty.[21] Interestingly, you are no better off if your mother remarries, or if your grandmother moves in. As adults, people from single-parent families are more likely to die young, and to get divorced themselves.[22]

Some children of course never live with their father: they are born to a single mother. The impact of this experience is broadly the same as when a father is present at first and then leaves.[23]

I have dwelt at some length on the effects of family break-up or being born without a father at home because half of all American children end up living with only one of their original parents by the age of fifteen. And 30% of all American children (of all ages) are in that position.

There are three main reasons why it is bad for children to live with only one parent.[24] One is simple poverty — family income drops by a half or more. This may explain half of the damage done. But there is also a decline in parental input and supervision, and often the disruption of friendships when the family has to move, as so often happens. Finally, there is the feeling of betrayal. In the United States about one-third of absent fathers never see their children in a year. Though another third see them every week, that too can sometimes be conflictual or bittersweet.

Adult Life

We now come to the effect of adult life itself upon each one of us. What are the features of our life that make the biggest difference to our happiness?

What doesn't matter

We can begin with five features that on average have a negligible effect on happiness. The first is age: if we trace people through their life, average happiness is remarkably stable, despite the ups and then downs of income, and despite increasing ill-health.[25] The second is gender: in nearly every country men and women are roughly equally happy.[26] Looks too make little difference.[27] Likewise, IQ is only weakly correlated with happiness, as are physical and mental energy (self-rated).[28] Finally, education has only a small direct effect on happiness, though of course it raises happiness by raising a person's income.[29]

The "Big Seven"

So what really does affect us? Seven factors stand out: our family relationships, our financial situation, our work, our community and

objective-ish

reminiscent of Nussbaum

62

friends, our health, our personal freedom and our personal values. Except for health and income, they are all concerned with the quality of our relationships.

To focus the mind, I will call these factors the Big Seven. The U.S. General Social Survey enables us to put the first five in order of importance. It asks people how happy they are in general, and also how satisfied they are with the different dimensions of their life (family, finance, work, community and friends, health). From their answers we can disentangle which dimensions of life are the most important. The results are shown in the following box, together with the two other key factors: personal freedom and personal values.[30]

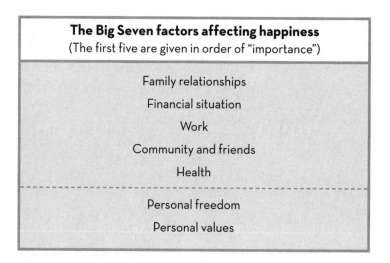

The Big Seven factors affecting happiness
(The first five are given in order of "importance")

Family relationships

Financial situation

Work

Community and friends

Health

Personal freedom

Personal values

As in every study, family relationships (and our close private life) are more important than any other single factor affecting our happiness. But we need more detail on all these factors. We can get it from the World Values Survey that has been carried out four times since 1981. It has been well analysed by John Helliwell of the

Effects on happiness

	Fall in happiness (points)
Financial situation	
Family income down by a third	2
Family relationships	
Divorced (rather than married)	5
Separated (rather than married)	8
Widowed (rather than married)	4
Never married (rather than married)	4.5
Cohabiting (rather than married)	2
Work	
Unemployed (rather than employed)	6
Job insecure (rather than secure)	3
Unemployment rate up 10 percentage points	3
Community and friends	
"In general, people can be trusted" Percentage of citizens saying yes down by 50 percentage points	1.5
Health	
Subjective health down 1 point (on a 5-point scale)	6
Personal freedom	
Quality of government Belarus 1995 rather than Hungary 1995	5
Personal values	
"God is important in my life" You say no to this rather than yes[3]	3.5

University of British Columbia and his results cover 90,000 people in forty-six countries.[32]

In the survey a person reports his happiness on a scale from 10 to 100, and he also reports the various features of his life.[33] We can therefore use these features to explain his happiness. To avoid mistaken inferences, we must always look at the effect of each feature while holding the other features constant.[34] The effects are shown in the table opposite; it will be explained in the remainder of this chapter.

We begin with the effect of income. A fall in income by one-third (holding national income constant) causes a fall in happiness of 2 points on the scale of happiness (from 10 to 100). This is quite a small change in happiness, but it provides a standard against which we can measure the effect of some of the more important influences.[35]

Family relationships

Differences in family situation cause a huge difference in happiness. If someone is divorced, that person's happiness falls by 5 points. This is more than double the effect of losing a third of one's income. And if someone is separated (reflecting a more recent break-up of the relationship), things are even worse. Widowhood too is a major blow.

But in this analysis we are comparing different people, and there is always the risk that less happy people are more likely to get divorced and so on.[36] To pin down what is causing what, we have to follow the same people through their lives. The German Socio-Economic Panel has done this for over twenty years. From this we find that people generally become happier as a result of marriage, and this is true of both men and women.[37] In the two or three years before marrying they are already becoming happier (some are already living together), but the year of marriage is the peak of happiness. After that first year some habituation sets in, and people become a bit less happy. But they remain happier than they were four years before the marriage.[38]

The pattern for divorce is similar but in reverse. Before the divorce, people are becoming ever less happy. The year of divorce is the worst. After that year men return on average to their baseline level of happiness, but women continue to suffer. The effects of high divorce rates can be seen when we compare countries as well as individuals. We shall come to this later, but divorce rates have significant effects on the happiness of nations—and on the rate of suicide.[39]

What about the effects of having children? There is indeed great rejoicing when children are born.[40] Yet within two years parents revert on average to their original level of happiness.

The main benefits of marriage or cohabitation are obvious: you give each other love and comfort; you share resources, gaining economies of scale; you help each other. Married people also have better sex lives on average than single people—more of it and more satisfying.[41] Furthermore, married people are healthier and live longer.[42] Though cohabitation is becoming much more common, it has not so far proved as stable a form of relationship as marriage.[43]

But of course it is the quality and stability of relationships that matter more than their form. We need other people, and we need to be needed. Increasingly, research confirms the dominating importance of love. People who are in loving relationships with another adult have better hormonal balance and better health,[44] and are of course happier. Much of the world's greatest literature is about love, and there is no need for me to add to it.[45]

Work

We can be needed by our family, but most of us need more than this: we need to feel we are contributing to the wider society. Thus work provides not only income but also an extra meaning to life. That is why unemployment is such a disaster: it reduces income but it also reduces happiness directly by destroying the self-respect and social relationships created by work. When people become un-employed, their happiness falls much less because of the loss of income than because of the loss of work itself. Economists almost always ignore this reality, and some even allege that the extra leisure must be a benefit to the unemployed.

If you look at the previous table, you might of course ask whether the measured effect of unemployment simply reflects prior differ-ences between people, with less happy people becoming unem-ployed more often. But the German Socio-Economic Panel shows that for a given person the pain of unemployment is even higher, rel-ative to the pain of losing income, than appears in the table.[46]

The German survey also enables us to settle another important question. Some people think that the main evil is not unemployment but non-employment. In other words it is as bad to be "out of the labour force" and not looking for work as to be unemployed: you are not looking for work because you are discouraged. The data totally re-fute this. Moves between work and being "out of the labour force" in-volve much smaller changes in happiness than moves between work and unemployment.[47] And retirement is not bad for happiness either.

So unemployment is a very special problem. Moreover, it hurts as much after one or two years of unemployment as it does at the beginning.[48] In that sense you do not habituate to it (though it hurts less if other people are out of work too).[49] And even when you are back at work, you still feel its effects as a psychological scar.[50]

Moreover, even when in work, people fear unemployment, and when unemployment goes up, it has a major impact on the happiness of everybody including those in work.[51] Thus if unemployment rises, it has two effects. First, there is the direct effect, because more people are unemployed. Then there is the indirect effect on everyone. So low and stable unemployment must be a major objective for any society.[52]

Work is vital, if that is what you want. But it is also important that the work be fulfilling. Perhaps the most important issue is the extent to which you have control over what you do. There is a creative spark in each of us, and if it finds no outlet, we feel half-dead. This can be literally true: among British civil servants of any given grade, those who do the most routine work experience the most rapid clogging of the arteries.[53]

Community and friends

According to the Greek philosopher Epicurus, "Of all the things that wisdom provides to help one live one's entire life in happiness, the greatest by far is friendship." Friendship is one of the best things in life. Many of the closest friendships are formed in early life, but we go on making friends at work and through the community.

The quality of our community is crucial for whether we make friends and how safe we feel. Researchers call the quality of the community "social capital."[54] It is not easy to assess it, but one good measure is to ask people, "Generally speaking, would you say that most people can be trusted, or that you can't be too careful in dealing with people?" This is asked in the World Values Survey, and the proportion who say "Yes, most people can be trusted" varies from 5% in Brazil to as high as 64% in Norway.

You might worry whether the replies to this question mean

anything. Do they correspond to anything real about how people in that country behave? They do. Researchers have dropped wallets in the street in different countries, wallets that included the name and address of the owner. They then counted the proportion of dropped wallets that were returned to the owner—the highest was in Scandinavia. These proportions were then compared with how the citizens of the country replied about trust. It turned out that the two were closely related: so when we ask about trust, we do learn something about whether people can actually be trusted.[55]

Moreover, trust does affect happiness. The previous table confirms that living where you can trust others makes a clear difference to your happiness.

Health

This brings us to health. We care greatly about our health, but it never comes through as the top determinant of happiness.[56] This may be partly because people have a considerable ability to adapt to physical limitations.[57] Healthy members of the public generally overestimate the loss of happiness that people actually experience from many of the main medical conditions.[58] But people can never adapt to chronic pain or to mental illness—feelings that come from inside themselves, rather than limitations on their external activities.[59] The control of such suffering must be one of our top priorities.

Personal freedom

Happiness also depends on the quality of the government. In the West we take for granted two factors that are lacking in half the globe—personal freedom and peace. When we looked at happiness in different countries, we learned how miserable people were under

Communism. The previous table uses a sophisticated measure of the quality of government reflecting six different features: the rule of law; stability and lack of violence; voice and accountability; the effectiveness of government services; the absence of corruption; and the efficiency of the system of regulation. It thus covers the three main dimensions of freedom: personal, political and economic. The result shows a huge difference in happiness associated with a government such as that of Belarus, which is still Communist, compared with that of post-Communist Hungary. We should never forget the importance of the freedoms we enjoy in the West.

A recent study of democracy in Switzerland has produced remarkable results. In every Swiss canton (or region) policies are often decided by referendum. But in some cantons citizens have more rights to demand referendums than in others. It turns out that people are much happier where they have more rights to referendums. If we compare those cantons where these rights are the most extensive with those where they are the least extensive, the difference in happiness is as great as if they had double the income.[60] These findings are highly relevant to the role of local democracy.

Of all social ills, the one that can cause the greatest misery is war. The terror and personal loss that it unleashes is impossible to measure. But in the last century over 100 million people died because of war.[61] For obvious reasons the effects of war could not be included in our table.

Explaining differences in happiness between countries

It is time to take stock, looking now at countries rather than mainly at individuals. As we saw in chapter 3, average happiness differs among countries. So how far do the kinds of factors we have been discussing help to explain this? Surprisingly well. Using the World Values Survey we can compare happiness in fifty countries in up to four different years. It turns out that six factors, closely linked to our Big Seven, can explain 80% of the variation in happiness.[62] The factors are the

- divorce rate

- unemployment rate

- level of trust

- membership in non-religious organisations[63]

- quality of government[64]

- fraction believing in God

Even so some sceptics still question whether the intercountry differences mean anything. One answer is to say that something which can be so easily and sensibly explained must really exist. But there is further evidence. The suicide rate is a more objective statistic than replies to questions about happiness. If our six factors really do explain happiness, they should also explain suicide. They do explain 57% of the variation.

They also help to explain the scale of deaths on the road. As is well known, a calm mind leads to calmer driving. So it is not surprising that when we compare countries, these same factors again explain a fraction of the differences in deaths on the road.[65]

Personal values (Philosophy of life)

Finally, and crucially, our happiness depends on our inner self and our philosophy of life. Obviously, people are happier if they are able to appreciate what they have, whatever it is; if they do not always compare themselves with others; and if they can school their own moods. The psychologist Daniel Goleman is right about emotional intelligence: it exists and it can be taught by parents and teachers.[66] You may know Sir Henry Wotton's description of the happy man, which ends:

> This man is freed from servile bands
> Of hope to rise or fear to fall,
> Lord of himself, though not of lands,
> And having nothing yet hath all.[67]

Different people have different ways of disciplining their minds and their moods—from cognitive therapy, to Buddhist mindfulness, to the Twelve Steps of Alcoholics Anonymous, to the *Spiritual Exercises* of Saint Ignatius. People find comfort from within, in all sorts of ways, but these generally include some system of relying for help on the deep positive part of oneself, rather than on the efforts of the conscious ego.

Some people call this source of comfort "divine," and the previous table reports one of the most robust findings of happiness research: that people who believe in God are happier. At the individual level one cannot be sure whether belief causes happiness or happiness causes belief. But since the relation also exists at the national level, we can be sure that to some extent belief causes happiness.[68]

So much for the way we school ourselves. But how we interact with others is equally important. We shall return to both these themes in later chapters. Enough to say here that people who care about other people are on average happier than those who are more preoccupied with themselves.[69] More anxiety comes from striving to "do well" for yourself than from striving to "do good" for the rest of the world.

Our Goals

What is sure is that our frame of mind has a profound effect on our happiness. We are not blank slates on which our situation operates to make us happy or sad. We are active agents who both shape our situation and control our response to that situation. As the saying goes, what matters is not what life brings to you, but what you bring to life.

Psychologists have always known this, but unfortunately some of the early students of the quality of life had a rather simple model of how to be happy.[70] Happiness, they said, depends on what you have (in different domains) relative to your expectations. If this were true, the simplest way to be happy would surely be to lower your expectations and your goals. Rightly, many thinkers have reacted adversely to this conclusion, especially radicals from the Left (who want more justice) and from the Right (who want more excellence). Indeed, the thought that you can be happy in that way has led many people to reject altogether the idea of happiness as a goal.

These people should not have worried, because the theory is false. We could not be happy without setting ourselves goals. Children test themselves—they see how fast they can run, how high they can climb. Every happy adult does the same—seeks new understandings, new achievements. Prod any happy person and you will find a project.

If our goals are too low, we get bored. But if they are too high, we get frustrated. The secret is to have goals that are stretching enough, but not too stretching.[71] Unattainable goals are a well-known cause of depression.[72] But so too is boredom.

In the 1970s the economist Tibor Scitovsky wrote a book called *The Joyless Economy* in which he tried to explain why so many people were unhappy, even though they had plenty of money. His explanation was boredom.[73] They had chosen comfort instead of stimulation. They had failed to find active interests that would engage them outside their work.

His diagnosis has an important element of truth. Even though many people feel under tremendous pressure, the average American or Briton still finds three and a half hours a day to watch television. People no longer have to struggle to keep alive, as they have done for most of human history. So we have more choice over our goals. Getting them right is the problem.

In the same vein the great economist Lord Keynes wrote, "To those who sweat for their daily bread, leisure is a longed-for sweet—until they get it." He quoted with chagrin the traditional epitaph written for herself by the old charwoman:

> *Don't mourn for me, friends,*
> *Don't weep for me never,*
> *For I'm going to do nothing*
> *For ever and ever.*

Both Keynes and Bertrand Russell considered boredom the biggest danger for humans, once economic scarcity had been overcome.[74] This is an overstatement, but the converse is certainly true: the greatest happiness comes from absorbing yourself in some goal outside yourself. The psychologist Mihaly Csikszentmihalyi uses the word "flow" to describe the experience when you are so absorbed in what you are doing that you "lose yourself."[75] You may be playing tennis, singing in a choir, painting a picture, watching football, writing a book or making love. We all have such experiences where we lose our sense of time. And we carry those experiences with us for the rest of our life. They are vital.

objectiv.

But they are only a part of our experience. It is the totality that we have to explain. There we face the paradox. In many ways life is better than fifty years ago: we have unprecedented wealth, better health and nicer jobs. Yet we are not happier. Is it because there are other new features of our experience that are bad and offset the new features that are good?

"I think the dosage needs adjusting. I'm not nearly as happy as the people in the ads."

What's going wrong?

*Whoever said money can't buy
happiness isn't spending it right.*

In 1998 the king of Bhutan, the small, idyllic Buddhist kingdom nestling high in the Himalayas, announced that his nation's objective would be the Gross National Happiness. What an enlightened ruler!

Yet one year later he made a fateful decision: to allow television into his country. Until then TV had been banned, as had all public advertising. But in 1999 the ban on TV was lifted, and licenses were given to more than thirty cable operators. The most successful operator provided forty-six channels, including Rupert Murdoch's Star TV network. And so the Bhutanese could see the usual mixture of football, violence, sexual betrayal, consumer advertising, wrestling and the like. They lapped it up, but the impact on their society provides a remarkable natural experiment in how technological change can affect attitudes and behaviour.[1]

Quite soon everyone noticed a sharp increase in family break-up, crime and drug taking. In schools violence in the playground increased, so that one principal's annual report had to include a new section called "Controversies," which reported "marathon staff meetings" to discuss these new problems. The "impact study" by some local academics showed that a third of parents now preferred watching TV to talking to their children.

One should of course be cautious in generalising from only one episode. But this striking tale reinforces the commonsense view that TV is a major independent force in our lives and not simply a reflection of what we already are.

In this chapter I want to argue that science and technology are the prime source of the changes that affect our attitudes and feelings. They explain the huge growth in our national wealth and the remarkable improvement in our health—all of which are blessings. Yet they also explain some of the negative trends that offset these blessings.

If we review our Big Seven sources of happiness, some of them have improved in the last fifty years: health, income and the quality of work. But some have deteriorated: family relationships, the strength and safety of communities and the prevalence of unselfish values. The first step is to document these deteriorating trends. After that I shall show how science and technology help to explain them.

Adverse Trends

Broken families

As we have seen, family break-up is generally bad for the children and for their subsequent happiness. In 1950 divorce was extremely uncommon, but now only a half of all American fifteen-year-olds are living with their biological father.[2] In Britain and Germany the figure is two in three.[3] Since second marriages break up faster than first marriages, many children now go through two or even more divorces.

The main change in divorce happened between 1960 and 1980. In America divorce peaked in 1980, while in Britain it continued rising slowly after that.[4] But more and more children are now born outside marriage—currently a third or more, as the table shows. In these cases a quarter of the mothers in the United States are living with the father, and two-thirds in Britain.[5] Some cohabitations are of course stable, but unmarried parents are on average twice as likely to split up as married parents.[6]

Divorce has been identified as the clearest reason for rising youth suicide in the United States.[7] But of course it also hurts the parents. Since more and more people are separated, divorced or never married, this exerts a steady downwards pressure on the average level of happiness.[8]

Family problems		
Divorces per year (as a percentage of all married couples)	Out-of-wedlock births (as a percentage of all births)	Families headed by a single parent (as a percentage of all families)
United States		
1960 0.9	5	9
2000 1.9	33	27
Britain		
1960 0.2	5	6
2000 1.3	40	21

Increased crime

The clearest failure of community life is the enormous rise in crime since the Second World War. This is hugely significant in two ways. First, it reflects a massive alienation in parts of the community. Second, it reduces the well-being of the victims, and the security of all of us. Roughly one-third of Britons feel unsafe walking outside after dark.[9] In public opinion polls in Britain and the United States, crime regularly figures as one of the top problems facing the country.[10]

At this point many people will say that crime is all due to inequality and unemployment. If only it were so simple. The fact is that the main rise in crime in the United States and in Britain occurred between 1950 and 1980, when inequality was generally falling and unemployment unusually low. Over this period all the main types of crime grew—violence, fraud, burglary, car theft, other theft and criminal damage. The overall rise in recorded crime was 300% in the United States and 500% in Britain.[11]

In the United States the tide turned in the early 1980s, when unemployment was higher than before, and economic growth slower than in the previous thirty years.[12] In Britain the tide turned around 1995.[13] But crime is still many times higher than it was fifty years ago. Many factors affect the ups and downs of crime, including the number of policemen and the number of criminals in prison. But the main factors relevant to this book are the social and moral influences at work.

Decreased trust

Lying behind higher crime and family break-up is a profound change in attitudes to the self and society. Moralists throughout the ages have argued that the world was going to pot. So one should be careful about any kind of alarmist talk. But surveys reveal fundamental changes for the worse.

We can begin with trust. At various times people have been asked, "Would you say that most people can be trusted—or would you say that you can't be too careful in dealing with people?" In 1959, 56% of Britons said yes, most people can be trusted. By 1998 that figure had fallen to 30%.[14] Similarly, in the United States the figure has fallen from 56% in the mid-1960s to 33%.[15]

I do not want to sound like an old fuddy-duddy or a Cassandra, and certainly don't want to be one, but the following evidence seems important. In 1952 half of all Americans thought people led "as good lives—moral and honest—as they used to." There was no majority for the view that things are going to the dogs. But, as the table shows, by 1998 there was a three-to-one majority for precisely that view—that people are less moral than they used to be.

Percentage saying that people lead "as good lives—moral and honest—as they used to" (United States)	
1952	51
1965	43
1976	32
1998	27

Also, fewer and fewer people in the United States now belong to associations of their fellows—be they organized around sport, politics, service to the young and elderly, religion or common ethnicity.[16] More and more people are going it alone, even when they go bowling. Noticing this, the sociologist Robert Putnam of

Harvard University studied carefully how many organisations people belonged to in the United States and showed how the number had fallen. He aptly titled his book *Bowling Alone*.

All these trends seem to be stronger in the United States than in Europe. In Britain, membership in associations has not fallen. On the European continent levels of trust have actually improved (or not fallen) in every country since 1980. By contrast, in the United States each new generation has begun its adult life at a lower level of trust than previous generations.[17]

These trends in family life and community trust are seismic changes and help to explain why happiness has not risen. To explain the trends is not easy. Economic growth as such provides no explanation, because economic growth has occurred for the last 150 years, but family break-up, higher crime and weaker moral values are a feature of only the last fifty. So in a search for explanations, one naturally looks at changes that have been specific to the last fifty years. I shall focus on three big changes: the change in gender roles, the spread of television and the growth of individualism. In each case I shall show how science and technology has been the ultimate driver of change.

Gender Roles

In 1950 20% of U.S. mothers went out to work.[18] Today it is over 70%. Similar, though less dramatic, changes have happened in Europe. This is a revolution. What has caused it?

In the 1870s half of all the children born in Chicago died before the age of five.[19] Mothers had to have up to ten children to be reasonably sure that two would survive to be adults. So there was no way that most mothers could work outside the home.[20] But when technology delivered better living standards and better medical care, child mortality fell drastically. In response women had fewer and fewer children. At the same time, over the last century, women's life expectancy was rising, from about fifty years to eighty. So the position of women was totally changed: once they spent most of their adult life bearing children; now they had few children and a much longer life to look forward to. As the South African writer Olive Schreiner forecast at the beginning of the twentieth century, these changes would totally alter the role of women.[21] Motherhood would no longer be enough, if it ever was.

Moreover, housework was becoming much easier owing to labour-saving technology. One has only to picture a world without electricity, central heating, vacuum cleaners, washing machines and convenience foods to see how those inventions have reduced the need for labour in the home.

Thus it became more possible for women to go out to work. In addition, the world of paid work became more inviting. Productivity growth raised women's wages steadily in real terms—and since the 1970s raised them faster than men's, as the need for male muscle power was replaced by machinery. So more and more mothers took jobs.[22]

This had profound effects for the family. First, the roles inside the family changed. There was no longer the old division of labour, where the husband earned the money and the wife cared for home and family. Wives now became paid workers as well as homemakers. This was in many ways liberating. But because most women continued to do more of the housework and parenting, this change created an extra strain. At the same time many men felt they got less attention than before from their wives.[23] From both sides there was greater potential for dissatisfaction.

It was also becoming easier to split up. Mothers could more readily contemplate the break-up of the marriage because they could earn better money than before, if they needed it. Or if they did not work, they could get more help from the state. This reduced the financial pressure on the wife to stay in an unhappy marriage, and likewise the moral pressure on the husband to remain.

Equally important was a quite different technological revolution: the control of childbirth. The pill, introduced in the 1960s, separated sex from the likelihood of pregnancy. Then legalised abortion (in the late 1960s and early 1970s) separated pregnancy from the necessity of childbirth. This new safety, supported by trends in popular culture (remember the Rolling Stones), led to the sexual revolution. Sex before marriage became widely accepted. And after a couple married, these developments made extramarital affairs a lot safer. At the same time men and women had new opportunities for meeting through the work-place.

Thus new dangers to marriage arose just as women's economic opportunities made splitting up less financially devastating. Attitudes also changed. In the early 1960s half of all American women felt that "when there are children in the family, parents should stay together even if they don't get along." By 1977 the proportion who felt this way was below a quarter.[24]

More and more people sought divorce, and at the same time the law became easier. In every country except Sweden, divorce, if allowed at all, had normally required a "matrimonial offence." In reality this "offence" was often an agreed fix-up, bringing the law into disrepute. So under pressure from lawyers among others, the law in the United States and Britain moved in the late 1960s and early 1970s to allow divorce by consent, or divorce on grounds of marriage breakdown. These changes in the law were not the main influence on family break-up, but they added further impetus to trends already under way.

Percentage of married people describing their marriage as "very happy" (United States)		
	Men	Women
1973–75	70	67
1996–98	64	62

One would have hoped that as divorce became easier, the marriages that continued would have become happier—just as your average score improves when you leave out the worst ones. Unfortunately, this has not been the case. In the United States, as shown above, both men and women are less satisfied with their marriages; the same is true in Britain.[25]

Thus have science and technology changed the relations between the sexes. Women are now as educated as their husbands and have the same need to use their brains. In many families the problem is simply lack of time. In the United States a quarter of all families take the evening meal together on fewer than four days a week; only 28% do it every day, compared with 38% in Britain.[26] Clearly, we need a more family-friendly lifestyle, one that is better adjusted to the new gender roles. This will mean more flexible hours of work, more parental leave and better child care.

Television

In 1950 there was no television in the home. By the 1960s it was practically universal in the industrialised world. Television has revolutionised our lives in the same way as printing once did. It has widened our experience immeasurably—with much greater immediacy than the printed word. It has also transformed the way we spend our time.

Social life

The typical Briton watches television for three and a half hours a day—roughly twenty-five hours a week.[27] Over a lifetime a typical Briton spends more time watching television than doing paid work. The figures are much the same in the United States.[28] In most European countries viewing rates are somewhat lower but generally average above two hours a day. These are not figures for how long the set is switched on; they are what individual viewers say about their own viewing.

This viewing time has to come from somewhere, and it mainly comes from social life. In 1973 there were still communities in Canada that had no TV. So an enterprising research group monitored what happened when TV was introduced into a particular town.[29] As you would expect, social life was reduced, especially for older people. And people stopped playing so much sport. Because television is so passive, it also reduced the measured creativity of people, both young and old.[30]

Originally of course television provided a common focus for the family, when there was only one set. Then the children got their own sets, which hastened the demise of the family evening meal. As Robert Putnam argues, television must be one of the reasons for the decline of community life in the United States.

Violence and sex

But if television reduces our social life, it also widens our experience in many ways. So how does the content of television affect our feelings about life, and our behaviour? If television simply mirrored life as it is, it would be unlikely to have much effect. However, it does not simply mirror life—that would be boring. Television focuses far more on the extremes. It contains far more violence, sex and chaotic relationships than ordinary life does, and it contains far more wealth and beauty. The results of these two phenomena are different. Chaos on the screen tends to desensitise—to make people more willing to engage in violence themselves and in illicit sex. At the same time wealth and beauty create discontent with what people have—an itch to earn or steal more wealth, or to find a more beautiful partner. Let us look at the evidence.

For forty years people have argued about the effect of violence in television upon violence in real life. To me the evidence is fairly persuasive.[31] First, there are standard experiments. If you expose children to violent films, they behave more violently in the playground. These "laboratory" experiments are confirmed by real world "experiments." For example, for two days after heavyweight prizefights in the United States, there is 9% more homicide than otherwise.[32] And after a reported suicide or a suicide in a television drama, more people actually take their lives.[33]

A second approach is to trace the development of children—to measure their level of aggression when they are young, then monitor their television watching and finally remeasure their level of aggression. This shows that the more television a child watches, the more aggressive he becomes.

However, there is always the question of why some children watch more television than others, and thus of what is causing what. Ideally, we want a real-world experiment, more substantial than a prizefight or a reported suicide. Again we can look at what happened in that particular Canadian town when TV was introduced in 1973. The researchers measured the change in children's aggression in the two years that followed and compared it with the change in similar towns that already had television. This showed conclusively that the introduction of television increased aggression,[34] exactly as in Bhutan.

Interestingly, when TV was first introduced in the United States in the 1950s, it did not increase violence.[35] This was because the level of violence on TV was then very low. TV only has an effect if it shows us something different from our own experience. It now does. Television programmes now contain much more violence and more illicit sex than are contained in real life. As a result people who watch more television believe there is more crime in real life and more adultery than there is.[36] They become desensitised to those activities and more willing to contemplate them for themselves. In these ways television, for all its blessings, has contributed in some degree to the decline of family and community life and the increase in crime.

Wealth and beauty

Television also affects our happiness through quite another channel: by raising our standards of comparison. It affects the norms we use to judge our income — and our spouse. Without films or television, people's experience of life was largely limited to people like themselves. A weekly trip to the movies widened people's horizons — but nothing like watching twenty-five hours of television each week.

Television takes us into the parlours of millionaires. It also exaggerates the number of millionaires around the place. In 1982 nearly half of all the characters in prime-time social dramas were millionaires.[37] And while two-thirds of real Americans work in blue-collar or service jobs, only 10% of television characters do. Advertising has similar effects, showing us worlds where people tend to live better than average.[38]

Does it matter? It does. The more television people watch, the more they overestimate the affluence of other people.[39] And the lower they rate their own relative income. The result is that they are less happy. For as we have seen, happiness depends much more on how you perceive your relative income than on what your relative income actually is. Since television has a negative impact on your perceived position, it is bad for your happiness.[40]

There is also the evidence of behaviour: on one estimate an extra hour a week watching television causes you to spend an extra $4 a week—on "keeping up with the Joneses."[41] So we have surely found another clear channel through which television reduces our happiness: it reduces our happiness with our possessions.[42] This point will be self-evident to many: not without reason do consumer-product companies spend billions on television advertising.

The most impressionable viewers of advertisements are young people; it is they the advertisers target most assiduously. Because children see the same advertisements as their friends, they need the same things as one another in order to keep up. That pressure, which is deep in human nature anyway, is inevitably increased through television.

Viewing may also reduce our happiness with our bodies, and with our spouses. The psychologist Douglas Kenrick showed women a series of pictures of female models.[43] He evaluated their mood before and after they looked at the pictures. After seeing the models, the women's mood fell. So how must women's moods be affected by television? In three hours of viewing television each day you cannot fail to see a parade of beautiful women.

What about the effect on men? As part of the same series of experiments, pictures of models were shown to a sample of men. Kenrick evaluated their feelings about their wives before and after each presentation. After seeing the models, most men felt less good about their wives.[44]

Thus television creates discontent, by bombarding us with images of body shapes and riches we do not have. What a paradox! This wonderful invention of science, which brings us so much understanding and entertainment, a blessing to the old and infirm and provider of a culture that connects one person to another, is at the same time a bringer of discontent and a solvent of community life. We should not go back to a world without television, but we can surely use our television better than we do now.

Moral and Spiritual Values

If we are trying to explain our values, by far the biggest change in the twentieth century was the decline in religious belief. This was largely due to the progress of science. Before Darwin, most Westerners believed that God created the world, that he set the rules of moral conduct and that there was an afterlife in which virtue would be rewarded and sin punished. Now these are minority views, at least in Europe. Most people accept the theory of evolution by natural selection: humans, like stars, are products of the basic laws of physics. And the earth is a planet with a finite lifespan, which could well have been destroyed before humans ever existed.

As regards morality, people differ, but many people, if pushed to explain their views, consider morals to be produced by human responses to the problems of living together. They no longer consider moral principles to have divine sanction backed by the threat of eternal punishment. While traditional beliefs and practices have been more tenacious in the United States than in Europe, the changes everywhere have been profound.

They have affected both how we behave and how we feel about our lives. They are in many ways a liberation—a liberation from false guilt. But they are also an invitation to license, unless a strong social ethic replaces the old religious sanction. For some time left-wing thinking provided a social ethic for many people, especially in Europe. It said there is something greater than ourselves, which we should respect and work for. In Europe these ideas provided a breath of afterlife to the old religious notions of social obligation, and similar ideas were espoused by the right-wing European parties known as Christian Democrats. Meantime, in the United States traditional religious ideas survived much longer and were buttressed by the strong philosophy of community action for which the United States was famous.

But over the last twenty years left-wing ideas have been in retreat, and community action has plummeted in the United States. Rampant individualism has become increasingly the norm.

This movement has come mainly from the libertarian Right, but it has blended invisibly with a completely different tradition led from the Left. That is the tradition of human rights. The basic idea of equal rights derives in modern times from Protestantism, which stressed that all Christian believers are equal in the sight of God. This led eventually, through concepts of natural law and natural rights, to the introduction of democracy throughout the West, and eventually to the death of deference. Thus ended the old order in which each person had an ordained position and could expect the appropriate respect.

Today we rightly refuse all deference to inherited position. But increasingly young people have withdrawn respect from those who should normally receive it: from schoolteachers, policemen and even parents. Where once young people went directly from the care of their parents to an adult relationship with an employer, they now enter an intermediate "youth culture" unrelated to the adult world and only partly influenced by adult values. This is the result of affluence, earlier puberty and longer education. Most children emerge relatively unharmed, but many are uncertain of their role in society.

The goal of self-realisation is not enough. No society can work unless its members feel responsibilities as well as rights. This raises a fundamental question: "Why should I feel responsible for other people?" It is a totally reasonable question. Unless we can offer an answer to that question, we cannot hope to create a happier society.

Unfortunately, our current culture provides no clear answer. The decline of orthodox Christianity and then of social solidarity has left a moral vacuum. The two dominant ideas in the West are now Charles Darwin's "natural selection" and Adam Smith's "invisible hand." From Darwin's theory of evolution many people now conclude that to survive you have to be selfish and to look after No. 1: if you don't, you'll only get taken for a ride. From Adam Smith they also learn, conveniently, that even if everyone is completely selfish, things will actually turn out for the best: free contracts between independent agents will produce the greatest possible happiness.

. . .

These ideas need a direct challenge, and in the next three chapters they receive it. First, I challenge social Darwinism and show how people can cooperate in pursuit of a common good. Next, I propose "the greatest happiness" as our concept of the common good. And then I show how Smithian laissez-faire (even as modified by modern economics) is not sufficient to achieve that objective.

Can we pursue a common good?

Always go to other people's funerals —
otherwise they won't come to yours.
YOGI BERRA

I always see the other person's point of view —
it can be a damn nuisance.
MY UNCLE PIP

Two youngsters are playing in the woods. They see a bear approaching. One of them reaches for his running shoes. The other says, "Why bother? You'll never outrun the bear." The first replies, "Perhaps not, but I'll outrun you."

That is the fundamental Darwinian idea. One of the two will be eaten, and the only issue is who. There is a limited number of niches in the world, and whoever is fittest to inhabit each survives. It is a world of "zero-sum games." Resources are fixed. Either I get them or you do. But whatever we do, the total that is available cannot be changed. All our efforts will produce zero-sum change in the total. It is the war of all against all.

Some of human life is of course like that. But much of it, its better part, consists of non-zero-sum interactions between people — ones that add to the total of our well-being. (Darwin himself realised this.[1])

Some of these fruitful interactions are "arm's-length," like when I buy my groceries; these market exchanges are the subject of chapter 9. But there is another type of interaction that is more "up close" and involves direct cooperation in a common endeavour: You and I agree to pursue a common goal, even if it involves a sacrifice of short-run advantage. If human beings were not capable of this type of behaviour, there would be no point in even discussing the principles of moral action, as we shall do in chapter 8. So this chapter is a lead-in to that discussion. It is about how far people can cooperate for their common long-term benefit.

The Dilemma

In any cooperative venture my selfish interest is clear: you should do the work and I should take it easy, reaping the fruits of your labour. In other words I would like to have a "free ride." But if you also took the same approach, nothing would get done.

This dilemma has faced mankind since we first evolved in the African savannah. I should like to illustrate it by a practical story set in the savannah — because it is there that natural selection laid down the biological basis of our human nature.

One can imagine the following situation. Two of our ancestors meet and discuss a hunting expedition to kill some deer. Call these ancestors "you" and "me." The takings from the hunt will depend crucially on whether each of us plays our part. Either I can cooperate, helping to round up the deer and sharing the takings, or I can cheat, letting you do the work but then stealing the prey. You too face the same alternatives: you can cooperate or you can cheat.

If we stick together, we will get the largest catch—two deer for each of us. But if you cheat and I do not, you will get three deer, while I get nothing. The reverse applies if I cheat and you do not. Finally, if we both cheat and go off on our own, we will end up with only one deer each.

These four possibilities are shown in the following table. As you and I debate whether to go on the hunt, we know that any of these behaviours is logically possible. But before we decide about whether to go on the hunt, we obviously form a view about which behaviour is the most likely.

What do I expect? If I do not know you and have no reason to trust you, I note that, whatever I do, you do better by cheating. For as the table shows, if I cooperate, you get more by cheating (3 deer rather than 2), and if I cheat, you *also* do better by cheating

Possible outcomes of the hunt			
Behaviour		Takings (deer)	
I	You	You get	I get
Cooperate	Cooperate	2	2
Cooperate	Cheat	3	0
Cheat	Cooperate	0	3
Cheat	Cheat	1	1

(1 rather than 0). So I infer that you will cheat. For the same reason you infer that I will cheat. So each of us knows that the other will cheat, in which case the expedition will only yield us one deer each. That may well be too little to justify the effort involved.

By contrast, if we know and trust each other, we can promise to cooperate and expect to be believed. In that case it is worth our while to go on the hunt, because we will each get two deer. This will certainly be worth the effort of going on the expedition.

So if we trust each other, we have better possibilities open to us—the total take will be higher. The result of the cooperation is not zero sum; it is a win-win activity. If human beings had not been able to cooperate in this way, they would probably not have survived the rigours of the savannah—or subsequently of regions a lot colder. At best their life would have been, as Thomas Hobbes put it, "solitary, poor, nasty, brutish and short."[2] We survived because our genes gave us the ability to cooperate.

The so-called prisoner's dilemma that I have described arises constantly in human life.[3] Sometimes there is so little trust that cooperation is not achieved—consider Europe in 1914, or Palestine and Israel at the time of this writing, or the situation in many workplaces and families. But in much of life cooperation is the order of the day, and people do ignore their private short-term interest in pursuit of a common goal from which all parties gain.

Cooperation is all around us. People are trusted with money where no one can check on them. Indeed, there cannot be any complete system of checking, for who can ultimately check those who check the checkers, who check the checkers and so on?[4] So how does this miracle happen? It comes from a variety of mechanisms, some more selfish in motivation and some more altruistic. There is a spectrum, and we shall start from the selfish end.

Punishment

As Thomas Hobbes pointed out in the seventeenth century, much good behaviour occurs simply because bad behaviour is punished by the courts. The courts enforce contracts and punish crime. Social scientists differ about how far the fear of punishment controls crime, since so few criminals are caught.[5] But there is clear evidence that conviction rates do affect the volume of recorded crime,[6] and the labelling of what conduct is criminal also inspires a natural hesitation to offend.

Even so, most moral action does not arise from fear of the criminal law. So there must be voluntary ways in which people cooperate, so as to produce a decent life for all parties.

Reputation

First, there is the rational calculus that leads us to value our reputation. We know there is someone "out there" who is looking for a cooperative person with whom to achieve a win-win situation. So it pays to develop a reputation for cooperation — for team-playing and reliability. We choose not to take money from the till, because if we got caught, the news might travel and spoil our future chances of fruitful employment. In this case it is the hope of reward that makes us cooperate.

The cooperation is not of course unconditional. If someone cheats us, we hit back. That is the strategy called tit for tat. If two people repeatedly face the choices like those in the table, the best strategy is in fact tit for tat.[7] This means that I cooperate in the first round of the game, but after that I simply follow what the other person did in the previous round. If he is selfish in the first round, I act selfish in the second round and so on. People do not necessarily choose this strategy on logical grounds; they may in fact do it through instinctive reactions developed by natural selection.

So reputation-building undoubtedly explains a lot of apparently moral behaviour. It is of course a primarily selfish affair and reflects the strong element of human selfishness revealed in a host of experiments conducted by the economist Ernst Fehr and others.[8]

Approval

However, there is more to moral behaviour than purely rational calculation. By the age of two many children will run and comfort another child who is hurt.[9] People grow up in families and that is where they first learn to cooperate. The driving force here is the continual desire for approval. Children want the approval of their parents, and of other children. Parents and friends naturally approve when you are nice to them. Wanting their approval, you behave as nicely as you can manage.

This desire for approval is more than the desire for a good reputation. It reflects a desire to be in harmony with those around us.[10] (Reputation, in contrast, can be sought with quite impersonal objectives in mind.) So good behaviour is in part an expression of our sociability. We like to have good relationships, not only as a means to other ends (the rational calculus), but also for the direct satisfaction they provide.

The Sense of Fairness

Thus much of our behaviour is driven by wanting the help or good opinion of others—now or in the future. But in a world of increasing mobility, where we constantly change our associates, the force of such motives is steadily diminishing. Cooperation is bound to rely increasingly on something else: our moral sense.[11]

The clearest evidence that this exists is the help we give to people we will never meet, or never meet again. We return lost property, give money to Save the Children and dive in to save a drowning stranger. Why? It comes from the deep sense of mutuality we feel for other people, a feeling that we should treat them as we would like them to treat us. This idea of fairness is at the heart of morality.

It varies considerably across people. It is not felt by the 1% or so who are psychopathic and lack moral feeling.[12] But in every human society there are concepts of right and wrong, of fairness, of rights and obligations.[13]

Anything so universal is likely to have a genetic element that is amplified through learning. We see it in young children. First, they want everything for themselves (except for what they give away). But bit by bit they recognise the concept of the fair share, and it is only on that basis that they make a claim. Interestingly, the trait of conscientiousness has a clear genetic component, being, in the language of geneticists, 40% heritable.[14]

Behaving well can of course make you feel good. Though the philosopher Immanuel Kant believed that doing the right thing should give no pleasure, the MRI scanner shows that it does. In one experiment people were asked to play the game shown in the table on p. 97 for real money in a series of plays against the same opponent. As we have seen, cooperation is risky because the other person may cheat. But when people cooperated in response to previous cooperation by the other player, their brains lit up in the standard areas that light up as a result of a rewarding experience. And this was before they knew whether the other player would play fair at the same time and thus whether they would themselves benefit. In this sense, virtue was its own reward. So, at least sometimes, our wiring makes us feel better when we behave well.[15]

If all humans were the same, it would be easy to tell a tale of how we get our sense of fairness. For example, suppose the main problem facing humans is how to divide a daily ration between two people. What kind of humans will do the job best? Suppose both of them demand more than half. They will not be able to agree, in which case they may fight and both starve. Now along comes a type of human who each demands 40%. These people will easily agree. But then a chance mutation produces a type who each demands 45%. They will get more to eat than the more modest type of person. In evolutionary terms they will be stronger and will displace the more modest inhabitants. Eventually they in turn will be displaced by a type of human who practises 50:50. This is the most ambitious type of people who can live effectively upon the earth, and they will come to inherit it.[16] (A world peopled by such humans is called an "evolutionarily stable equilibrium," and its inhabitants are people whose "strategy" is evolutionarily stable.)

This theory is a fairly commonsense "functional" explanation of the sense of fairness, couched as it should be in the context of a theory of evolution based on natural selection. And sharing was of course critical to our early survival when supplies of food were so irregular. It is quite a good positive theory of how we got our sense of fairness. It explains why there is an element of decency and reliability in most people, a feeling that we should give as much as we take, and do as we would be done by.

However, people vary enormously in their moral sense. So don't the wicked prosper—by cheating on the rest of us? In general they do not. On average, people with a strong moral sense do better than others, even economically.[17] This is because they are more trustworthy and so get more responsibility. This only happens because trustworthy people can be recognised as such from the way they naturally behave. If they normally behave well—including to strangers—this can be seen and will attract good opportunities in life.

One key feature of good behaviour is that you stick to a bargain—if you say you will do it, you do it, even if you would later prefer to do something else. That is what we call commitment. Let us explore this idea.

Commitment

As our original hunting example illustrated, a society cannot flourish unless people can make commitments; they must keep their promises, even when it no longer suits them to do so. The law and even the need for reputation are inadequate mechanisms to enforce this. A more effective mechanism is the inner compulsion of self-respect, which is the converse of guilt.

So here is a person facing an inner struggle between the desire for immediate gratification and his long-term interest. The temptation to seek instantaneous advantage seems to be deep in our natures. There have been countless studies along the following lines. People are first asked to choose between getting £100 today and £101 in a week's time. Most choose £100 today. Then they are asked to choose between £100 three weeks hence and £101 four weeks hence. Faced with this choice, most opt for £101 four weeks later. Thus when the immediate present is at issue, people press for immediate gratification, even though when the choice lies in the future they take the more long-term view.[18] This compulsion appears to be wired into our genes, since similar choices have been offered to pigeons, rats, cats, dogs, guinea pigs and hogs, all with similar results.[19]

But the pressure to gratify immediate self-interest can be offset by a feeling that is stronger still. In almost all human decisions, emotion is a necessary ingredient.[20] To offset the pressure for immediate gratification, it may well take more than the calculation of long-term advantage. A strong moral sense can do the trick. And this feeling will on average benefit us in the long run, by making us more reliable.

People who have a moral sense can be recognised by other people—from what they do and how they look and talk. In psychological experiments with games requiring cooperation, people who are given thirty minutes beforehand to talk to other strangers are quite good at forecasting how well the others will behave when the game is played.[21] Humans are not bad at distinguishing between who can be trusted and who cannot.

Trustworthiness is crucial in any venture, and no long-term contract can flourish except on the basis of commitment to the common goal. This applies in business, in friendship or in marriage. Unfortunately, the growth of individualism has encouraged a short-term version of *contractarian* thinking, where more and more decisions are conducted on the basis of a short-term quid pro quo.[22] Even in marriage people increasingly think of bargaining as the way to make short-term decisions.

In his *Treatise on the Family*, the Nobel-laureate economist Gary Becker of the University of Chicago explained that both marriage and its continuance are determined by simple contractarian principles.[23] People get married because each of them prefers to be married to the partner than to be apart; when either partner prefers to be apart, the marriage comes to an end.

In this environment of continuous reoptimisation, it is not surprising that, as we have seen, people are less satisfied with their marriages. There is also clear evidence that when spouses arrange the details of their lives on the basis of quid pro quo, they are less satisfied with the marriage than when it is based on the concept of giving.[24] This is true for both men and women. The evidence also shows that when one spouse does something and the other spouse reciprocates, the first gets less satisfaction than when no direct reciprocation occurs.[25] This is because giving confers satisfaction, and can confer more satisfaction than taking.

Above all, we need to know that our partner has sufficient emotional commitment to the enterprise. If so, we know the partner will stick to the relationship, even when short-run advantage would say "Out." (The promises in the marriage ceremony cover *all* eventualities—in sickness and in health.) If both parties know that the other is really committed, each will invest more and the probability of success will rise.

In all walks of life, good behaviour by one person elicits good behaviour by others. An interesting illustration comes from a 1968 study in which wallets were left on sidewalks in Manhattan, with personal valuables in them plus $2 in cash and a cheque for $26.30 made out to "EMH Co." The wallets were enclosed in envelopes addressed to the owner, with a letter inside from a supposed finder. One set of supposed finders wrote glowingly about what a great pleasure it was to be able to return the wallet. Another set of supposed finders wrote complaining about the hassle involved. Of the first set of wallets (those that were paired with "generous" letters), 70% were returned intact, compared with only 10% of the second set (which had the "griping" letters). This simply illustrates how strongly people are affected by the norms of attitude and behaviour to which they are exposed.[26]

So despite our abiding selfishness, there is also a streak of goodness that makes us able to collaborate in pursuit of a common good. Yet some people say that we can only collaborate in order to fight some other group. Is this true?

Tribalism

When our Stone Age ancestors cooperated, it was often in order to defeat other clans.[27] Warfare appears to be an endemic feature of most primitive societies. As the chart shows, among many primitive peoples for whom we have records, over 20% of all male deaths happened through war.[28] By contrast, in Europe and the United States two world wars accounted for only about 2% of all male deaths in the twentieth century, even if we include the effects of wartime disease and starvation.

Thus the idea of the peaceful Noble Savage is a myth. Likewise the idea of a peaceful Merrie England in the Middle Ages. Seven hundred years ago the homicide rate in England was twenty times

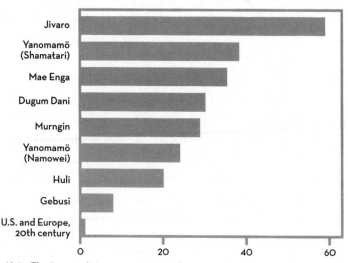

Percentage of male deaths caused by warfare

Note: The Jivaro and Yanomamö are in South America, the Murngin in Australia, and the other tribes in New Guinea.

higher than it is now.[29] So there has been progress in the range of people with whom we can cooperate peacefully.

Even so, tribalism still runs deep in our nature. A famous experiment organised by the psychologist Muzafer Sherif illustrates this. A group of eleven- and twelve-year-olds went to camp together. Originally, they were all put in one cabin and formed many good friendships there. Then they were put into two separate cabins, with most of the pairs of friends being split up. The groups from the different cabins soon began to taunt each other. They came to hate their former friends and to exaggerate the achievements of their newer friends. This process of group identification was entirely spontaneous. As time went on, rougher leaders emerged on each side. No parleys or informal meetings between members of the rival groups could break down the enmity that had developed.

Eventually, what broke the deadlock was a problem that could only be solved by both groups working together: the food truck got bogged down, and all the boys were needed to pull it out. After that the boys voted, surprisingly, to go home in the same bus together.[30] A common predicament is a great breeder of cooperation.

Thus Hobbes was wrong. It is not only the fear of higher authority that can stop us from fighting. As we have seen, many other motives besides the fear of punishment can lead to human cooperation: the desire for reputation and approval and, to a varying extent, the sense of fairness. These are motives that can lead to a widening circle of cooperation from which we can all benefit.

Most people do, after all, have a moral sense. They can detach themselves from their own interest and consider what is fair for the group as a whole. They can also widen their sense of the group to include, dare we hope, the interests of the whole human race.

So what could we do to improve our experience of life? That is the issue for the rest of this book:

- First, I define our objective: a clear concept of the common good, one that we could all accept and work for.

- Then I ask if existing economic ideas are adequate for promoting this objective.

- Next, I propose concrete public policies to increase our happiness.

- Finally, I turn to the private, inner life and ask what sources of comfort we can find to refresh and uplift our spirits.

One test of happiness is whether you feel the world is a friendly place. We need friends without, and friends inside ourselves. I shall try to deal with both of these needs.

PART II

What Can Be Done?

"Get serious, John, we're talking business ethics not ethics."

The Greatest Happiness: Is that the goal?

Create all the happiness you are able to create: remove all the misery you are able to remove.

Jeremy Bentham[1]

J eremy Bentham began life as a lawyer. But he was appalled by the lack of any rationale for the jumble of laws and punishments that then existed: a man could be hanged for stealing a sheep. Bentham insisted that all laws, and indeed all rules of morality, must be based on some unifying principle. Otherwise, how could they be consistent with one another?

As that principle, he proposed that all laws and all actions should aim at producing the greatest possible happiness. A society, he said, is good in so far as its citizens are happy. Thus a law is good if it increases the happiness of the citizens and decreases their misery; if it does not, it is bad. The same is true of the rules of morality—they should be designed to increase our overall happiness. Indeed, any decision, public or private, should be judged by its impact on the happiness of all those affected by it, each person counting equally. This is the principle of the Greatest Happiness: the right action is the one that produces the greatest overall happiness.[2]

Although this noble idea has inspired much of the social progress of the last two centuries, it has also come under serious attack. Thus, we now have a society in which there is no agreed philosophical basis for public policy or for private morality. Pragmatic policy-makers claim to be doing "what works," but works to what end? We are seriously in need of a clear concept of the good society, and of the good action.

I believe that Bentham's idea was right and that we should fearlessly adopt it and apply it to our lives. You can of course agree with much that is in this book without agreeing with Bentham. But a clear idea adds great power to a set of good intentions.

Bentham's principle involves two separate points: one about fairness and one about happiness. The idea about fairness is that everybody is equally important. I am no more important than you, and your "good" counts equally with mine. We discussed this in the last chapter. The other idea is that happiness is the ultimate good. Is it?

The Social Good

Why should we take the greatest happiness as the goal for our society? Why not some other goal—or indeed many? What about health, autonomy, accomplishment or freedom? The problem with many goals is that they often conflict, and then we have to balance one against the other. So we naturally look for one ultimate goal that enables us to judge other goals by how they contribute to it.

Happiness is that ultimate goal because, unlike all other goals, it is self-evidently good. If we are asked why happiness matters, we can give no further, external reason. It just obviously does matter.[3] As the American Declaration of Independence says, it is a "self-evident" objective.

By contrast, if I ask you why you want people to be healthier, you can probably think of reasons why—people should not be in pain, they should be able to enjoy life and so on. Similarly, if I ask you about autonomy you will point out that people feel better if they can control their own lives. Likewise, freedom is good because slavery, prison and the secret police lead to nothing but misery.

So goods like health, autonomy and freedom are "instrumental" goods—we can give further, more ultimate reasons for valuing them. And that is why we are sometimes willing to sacrifice one of these goods for the sake of another. To provide security on the streets, we lock up criminals (balancing the autonomy of the citizen against the freedom of the criminal). To reduce illiteracy, we levy taxes (balancing accomplishment against economic freedom).

To help us promote the greatest happiness, we obviously need to understand what conditions affect people's happiness, and by how much. This is now becoming possible on an empirical basis. We reviewed some evidence in chapter 5, and the Big Seven requirements there were similar to the personal "capabilities" that the Nobel laureate Amartya Sen has proposed as the goals of public policy.[4] But unless we can justify our goals by how people feel, there is a real danger of paternalism. We ought never to say: this is good for you, even though it will never make you or others feel better. On the contrary, if we want to measure the quality of life, it must be based on how people feel.

Brave New World?

But isn't there more to life than whether people feel good or bad? What about striving and aspiration? Isn't the Greatest Happiness principle an invitation to a life of pleasure, eating lotuses?[5] Actually, if everybody enjoyed eating lotuses and we could organise such a life for everyone, that would be a pretty good outcome: the miserable millions of the world would consider it a blessed delivery.

But in fact people are unlikely to be happy eating lotuses for long. As we have seen, they naturally set themselves goals that involve some challenge, and happiness depends on having goals that are sufficiently stretching but can also be accomplished. Goals give meaning to life. However, a sensible person chooses goals whose pursuit he enjoys. There is not much sense in trying to accomplish things that give no joy, and most people do not do it. Those who do end up depressed.

But what if there were a drug or a machine that could make you feel happier, even without a goal? In Aldous Huxley's *Brave New World* people take *soma* to make themselves feel better. This idea was meant to sound revolting and threatening. However, people have used drugs such as alcohol from the beginning of time. But most of the drugs we have found so far can have bad side effects. If someone finds a happiness drug without side effects, I have no doubt that most of us will sometimes use it. People argued against anaesthesia and aspirin on the grounds that they were unnatural; now everyone uses them.

What about the imaginary "happiness machine" discussed by the Harvard philosopher Robert Nozick?[6] This hypothetical machine could deliver virtual experience that would make an individual feel he was actually living an enjoyable, and therefore active, life while he was in fact inert. If offered the chance, asks Nozick, would you plug in? Of course many people would not, for all sorts of reasons. They would not trust the machine to deliver what it promised, and so they would prefer to keep their real autonomy. Or they might have obligations to others that they could not perform if they were inert. And so on. Thus it is a weak test case, especially because it describes a situation so far from our reality that we have almost become a different animal.

Private Ethics

So the greatest happiness is the right guide to public policy. It is also the proper criterion for private ethical decisions. When I am wondering what to do, I should seek the greatest happiness of everyone affected, each person's happiness counting equally. Indeed, in a democratic society where people vote on public policy, it would not be much good proposing a goal for public policy that people did not also recognise as governing their own private conduct.

Here we need a brief digression into prehistory. Obviously the rules of private moral conduct were not invented by philosophers or thinkers of any kind. We discussed in the last chapter how people acquired rules for interacting with each other, which led to the survival and growth of our species. These rules were transmitted through the interaction of our genes with social learning. Thus we developed basic rules about promise-keeping, truth-telling and consideration for others. People vary in their commitment to these principles, but much of the time we apply them without much thought.

However, there are times when we need to reflect. For example, I may have promised to go to my daughter's play, but my mother is taken to hospital. How should I use my time—to keep my promise or to show consideration to my mother? Obviously I should figure out whose feelings would be most hurt if I did not come. That is the Benthamite solution.[7]

Ethical principles have to cover much more than "don'ts." They must guide us on how to use our time and our talents. Take the huge issue of which career I should adopt. I should obviously think about what I would enjoy, but I should also think about what would make the most difference to the welfare of others. The ordinary "rules of morality" provide little guidance in such a momentous moral choice, yet this is one of the most important moral decisions anyone makes. The sin of omission can be as bad as the sin of commission.

Or take problems of family conflict and break-up. How can these be considered except in terms of the feelings and welfare of all concerned?

But why should I consider anyone's happiness but my own? This is one of the oldest questions in philosophy. At one level I would like everyone else to behave unselfishly, while behaving selfishly myself. That part of myself would like to consider only my own feelings. But I also have a moral sense that tells me I should take a wider view. I feel there are things I ought to do, and I reflect on what they are by taking the view of an "impartial spectator."[8] If I am wondering whether to do this or that, I ask which set of outcomes would appear best to someone who was neither me nor anyone else affected by my decision. This impartial spectator, being human, knows that everyone wants to be happy, and he therefore judges the two outcomes in terms of the total happiness of all those affected.

The principle of impartiality or anonymity is fundamental to all moral ideas. In a situation involving A and B, the morally correct action for A must be the same whether you are A or you are B.

It should be determined by giving equal importance to the interests of A and B. That is the golden rule of the New Testament: *Love your neighbour as yourself, and do as you would be done by.* There is to be complete symmetry.[9]

Of course some of us are more moral than others. So a realistic view of what happens is this: I do take others into account, partly out of pure selfishness (expecting them to reciprocate) and partly out of genuine sympathy, and partly out of principle. Almost no one behaves as well as the impartial spectator would prescribe. But most of us behave better than we otherwise might, because we think about moral principles. That is why these principles are so important. They can also be genuinely comforting. If I fail to get a job and it goes to another competent applicant, I can reflect that my disappointment is balanced by his rejoicing.

Such thinking goes beyond our basic animal nature, to one that is more suitable now that we are no longer struggling to survive. A happy society has to be built on two foundations: first, the greatest level of sympathy for others, and, second, the strongest moral principles of impartiality. Unless we can widen our sympathies, we may fail to advance our happiness despite our growing affluence: the cancer of envy will eat up all the gains. If we can enjoy the well-being of others, we shall all be happier. We shall help those who can most benefit, and in addition we shall gain by enjoying their success.[10] The Bible says, "It is more blessed to give than to receive," but in fact both are good.

Objections

Although the principle of the Greatest Happiness is so compelling and so widely used, it has been subject to fierce attack by philosophers, including in recent decades Amartya Sen and Bernard

Williams.[11] I have already dealt with the objection that other things matter besides happiness. But there are plenty of other objections. I believe they are misconceived.

Qualities of happiness

The first critique came from Bentham's godson, the great philosopher and economist John Stuart Mill. His father had been a protégé of Bentham, and the Mills lived for a time in the garden cottage of Bentham's London house in Queen's Square. Mill's father had high hopes for his son, both as a scholar and as a moral person, and on both scores his hopes were realised. By the age of four the young John Stuart could read Greek texts, and by his teens he had fully mastered the philosophy of the greatest happiness to which his father subscribed. Then at twenty he had a two-year-long depression, which he eventually attributed to the unfeeling content of his upbringing. In particular he came to believe there must be something wrong with the Benthamite philosophy. By the time he wrote his own book on what by then was called Utilitarianism, he felt he had pinpointed the problem. There are, he said, higher and lower forms of happiness: otherwise we should have to believe that a satisfied fool was in a better condition than a dissatisfied Socrates.

This conclusion is wrong. In his own life the satisfied fool would indeed account for more happiness than a dissatisfied Socrates. But we also have to allow for the results of Socrates' work—and the millions of other people whose happiness it has increased. There are many heroes who have suffered that others might benefit. Of course the scale of those benefits is difficult to evaluate, but it is those benefits that justify the actions. The suffering *in itself* ought not to be considered a good.

The paradox of happiness

A second argument is that the pursuit of happiness is self-defeating: the only way to become happy is to do something else—happiness is a by-product.[12] Thus, it is argued, the principle of the Greatest Happiness involves an internal contradiction: the so-called paradox of happiness.

There is an important psychological insight here. For most of our working lives we are pursuing particular projects—walking in the country, plying our trade, playing squash, eating, making love. We are not explicitly trying to be happy. Yet we do most of these things either because we enjoy them at the time or because they provide us with the indirect means of obtaining enjoyment (by, for example, not starving to death)—or because we believe they help others. We often do things we would rather not do, but we do them for the sake of some future good. Most people would like to do less work than they do, but the extra earnings buy them other sources of satisfaction. So there is nothing wrong in the notion that people want to be happy, and that life is in many ways a quest for activities that give more satisfaction. In a properly educated world these activities include pursuing the happiness of others.

Consequentialism

Another criticism is that the Greatest Happiness principle only takes into account the consequences of actions and ignores the nature of the action itself. It thus sacrifices the means to the end.

This is a simple misunderstanding. If I decide to do something, everything that follows is a consequence, including the action itself. For example, suppose I am an employer who is worrying about whether to sack someone. The act of sacking someone has a special quality—a massive exercise of power of one person over another. I would rather avoid it. But when I decide what to do, I include that aspect in my evaluation, as well as the effects on the employee and upon the operation of the business. I do consider the means as well as the end.

Some people argue that consequentialism involves an infinite regress, since the immediate consequences have further consequences and so on. The ultimate consequences are thus infinitely far ahead. This is an absurd line of argument. The relevant consequences of an action are the changes in human happiness, beginning from the moment the action is taken. These changes continue on into the infinite future, with increasing uncertainty the further ahead we look. Forecasting is of course difficult in ethical decisions as it is in business decisions. This is no argument against forecasting, but clearly we should give special weight to the earlier and more forecastable results. In fact it is difficult to see how any responsible person could take a decision that was not based upon its consequences.[13]

Adaptation

Another objection: human beings adapt. To an extent, they adapt to poverty and oppression. Thus some who fight for human rights oppose the Greatest Happiness principle because they think it too easily accepts poverty.[14] On the contrary, adaptation is even greater on the upside and explains why the rich gain so little from their extra wealth. Moreover, as we have seen, the gains to the rich can be directly compared with the greater gains which the poor would experience if the money were spread more widely. It is precisely this comparison that provides the strongest argument we have in favour of redistribution.[15] So the principle of Greatest Happiness is inherently pro-poor. It would be unlikely to support tax-cutting in the United States.

In fact if people did not dislike being poor or oppressed, would we worry about poverty and oppression? But they do dislike it. American slaves wanted their freedom, not because it would give them higher incomes,[16] but because of the humiliation of being a slave. Slavery offended their feelings, and that is why slavery is wrong. Ethical theory should surely focus on what people feel, rather than on what other people think is good for them. If we accept the Marxist idea of "false consciousness," we play God and decide what is good for others, even if they will never feel it to be so.

Instead, we should try to discover what people cannot adapt to, and what they can adapt to. We ought to be specially concerned about those misfortunes to which it is difficult to adapt. For example, persistent mental illness is impossible to adapt to. But most people adapt quite well if taxed to help the mentally ill.

Fairness

According to the Greatest Happiness principle, the only thing that matters is the feelings of everyone concerned. But how should we weigh the happiness of the different people involved? Bentham believed that all should be considered equally, and so we should simply add up the happiness of all concerned. If one policy produces more total happiness than another, it is better.

In one sense this is fair: a change in each person's happiness counts equally, whoever he is. In another sense it is not fair. For suppose there was a new policy that would affect two people, one of whom was already happy while the other was miserable, and this new policy would make the happy person happier and the miserable person even less happy. Provided the gain to the happy person was bigger than the loss to the person who was miserable, Bentham would approve the policy.

But this seems too extreme. The impartial spectator would surely care more about what happened to the miserable person than to the person who was already happy. He would therefore give a different "weight" to changes in happiness according to how happy the person was already. But how much extra weight? That is a value judgement.[17] Until recently it was pretty artificial to discuss these issues, since there was no way of measuring the changes in happiness in the first place. But this is now beginning to be possible. So the time is ripe for a serious debate on the "weights" to be given to changes in happiness when people differ in their existing level of happiness.[18]

From these considerations we conclude that it is more important to reduce suffering than to generate extreme happiness. Another reason for the same conclusion is that we understand better what causes misery than what causes extreme happiness.[19]

Oppression is one of the most potent sources of misery. Consequently, the Greatest Happiness principle would strongly condemn the oppression of any group or individual.[20]

Expediency

But the Greatest Happiness principle is sometime criticized on the grounds that it puts expediency above rules—for example, that it allows the killing of an innocent person as an example to others. The criticism is wrong. A happy society has to live by rules—sparing the innocent, telling the truth, keeping promises and so on. People need to honour those principles and to find it repugnant to break them. But sometimes the rules conflict, and then the

Greatest Happiness principle has to decide which particular action is best.

So the Greatest Happiness principle involves a two-stage approach[21]—first to help us choose the "rules," and then to help us choose the "action" when the rules conflict. But rules are crucial.

Rights

That is why it is so important that basic rights are well defined and well entrenched in the constitution and laws of a country. Any human right has to be justified as a way of preventing suffering (or promoting happiness). To become a right it has then to be enshrined in a law.[22] All the basic human rights, like equality before the law, freedom from arbitrary arrest, rights at work and so on, can be justified in this way.

The constitution and laws we live with are crucial to our happiness. They have to be justified by the Greatest Happiness principle, but once established they should not normally be broken, even if that would sometimes produce more happiness in the short run. For it would undermine the longer-term gain we derive from having these laws.

Constitutions and political processes are so important that some thinkers have argued that the main role of the Greatest Happiness principle is to help us devise the best constitution: after that we should just accept whatever policies the political system delivers.[23] This would be a great error. There is a crucial role for public debate about which specific policies are best, and this debate too should be guided by the principle of the Greatest Happiness. The analysis is always difficult, but it will become easier as our knowledge progresses. To proceed in any other way could only lead to worse, more ill-informed decisions.

An Overarching Principle

So we come back to the central idea of a humane ethic that values what people want for themselves, for their children and for their fellow citizens. And that is their happiness. It is of course impossible to evaluate all the ways in which our actions affect happiness. That is why we have rules that we follow much of the time without even thinking about them—truth-telling, promise-keeping, kindness and so on. But we desperately need a single overarching principle, for at least three reasons.

First, there may be a *conflict between the rules.* If a Nazi stormtrooper asks us where we think a Jew is hiding, we would surely invent a plausible lie.

Second, we need to be able to *review the rules.* Thomas Jefferson's rules of thumb permitted slavery. More detached analysis of what slavery involves rules it out. Moreover, as facts change, so should the rules. But that is not moral relativism. The unchanging objective should be the greatest happiness, whatever the circumstances. Other moral philosophies are far more liable to change over time.

Third, there are many major choices where *rules provide little guidance.* There are public choices like how to treat criminals, or how to solve traffic problems. Simple appeals to principles of freedom or loving-kindness will help little here. There are private choices too, like what career to pursue or how to spend one's money. The answer can only be found from the overarching objective of maximising human happiness. By contrast, most moral codes are much stronger on don'ts than on do's. They are not good at preventing sins of omission.

None of us can take responsibility for the whole human race—

we do not have the knowledge, nor will we get the same happiness ourselves from helping an unknown stranger as from helping our children. Thus charity begins at home. But as knowledge expands and morality progresses, it should embrace an ever widening circle.[24]

Nevertheless, some people still argue that, rather than look for a clear philosophy, we should just stick with our various different moral intuitions. I answer thus. That was not the way we progressed in our understanding of nature. We were dissatisfied with our partial, intuitive concepts of causality. We sought desperately for a unified theory that could cover all kinds of disparate phenomena—the fall of the apple *and* the rotation of the moon.[25] Similarly, we can make moral progress by searching for an overarching moral principle, and working out its implications. Our understanding will never be exact, like the laws of physics, but there is no other way to progress. And I do believe that progress is possible.[26]

In the West we have a society that is probably as happy as any there has ever been.[27] But as we have seen, there is a danger that me-first may pollute our way of life, now that divine punishment no longer provides a general sanction for morality. If that happens, we shall all be less happy. So we do need a clear philosophy. The obvious aim is the greatest happiness of all. If we all really pursued that, we should all be less selfish, and we should also be happier.

So my argument is this. People want to be happy. But we also have a moral sense, which tells us to consider other people as well as ourselves. Our reason helps us think how to do this, so that we come to value the happiness of everyone equally. That should be the rule for private behaviour and for public choice. We shall not always do what is right, but if everyone tries to, we shall end up happier. Bully for Bentham, I say.[28]

"There, there it is again—the invisible hand of the marketplace giving us the finger."

Does economics
have a clue?

Economists are like computers.
They need to have facts punched into them.
KENNETH BOULDING

So how then should our social life be organised to make us happy? Can economics help? Standard economics favours the market economy because it is efficient. Economic theory predicted the failure of Communism, and it proved right. Moreover, when it comes to government activity, economics offers the sophisticated tool of cost-benefit analysis to tell us what government should and should not do. So does economics have the answer?

Yes and no. The framework is terrific. We start from the individuals and their wants. Then we have the market where they interact — and where their wants get satisfied, either more or less. What is wrong is the theory of human nature, which is largely based on an outdated version of behaviourism.

Behaviourism says that we can never know what people are feeling: we can only watch how they behave. In the middle of the last century its dominant figure was B. F. Skinner of Harvard University, he of the Skinner box in which he tested the conditioned reflexes of rats. The story is told that when he was teaching, Skinner used to walk back and forth along the lecture platform. Applying his ideas, the students agreed that whenever he walked to the left of the platform, they would look down and frown, and whenever he went to the right, they would look up and smile. After a short time they had him falling off the right-hand end of the platform.

One up for behaviourism. But if we cannot know what people feel, we cannot organise things so that they are happy. Fortunately, psychology has now returned to the study of feelings. But psychology lacks the comprehensive framework for policy analysis that economics provides. So in this chapter I want to look at the strength and weakness of economics and show how economics could help us much more if it incorporated the findings of modern psychology.

Voluntary Exchange

We can start with the existing economic theory of the free market. A free market works through voluntary exchange. The simplest case is barter. I have bread but no jam, and you have jam but no bread. I swap some of my bread for some of your jam. We are both better off, for otherwise we would not have agreed to the swap. We have both experienced "gains from trade." These can occur between individuals and also of course between countries.

Today most exchange is for money, but the principle is the

same. I work for you because it makes both of us better off. You sell the output to your customers, again because it makes both parties better off. It is a win-win situation.

All this comes about through the naked pursuit of self-interest. The famous words of Adam Smith cannot be quoted too often:

> It is not from the benevolence of the butcher, the brewer, or the baker that we expect our dinner, but from their regard to their own interest. We address ourselves not to their humanity, but to their self-love, and never talk to them of our own necessities, but of their advantage.[1]

This is not cooperation of the kind we talked about in chapter 7. It is an arm's-length arrangement that has its own way of working in a completely impersonal way.

Such exchanges are the central feature of any free market economy. A person brings to the market whatever talents or wealth he has and exchanges them for something he wants more.

Efficiency

The result is marvellously efficient. Every exchange that can benefit those concerned will happen automatically—provided the market is truly "free." So all the possible "gains from trade" will be realised. After that it would only be possible for someone to benefit at the expense of someone else. All obvious waste has been eliminated, and the situation is in that sense fully efficient.[2] It may not be a fair situation if the people started off very unequal, and it may not be a very desirable one if people have tastes which are hard to satisfy. But given people's starting points, it is efficient.

The efficiency of the free market is its enormous strength. It eliminates much of the waste that would happen under any other system. However, it is only efficient if three conditions are satisfied.

First, the market must be truly free so that new entrants can come into the market and sell at whatever price they like. Price-fixing by cartels of firms must be banned, and if there is a natural monopoly, the authorities will need to regulate it or even provide the service itself, like the police service or a local school. Between companies it is competition that we need, not cooperation— competition which also provides the spur to innovation, cost-saving and customer care.

Next, buyers and sellers must have the same information about what is being sold. If the buyer is ill-informed through no fault of his own, he needs consumer protection.

Finally, and crucial to our argument, voluntary exchange works well if each deal affects only the parties to the exchange. If a deal affects other parties adversely, there may in fact be net losses to society as a whole even though there are gains to the parties involved in the deal. The classic example is the factory chimney. A mill owner produces cloth or steel that he sells to a willing buyer, but in the process he belches out filthy smoke on the surrounding residents. In economic jargon this is an "external effect" or "externality." When the mill owner laid his production plan, he calculated his own receipts and costs, but he did not take into account the costs he imposed on the unfortunate neighbours. So he almost certainly produced too much smoke. To make his plans efficient, we must tax him for the costs that his smoke creates. He will then "internalise" these costs and treat them as his own. A cruder alternative is to regulate his smoke emissions.

Externalities are pervasive in our social life: when my colleague is given a raise, this affects me even though I am not a party to the exchange. In principle, economics can allow for all these interactions to be taken into account, but in practice it allows for very few of them. We shall come back to this.

Cost-Benefit Analysis

But first we need to explore a second strength of economics: cost-benefit analysis.[3] Because of the limitations of voluntary exchange, we have public policies about most areas of our life: defence, law and order, education, health, transport, the environment and so on. To help us think about these policies, economists offer cost-benefit analysis. Change the policy, they say, if the benefits of doing so exceed the costs; if they don't, stay put.

But how to measure the benefits and costs? To answer this we have to start with an individual engaged in voluntary exchange. Suppose he is considering buying something that costs $10. If he is willing to pay up to $12, he will buy it. He is in effect comparing the benefits with the costs, and the benefits are measured by how much he is willing to pay—$12 in this case. So the basic concept of economic benefit is "willingness-to-pay."

Now suppose the government is thinking of building a new freeway above an urban ghetto. The planners will list the benefits and costs—the benefits to drivers, the environmental costs to the inhabitants of the ghetto and the cost of constructing the freeway. They will measure the benefits to drivers by calculating how much they would be willing to pay for the quicker journey. They will measure the costs to the ghetto dwellers by how much they would be willing to pay to prevent the freeway from being built. And the costs of construction will be the taxes needed to pay for building the freeway. (Of course some ghetto dwellers are also taxpayers and some are drivers, but here we are looking at people in terms of their roles.)

Next the planners will add up all the estimated benefits and costs. If the benefits are greater than the costs, they will decide in favour of the freeway; it is efficient, they will claim, to build it.

What makes them say this? Their answer is that the gainers are gaining more than the losers are losing and therefore they could easily compensate the losers and still be better off themselves. Thus, as a result of the project, it would be possible for some people to gain while no one lost. This, they say, is a gain in efficiency, and not to do it is a waste.[4]

But wait a moment. Suppose the ghetto dwellers and the taxpayers were not *in fact* compensated. Then the project would have generated some gainers *and* some losers. This could not be called an improvement in efficiency, for the only test that has been passed involves *hypothetical* compensation, not actual compensation.

So what has gone wrong in the reasoning? The original idea was excellent: in making decisions, we ought to compare the benefits and costs. But these benefits and costs ought to be measured in terms of happiness as Bentham proposed. Using money is no adequate substitute, for, as we have seen, money matters more to some people than to others. So we need to know who the gainers and losers are, in order to know how much money matters to them. We can then follow a two-stage approach: first calculating for each group the changes in terms of their "willingness-to-pay," and then weighting these changes by how much money matters to each group. (In addition, we should give particular weight to changes in happiness affecting the most miserable people.)

This approach points the way to a better cost-benefit analysis that builds on the old approach but uses the new psychology to do it better—rather than cribbing the Benthamite idea and then perverting it.

The National Income: A Sorry Tale

This brings us to the question of the proper measure of national welfare. Clearly, we need to measure the average happiness of the population (adjusted to give extra weight to the least happy).[5]

Instead of this, governments currently focus on the national income, or gross national product (GNP), in which everybody's dollar counts equally. The concept was developed in the 1930s for a very good purpose—to help think about fluctuations in unemployment, and it has been crucial in the effort to control boom and bust. But very quickly it got hijacked to become a measure of national welfare, and nations now jostle for position in the national income stakes.

This hijacking was inevitable once economics had been captured by behaviourism in the 1930s. It is actually a rather sorry tale. In the late nineteenth century most English economists thought that economics was about happiness.[6] They thought of a person's happiness as in principle measurable, like temperature,[7] and they thought we could compare one person's happiness with another's. They also assumed that extra income brought less and less extra happiness as a person got richer.

Their system was not fully operational, but it was a forward-looking agenda. It was also in tune with late nineteenth century psychology like that of William James, who was actively studying the strength of human feelings. Then psychology turned behaviourist. Along came John Watson and Ivan Pavlov (followed by Skinner), who argued that we can never know other people's feelings, and all we can do is to study their behaviour.

So behaviourism became the intellectual climate, and in the 1930s it took over economics.[8] This led to a much narrower concept of happiness. For if all we care about is a person's behaviour, this depends simply on which situations are available and which of those situations a person likes best. It is unaffected by how intensely he prefers one situation to another.[9] Since he will always choose the most preferred situation open to him, we can infer his preferences from his behaviour. But we can say nothing about how intense these preferences are, or how happy he is with what he obtains.

How does this lead to national income as a measure of national welfare? There are two steps. First, the individual. We assume that his preferences do not change over time. So if he can now consume more than before, he must be better off. We do not know how much better off, but better off he must be. That is all we can derive from the measure of income. Second, the group of individuals. How can we compare one person's rise in income with another's fall? You might think that on behaviourist assumptions, it was impossible. But no. The hypothetical compensation test appears as a magic wand, and tells us that national welfare has indeed increased if the gainers could compensate the losers—in other words, if national income has increased.

It is all very distressing. Let me hasten to say that most economists recognise some weaknesses in the GNP as a welfare measure. Most obviously, some nations choose to work longer hours than others. For example, hourly wages are currently the same in Germany and in the United States, but Americans choose to work much longer hours. Accordingly, national income per head is higher in the United States. However, most good economists would say that true income is the same in both countries since their purchasing power (over goods *and* leisure) is the same. Similarly, economists have tried to allow for environmental quality as well as leisure in a better measure of national income.[10]

But the real problems with economics are much more profound. They arise because economists have no interest in how happy people are and focus instead on their combined purchasing power, assuming their preferences are constant over time. Instead, we need a new economics that collaborates with the new psychology. There are at least five main features of human nature that must somehow be included in this new vision of how our well-being is generated.[11]

- **Inequality.** Extra income matters more to poor people than to rich.

- **External effects.** Other people affect us indirectly and not only through exchange.

- **Values.** Our norms and values change in response to external influences.

- **Loss-aversion.** We hate loss more than we value gain.

- **Inconsistent behaviour.** We behave inconsistently in many ways.

Inequality

I take inequality first, because it is the area where economists are already the most active. (Indeed, there is an army of them studying why so many people live below the poverty line.) But what if raising up the poor means bringing down the rich, so that they lose more in dollars than the poor gain? What metric can we use to value the gains of the poor compared with the losses of the rich?

The question has already been answered in theory by a brilliant group of economists in the 1960s, including the Nobel Prize winners James Meade, James Mirrlees and Amartya Sen.[12] They start from the point that an extra dollar gives more happiness to the poor than to the rich. So we should tax the rich for the benefit of the poor. But as we do this, we blunt the incentives facing both rich and poor. Thus, as we raise the tax rate, the total size of the cake falls. So we should stop raising the tax rate well before we reach complete equality. The optimum is where the gains from further redistribution are just outweighed by the losses from the shrinking of the cake.[13]

This type of analysis has been applied in many contexts and even in some cost-benefit analysis. However, it has never entered mainstream economic practice, because these brilliant economists never commissioned any empirical work to discover the speed at which the value of an extra dollar falls as a person gets richer.

Modern psychology is now beginning to make this possible. To get good evidence will take time. In the meantime we really must treat the dollars of rich and poor as of different value—using a range of possible ratios.

Against this you often hear the following argument. We should never pass up an opportunity to increase GNP because once we have got the maximum GNP, we can always redistribute it. This argument, often put by economists, misses the whole point: it *is* costly to redistribute the GNP—the more we do so, the more the GNP falls, owing to blunted incentives. The pie shrinks as it becomes more equally distributed. At some point this efficiency cost of further redistribution will outweigh the gain in fairness. At this point, we should stop any further equalisation, even though the rich man's dollar is still less valuable than the poor man's dollar.[14]

It is against that background that cost-benefit analysis of other government policies has to be done. Hence in doing it we should assign a lower value to monetary gains and losses accruing to the rich, and a higher value to equal gains and losses accruing to the poor. If we then analysed all the possible policy changes one by one, we could ultimately arrive at the best overall outcome, given our initial resources.[15]

A good proportion of economists would agree with this approach in principle (even though it is rarely practised); and these issues are much discussed. Much less are the next two, which I consider fundamental.

External Effects

External effects are everywhere. Almost every major transaction we make affects other people who are not a party to the transaction. When someone buys a Lexus, he sets a new standard for the street. When a firm advertises a Barbie doll, it creates a want that was not there before. If we take our Big Seven factors affecting happiness, each of them is profoundly affected by the behaviour of other people.

That will be the theme of the next two chapters, which document the main challenges to current economic thinking. This chapter provides a preview. Here are some examples of external effects.

Income. If other people's income increases, I become less satisfied with my own income.

Work. If my friend receives a performance bonus, I feel I should have one too.

Family life. If divorce becomes more common, I feel less secure.

Community. If a transient population moves into my neighbourhood, I am more likely to be mugged.

Health. If more social networks form in my neighbourhood, I am less likely to become depressed.

Freedom. If people cannot speak their mind, I am impoverished.

Values. If other people become more selfish, my life becomes harder.

These examples may seem rather obvious, even banal. But such interactions are rarely considered when economic policy is at issue. Take as an example geographic mobility. Every government has an attitude to this and it is reflected in land-use planning, the distribution of central-government money to regions, the promotion of regional development agencies and so on. In recent years the general message from bodies like the Organisation for Economic Cooperation and Development (OECD) has been that workers should move more.

How would this score in relation to the Big Seven? It would certainly increase income, because people generally move from lower to higher incomes. But as we shall see, it would tend to destabilise the life of the community and family life. It would probably increase mental illness and would reduce the level of interpersonal trust. Economists do not consider these factors, because they have no expertise in them. Nevertheless, they still advocate more mobility.

Forming Our Values

Economists are especially cavalier about the formation of our values—or what they call tastes. By values I precisely mean that: which things and activities we value, and how much happiness each combination of them would give us.

Economists prefer to assume that values are universal and unchanging.[16] For if values were constant, changes in people's behaviour could be explained entirely by changes in their income or in the cost of different alternatives. It is a neat application of Ockham's razor: you reduce to the minimum possible the list of factors you consider. In many cases the approach works quite well.

But it does not even explain all behaviour: fashions change and so do moral codes. More important, it does not explain happiness. If someone could buy the same standard of living as his parents, we cannot assume that he would get the same happiness from it. In fact our evidence shows that he would generally get less happiness, because he expected a better standard of living.

This is illustrated in the following diagram. The traditional economist's view of the world is in the top half of the figure, and the new psychological view in the bottom. In the psychologist's

Two views of happiness[17]

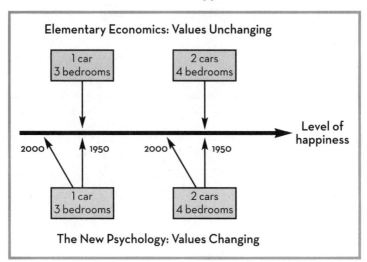

analysis, discussed in chapter 4, the same standard of living gives less satisfaction in 2000 than in 1950.

In the following chapters we shall investigate a whole range of factors that influences how happy a person is with a given standard of living. One factor is the salience he attaches to social comparisons. This is partly a matter of personal philosophy, but it is heavily influenced by the ethics of the society and by its reward system.[18] For example, if there is performance-related pay and everyone is ranked publicly against their colleagues, this makes people conscious of those comparisons for more of the time. It may also undermine the pleasure that a person derives from doing his job well for its own sake. Similarly, within a profession the existence of prizes (like the Nobel Prize) increases the comparative element in a person's self-evaluation. The number of rankings we create in our world is a matter of social choice, yielding benefits and costs that are discussed in the next chapter.

Another issue is the value we attach to money. When designing an organisation, economists almost automatically focus on "external" financial rewards, ignoring the role of "internal" rewards from a job well done.[19] This often leads to absurdly elaborate contracts that try to specify in advance exactly what the contractor should do in every possible circumstance. (This can happen whether the contractor is a chief executive officer or an outside company.) But even if you write a very detailed contract, you may need a third party to adjudicate on whether the contract has been performed. And how do you trust *that* person to do it right?[20] We get into an infinite regress, with growing numbers of accountants and lawyers. In the end no contract can cover all the eventualities, and at some point we have to rely on the contractor's professional pride.

Moreover, as we shall see, excessive focus on financial rewards can undermine that very professional pride.[21] It can also reduce happiness—the people who care most about money are less happy with a given amount of it than other people are.[22]

Economists do not of course believe in "homo economicus"—that a person will work for money until he can work no more. In fact most economists could earn a lot more doing something else; they value plenty of things besides money. Even so, they have a special competence when talking about money. So they generally think in terms of financial rewards. They also have great public influence and have thus inevitably helped to promote the public esteem in which money is held.

Then there is the issue of altruism. My celebrated economics tutor was always warning me against the pitfalls of do-goodery. Yet the happiness of a society is likely to increase the more people care about other people. If we get more happiness from the well-being of others, we shall do more to promote it and in turn benefit from their greater happiness.[23] This is profoundly important. Again it is not inconsistent with sophisticated economics, but if economists overextol the successes of selfishness, they are not likely to promote a happy society.[24]

Hence we need a fundamental reform: we have to implant the substantive findings of psychology into the framework of economics. And the most important new findings are those on external effects and the formation of values.

Loss-Aversion

There is another inconvenient fact about human nature, as we shall see: people hate a loss more than they value an equal gain.[25]

On average, if someone loses £100, his mood worsens twice as much as it would improve if he gained £100. That is why people are so averse to risky investments unless the financial gain from taking on the risk is likely to be substantial.

Loss-aversion is contrary to standard economic theory, which implies that if the stakes are small enough, people do not care about risk.[26] But the implications of loss-aversion go much wider, for people really dislike loss of any kind. This becomes critical when considering an economic reform. In the 1930s mass unemployment caused little political protest in Britain. But massive protests arose when the government rationalised the unemployment benefit system in a way that helped most unemployed people but hurt a few of them.[27] Even today there are many reorganisations that are good for average performance, but because of their impact on the losers they cause more misery than they remove. Politicians are generally more sensitive to these issues than economists, since they often know more about human nature.

Should we therefore avoid change? In any reform there will almost always be some losers, and in the short term they will suffer a lot. But after a while they will largely adapt. If the benefits of the reform will persist for many years, the short-term pain for the few may be justified by the long-term gain to the many. However, this would not happen if the reform were to be followed quite soon by yet another reform. We should therefore question policies of continuous change, since they involve repeated losses: the focus should be on finding policies that can last.

Inconsistent Behaviour

I have left to the last the problems caused by inconsistent behaviour,[28] which have been the main focus of "behavioural economics." These come from

- failures to forecast your future feelings

- ill-informed behaviour towards risk

- simple innumeracy

We have already seen how people fail to forecast the process of adaptation—they think the new house will make them happier forever, rather than just for a year or two.[29] A related forecasting failure comes from addiction to smoking, drugs, alcohol or gambling: when you start, you do not realise how difficult it can be to stop. With any bad habit, people often plan to give it up next month and then, when next month comes, they plan to give it up the following month. They are gripped by the desire for immediate gratification that blinds them to the fact that the same thing will be true next time round as well.[30]

In all these failures people are making themselves less happy in life than they could be. So there is a natural issue of whether society as a whole could help, even though it might of course involve paternalism.

A second inconsistency occurs in relation to risk. Loss-aversion is not inconsistent: it reflects precisely how people would feel if the bad outcome happened. But people have a very bad habit of underestimating the seriousness of really bad things that might happen. This appears from many experiments where people prefer to risk quite high probabilities of large losses in order to avoid the certainty of much smaller losses. As Daniel Ellsberg, who released the *Pentagon Papers* in 1971, has pointed out,[31] this is exactly what President Lyndon Johnson did in the Vietnam War. In 1965 Deputy Secretary of State George Ball made it clear to Johnson that although there was a small chance of success if he continued the war, there was a large chance of losing, with expected losses of around fifty thousand men. To avoid the certainty of being called bad names if he got out, Johnson took the risk of continuing. The losses were around fifty thousand.

People also tend to exaggerate small probabilities, which is the origin of many of the health scares to which modern society is prey. None of this is very surprising, for most people have a poor appreciation of any numerical magnitude. For example, people have been asked how much extra they would pay in taxes if this would reduce the number of road deaths by different amounts. In order to save three times as many lives, the average respondent was only willing to pay one-third more money.[32] Moreover, people's guesses about numbers are often based on quite irrelevant things. For example, a sample of people were asked first their Social Security number and then how many doctors there were in California. It turned out that on average the higher a person's Social Security number, the higher the number of doctors he thought there were in California. This illustrates the influence of the "frame" within which a question is considered.

How should these inconsistencies in human judgements and behaviour affect the way we view the economy? They suggest there are some crazy elements in what goes on, but often this has no clear policy implication because the direction in which it biases behaviour is not clear. Perhaps the main conclusion is this: that people may quite sensibly decide not to make every big decision for themselves but to hand some decisions over to experts or to the government, depending on whom they trust.

Where Next?

In public policy circles the economist is, to a large extent, king. Is this a good thing? The strength of economics is that it starts from the idea of people as self-determining agents. No reasonable analysis of what society we want should start anywhere else. Economics also provides a good general framework for policy analysis, by attempting to calculate and compare all the costs and benefits. However, the economic model of human nature is far too limited — it has to be combined with knowledge from the other social sciences.

So sensible policy development is quite difficult. How much easier it would be, for example, if economic policy affected income only, with no effect on family life. It could then be safely left to traditionally minded economists, and family life could be left to experts on the family, and so on. Such a nice convenient world is shown in the first diagram below.

Alas, it is not the world we live in. Almost every policy affects happiness through many channels. An example is our approach to geographical mobility, which we discussed earlier and is illustrated in the second diagram. More mobility increases income, so economists tend to favour it. But it may also undermine family life and the safety of our streets, as well as altering our values. All these factors need to be weighed against each other; the different experts need to put their heads together.

We need a revolution in academia, with every social science attempting to understand the causes of happiness. We also need a

The policy-makers' ideal world

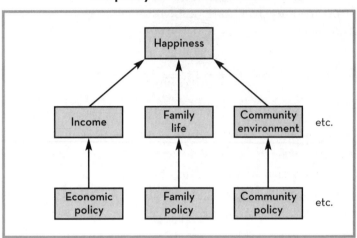

Reality

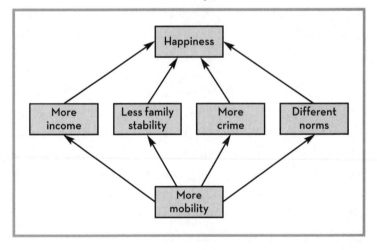

revolution in government. Happiness should become the goal of policy, and the progress of national happiness should be measured and analysed as closely as the growth of GNP.[33]

Plenty of evidence is available already on how to make good policy. We review it in the next two chapters, beginning with the problem of the rat race.

"I feel so good today I could almost turn down a tax cut."

How can we tame
the rat race?

What is this life if, full of care,
We have no time to stand and stare?
W. H. DAVIES[1]

We all want status—or at least respect. It is wired into
our genes and is a major source of satisfaction if we
get it. We know this from the remarkable studies of
vervet monkeys by Michael McGuire and his colleagues at
UCLA.[2] Their method was to manipulate the status of a male monkey by moving him from one group of monkeys to another. In each
situation they measured the monkey's level of serotonin, a neurotransmitter connected with feeling good. The finding was striking—the higher the monkey's position in the hierarchy, the better
the monkey feels.

When a monkey beats off his rivals, he not only gets more
mates and more bananas, he also gets a direct reward: being top

makes him feel great. This is a powerful motivator. So monkeys with the strongest desire for status get the most sex and therefore produce the most offspring. In this way the desire for status has got spread throughout the monkey population.[3]

If monkeys enjoy status, so do human beings. We want status not only for what else it makes possible, but also for itself. We hate falling short of others, and we like to excel. We want to entertain other people as well as they entertain us, and we want our children to have the things their friends have. These are not ignoble sentiments of envy; the desire for status is basic to our human nature.

You can see how important it is by looking at its effect on physical health. When monkeys are put in different groups so that their rank changes, their coronary arteries clog up more slowly the higher their rank.[4] Similarly, among British civil servants, those of higher rank secrete lower average levels of stress-related cortisol — one reason why they live longer. In fact people in the higher grades live on average four and a half years longer than those in the lower grades. In case you wondered, very little of this difference is due to differences in lifestyle — smoking, drinking, diet, exercise or kinds of housing. Likewise, as we have seen, Oscar winners on average live four years longer than Oscar nominees who lose.

The Race for Status

So the desire for status is utterly natural. But it creates a massive problem if we want to make people happier, for the total amount of status available is fixed. Putting it crudely, status is like the outcome of a race. There is number 1, number 2, number 3 and so on. If my score improves, someone else's deteriorates. My gain is his loss. In the jargon, we are engaged in a zero-sum game, since the sum of 1 + 2 + 3 and so on cannot be changed, however hard we try. As Gore Vidal once put it, "It is not enough to succeed; others must fail."[5]

The problem is that we all put massive effort into changing what cannot in total be changed. Thus everything we do to advantage ourselves imposes a "disbenefit" on somebody else. It is a bit like what can happen in a football stadium. Someone stands up to improve his view. This obscures someone else's view: he stands up. Eventually, everybody is standing. They all have the same view as before, but they also have the extra effort involved in standing.

Many things bring status, and money is one of them. If money was simply wanted for the sake of status, the quest for money would be totally self-defeating. For the number of ranks in the income distribution is fixed, and one person's gain would be another's loss. Fortunately, as we saw in chapter 4, people also want income for its own sake, and not only for its value relative to others'. One study quoted earlier found that people care about absolute income twice as much as they care about relative income.[6]

However, the struggle for *relative* income is totally self-defeating at the level of the society as a whole. If my income rises relative to yours, your income falls relative to mine by exactly the same amount. The whole process produces no net social gain, but may involve a massive sacrifice of private life and time with family and friends. It should be discouraged.

One solution would be a collective agreement to limit the race of all against all. Nations have sometimes agreed to abstain from fruitless arms races against each other, recognising that these are zero-sum games. So why can't people do the same? The answer is that there are just too many people to make such an agreement possible. We need to find some other way.

The Fallacy of Consumer Sovereignty

"Wait a moment," I hear you say. "Is there really a problem at all? I want my plumbing fixed, and I really don't mind whether the plumber is working to improve his status or to improve his absolute standard of living. In fact, surely the economy exists to satisfy the consumer, and it must be a good thing for the consumer if we can get people to work harder."

This is wrong, because the consumers are also the producers. If the consumers are to consume more, it is they who will have to produce it. If they work harder, they can indeed consume more but only at the sacrifice of something—their family life or their tennis or whatever. So it only makes sense for them to work harder if there is some overall net benefit. But as we have seen, people can have too great a work incentive, because one of their aims is to improve their relative income. Every time they raise their relative income (which they like), they lower the relative income of other people (which those people dislike). This is an "external disbenefit" imposed on others, a form of physical pollution.

If people do not take this pollution into account when they decide how much to work, they are behaving just like someone who stands up at a football match. The result will be too much work and a distorted work-life balance.

Taxing Pollution

At least that would be true if there were no taxes. But taxes provide a standard cure for pollution. They make it possible to charge people for the damage which they do to others—and so force them to take this damage into account. People will thus take note of external costs which they would otherwise ignore, and if the level of tax is right, the polluting activity will be cut back to the most efficient level.[7] Thus a tax on noxious emissions will reduce these emissions, and a tax on income from work will reduce work.

In both situations the tax is not distorting (by discouraging something that is desirable) but corrective (by discouraging something that is undesirable). This puts a completely new light on our existing taxes, because both economists and politicians have tended to look on taxes as distorting, even at very low levels of tax. But we have now seen that at least up to some point the taxes are performing a useful function that we were unaware of. They are helping to preserve our work-life balance.

Such thinking requires a revolution in what is called "public economics."[8] And it goes wider than that, since it provides an important new element in the case for progressive politics as such.

Libertarians object strongly to the argument. They say it panders to the ignoble sentiment of envy, which ought to be disregarded. This is an extraordinarily weak argument. Public policy has to deal with human nature as it is. The desire for status is after all ubiquitous, and we all recognise it. Greed is also common, and libertarians do not disallow it. So why should they disallow the desire for status? Both sentiments are features of human nature. We are not perfect, and public policy should help us to make the best of what we are.

I have put this pretty starkly. To avoid misunderstanding, let me stress that most people enjoy much of their work; they do not work for money alone but for comradeship and the enjoyment of work well done. Moreover, the element of struggle in a job is often about keeping it rather than making more money:[9] some of life's struggles are inevitable. But we can at least do something about the distorting effect of the struggle for status.

Taxing Addiction

There is also the distorting effect of unforeseen habituation. One reason why happiness has not risen, despite our higher standard of living, is that we get used to the higher living standard. At first, extra comfort gives extra pleasure. Then we adapt to it, and our pleasure returns towards its former level. Indeed, the pleasure is largely associated with the change in income rather than its level. To some extent it is like the classic forms of addiction, such as alcohol or drugs, where you have to increase the dosage all the time to get the same enjoyment.[10] How different these sources of pleasure are from deeper sources of satisfaction, like time with family or friends, which just keep on satisfying us.[11]

If we foresaw our habituation to income, our decisions would be undistorted by it. It would be just a fact of life, which we took into account. But in fact people who raise their style of living expect more happiness from it than they ultimately get.[12] The reason is that the new lifestyle becomes more or less a necessity—a fact which they did not fully anticipate.[13] It is like smoking. Only 32% of young people who start smoking expect to be doing it five years later. In fact 70% are still smoking. They have become addicted.

We usually deal with addictive expenditures by taxing them. We tax cigarettes heavily and rightly so. Taxes on smoking have been found to benefit potential smokers by cutting their smoking even though they pay more for what they smoke.[14] We should not hesitate to tax other unhealthy, addictive expenditures as well.

So we have two distortions that taxation can rectify: one from pollution and the other from unforeseen addiction. But how high should taxes be? The right level of tax depends on many considerations, including how much spending is justified on public services, and how much on redistribution. But if you had formed some view on this which did not allow for the arguments in this chapter and you now accept these arguments, you should revise upwards your view about tax levels.

The same point could be put in a more technical way. When economists think about taxation, they normally assume that all taxes on income or spending are distorting. This means that £1 collected in tax actually hurts more than the simple loss of £1—the difference being called the "excess burden" of the tax. This makes taxes harder to justify. However, if the tax is corrective rather than distorting, the excess burden is negative. So the case for public expenditure becomes stronger and so does the case for taxation.[15]

It would be nice to say how much stronger, but the evidence is not yet sufficiently precise. One thing is clear. We are not making a mountain out of a molehill: if extra income has done so little to produce a happier society, there must be something quite wasteful about much of it.

The findings in chapter 4 make good sense. We mentioned there some estimates of what happened to national happiness when someone earned and spent an extra pound. The earner gained in happiness. But owing to pollution, the rest of the society lost in happiness about a third of what the earner gained.[16] In addition, because of habituation, the individual himself lost in the next period about 40% of what he had gained in happiness the previous period, and much of this loss was unforeseen. These are strong negative effects. But they are surrounded with such huge margins of uncertainty that they do not yet provide an exact basis for policy.[17]

My conclusion about taxation is this. If you have not before considered the issues raised in this chapter, rethink your position. Taxes are clearly performing some useful function, beyond that of raising money to pay for public expenditure: they are holding us back from an even more fevered way of life.

If anyone replies that the average citizen should work harder, please ask him to think about it a little longer. In Europe we find it particularly irritating when American economists lecture Europeans about our shorter working week and our longer holidays. The majority of Europeans are happy with the hours they work, even though the GNP would be higher if they worked longer. A few may compare their incomes with those in America, but that is not a major problem so far.

Respect

We have talked thus far as though people mainly work for pay and status, but our motivations are much more complex than that. We also work to be respected by our fellows.

Respect is certainly given to status, but it is given to many other qualities as well. Thus a different way to deal with the status race is to increase the respect that is given to other things.[18] If the only thing we respect is status, we are in for trouble. I was shocked when I last visited the Department of Education and Skills in London and found two huge banners in the entrance hall saying, "Getting ahead." Is this really the aim of education? Instead, we should be cultivating respect for those who contribute to the welfare of others. That will increase the amount of kindness and cooperation in the world, leaving the amount of status (as it must be) unchanged. The last thing we want is to give even more attention to rankings, and that is why performance-related pay stirs up such strong feelings.

Performance-Related Pay

The idea of course is that by paying people for what they achieve, we provide the best possible system of incentives. Certainly, where we can measure people's achievement accurately, we should pay them for it—people such as travelling salesmen, or foreign exchange dealers, or racehorse jockeys.[19] Even where achievement depends on the effort of a team, we should reward the team, provided their performance can be unambiguously measured. If the team is small enough and the reward well specified in advance, peer pressure will make each person pull his weight. Going even wider, if we take a whole firm, there is much to be said for profit-sharing, which encourages workers to identify with the objectives of the firm.

But management gurus are after something more finely tuned than that. They want each individual to be paid for his specific contribution and are not happy with the older system where pay goes with the job—even though that provides quite powerful incentives to qualify for better-paid jobs. No, they want a year-by-year alignment between individual pay and performance. They rightly say that every individual should be given a clear set of goals, with an annual discussion of how he is doing.[20] But they want more than this: they want a person's pay to reflect his performance, year by year.

The problem is that in most jobs there is no objective measure of performance. People must in effect be evaluated against their peers. Even if the scores purport to be objective rather than relative, most people know how many people get each grade. The effect is to put employees into a ranking. If everybody agreed about the rankings, it would not be that bad. But studies have shown quite low correlations between one evaluator's rankings and another's.[21] Thus a lot of self-respect (and often very little pay) is being attached to an uncertain ranking process, which fundamentally alters the relationship of cooperation between an employee and his boss, and between an employee and his peers.

Is this process worth the trouble it involves? There are two main problems.

First, it gives greater salience to rank. In this sense it changes tastes in a way that is inimical to happiness. If people sacrifice more in order to improve their rank, that is a clear loss unless the gain in output outweighs the extra sacrifice. The growth of performance-related pay has been associated with a measurable increase in stress. For example, in 1996 the Eurobarometer survey asked employed people in each country whether in the last five years there had been a "significant increase in the stress involved in your job." Nearly 50% said it had increased, and under 10% said it had diminished. Figures for Britain were similar to the European average.[22] Some might argue that if you want to avoid stress, you can always change your job. That is true. But when a fashion has taken hold, it may be difficult to escape it.

Some comparisons between people are of course inevitable, since hierarchy is necessary and unavoidable. Some people get promoted and others do not. Moreover those who get promoted must be paid more, since they are talented and the employer wishes to retain them. He also uses pay as a recruiting device. So pay is important at key moments as a way of affecting people's decisions between occupations and between employers. But, fortunately, promotions and moves between employers are for most people still relatively infrequent. The associated changes in pay are not constantly salient in people's thoughts. But performance-related pay changes all that.

There is a second argument against performance-related pay. Economists and politicians have tended to assume that when financial motives for performance are increased, other motives remain the same. In fact, these motives can change, as was pointed out long ago in relation to the supply of blood.[23] Let me report three suggestive studies.

At a child care centre in Israel, some parents were often late in picking up their children, so fines were introduced for lateness. The result was a surprise: even more people were late.[24] They now felt it was all right to be late, provided that you paid for it.

In another study the psychologist Edward Deci gave puzzles to two groups of students.[25] One group he paid for each correct solution, the other he did not. After time was up, both groups were allowed to go on working. The unpaid group did much more extra work—owing to their intrinsic interest in the exercise. But for the group that had been paid, the external motivation had reduced the internal motivation that would otherwise have existed. They did half as much additional work on the puzzles.

A third example is a natural experiment in Switzerland in 1993, when two communities had been selected as potential storage sites for radioactive waste. An economist, Bruno Frey, arranged a survey of the inhabitants.[26] One group was asked, "Would you be willing to have the repository here?" Some 50% said yes. A second group was asked, "If you were offered a certain amount of compensation [which was specified], would you be willing to have the repository here?" To this second question, under 25% said yes. Focusing on financial rewards reduced people's willingness to act on the merits of the case.

Many more examples could be given.[27] So we have to consider quite seriously the argument that by upping financial incentives, we diminish a person's internal incentives to give of his best and to live up to the name of his profession. The overall effect is therefore uncertain. The professional ethic is a precious motivation that should be cherished. If we do not cultivate it, we may well not even improve performance, let alone produce workers who enjoy their work. Pay has useful effects on which careers people choose, and which employers they work for. But once someone has joined an organisation, he has peers whose respect is a powerful motivator. We should exploit this motivation.

In the light of all this it seems that governments over the last twenty years have made serious errors in their approach to the reform of public services. They have stressed ever more the need to reward individual performance, rather than providing proper pay for each grade and stressing the importance of the job and of professional norms and professional competence. It is not surprising that the reform of the public services is proving so difficult, when the wrong levers are so often pulled and the workers so often demoralised.

No sensible employer takes the tastes of his employees as given. He tries to develop their pride in their work, and their willingness to help each other. Highly tuned incentives so easily work in the opposite direction. If we want a better work-place, we should teach our children that job satisfaction comes from work well done and not from "getting ahead."[28] That approach is not "socialist": it derives rather from universal human experience.

Advertising

So values do matter. Advertising is clearly meant to change our values—how we like one product compared with another. But does the advertising experience make us happier? If advertising simply provided information, it would be hard to object. But a lot of advertising makes us feel we need something that we previously didn't need. The advertiser may have only wanted us to buy his brand rather than another. But the overall effect is to make people want more.

The most common advertising device is to show us that people of our sort have this thing—on the assumption that we will want to conform. The advert becomes a self-fulfilling prophecy. The most serious effect is on children, who put parents under intolerable pressure to buy the latest doll or the coolest make of footwear. The waste is extraordinary, and children get the idea that they need this vast array of spending just to be themselves. That is the reason why Sweden bans commercial advertising directed at children under twelve.[29] Every country should learn from this example. We should also consider stopping tax allowances for all pictorial advertising by business, since it can have such a negative effect on the happiness of those it puts pressure on.

It is sometimes said that capitalism depends on advertising to achieve full employment. According to this view, without advertisements less would be bought, and therefore there would be less work to be done.[30] This would cause unemployment. But this is a fallacy. It is true that less work would be done, but at the same time people would also *want* to do less work because they would want to buy less. So there would be no change in the balance between the demand and supply of labour. Unemployment would not rise. So advertising cannot be justified as an anti-unemployment device. If advertising lures us into an arms race of spending, we should have a serious debate about the appropriate response.

Compete or Cooperate?

At the school I went to, we sat in class according to our test results in the previous fortnight. We also ate meals and prayed in chapel in the order of our exam results in the previous term. This was clearly an excessive incentive. But should there be no use of competitions in school, and no honours?

As we have seen, a degree of rivalry is wired into our genes.

This competitive instinct enhanced our reproductive fitness in the wild. We also inherited another basic survival mechanism.[31] In the wild the people who survived were those who were not content unless they gave their all. To keep themselves up to the mark, these people used social comparisons and past achievements as norms against which to evaluate their current achievements: they were not content to achieve less than that norm.

These are genes we have inherited. This means that we are set up to be dissatisfied. But now that we have conquered scarcity, we need no longer be slaves to our nature. Centuries ago we decided to preserve the weak; we can also afford to give everyone a break from the relentless pressure to succeed. The basic problem with this pressure can be stated quite simply. Either you make it, in which case you breathe a sigh of relief—or you fail. There is no space where you can achieve your goal with ease and comfort.

A society obsessed by status is condemned to that condition. Success becomes the main object of thought and conversation: who will get what job; how much will he be paid? We have to escape that condition.

So should competition have any role? Of course it should. A degree of competition is a necessary motivator, and honours systems can be used to signal what we value. An element of competition adds interest to life, and games against other people can also be more fun than developing your skill in lonely isolation. Games are sociable, and thus consonant with our nature. Most physical sports are inherently competitive, and it is more fun to play chess against a worthy opponent than against a computer. It is also great fun to watch others competing.

Moreover, a good way to improve one's own performance is often to compare it with some benchmark. In schools and hospitals, using such measures (test scores, numbers of post-operative deaths) can be a powerful aid. But the information is much more valuable if it relates to absolute measures of your performance compared with other people's, rather than to where you rank in some order.

We are talking about a sensible balance, which means a balance that is less obsessed with rankings than at present. For our fundamental problem today is a lack of common feeling between people—the notion that life is essentially a competitive struggle. With such a philosophy the losers become alienated and a threat to the rest of us, and even the winners cannot relax in peace. Given this, it is not surprising that on many measures the Scandinavian countries are among the happiest. They do not, incidentally, have exceptionally high suicide rates,[32] but they do have the clearest concept of the common good. As the table shows, the cooperative ideology of a country does show up quite strongly in the quality of life its children experience.

Percentage of children aged eleven to fifteen agreeing that "Most of the students in my class[es] are kind and helpful"	
Switzerland	81
Sweden	77
Germany	76
Denmark	73
France	54
United States	53
Russia	46
England	43

Risk-Taking

I have focused on incentives to work. But there must also be incentives for risk-taking. When rich-country governments meet at the OECD in Paris, they always say that Europeans should be more willing to become entrepreneurs and to take risks. As I have explained, standard economic theory does not allow you to say that one set of predispositions is better than another. On that traditional basis these OECD statements are illegitimate. They are, however, easier to justify in terms of a happiness objective, where different tastes *can* be compared in terms of the resulting happiness. In this context entrepreneurs are essential.[33]

But as a society, how much risk should we expect the ordinary citizen to bear? For most people the desire for security is a central part of their nature. That is why we have social programmes and why, ever since the Second World War, governments and central banks have tried to dampen down the cycle of boom and bust. Of course there have been many bad policies—in some European countries income is still guaranteed even when people reject the work that is available.

But, what madness it is if, as we become richer, we also become less secure and more stressed. As Lord Keynes said, "We have been trained too long to strive and not to enjoy."[34] Both security and a quiet mind are goods that should increase, not decrease, as people become richer.

Yet many in the Anglo-American elites glorify change and novelty for its own sake. Nothing is good unless it is "innovative." Bureaucrats gaily reorganise the public services, oblivious of how each reorganisation destroys a major channel of personal security and trust. I believe that Anglo-Americans have a lot to learn from "old Europe," where the value of stability is better understood.

So what does affect our sense of security?

Can we afford
to be secure?

*The biggest disease today is not leprosy or
tuberculosis, but rather the feeling of being unwanted,
uncared for and deserted by everybody.*

Mother Teresa[1]

Suppose you were offered the following bet. On the toss
of a coin you would either lose £100 or gain a larger sum.
How large a sum would be necessary to make you accept
the bet?

Daniel Kahneman of Princeton University has studied how
people answer this question. (He is the only psychologist to have
won the Nobel Prize in economics.) He finds that the typical answer is around £200.[2] People need the prospect of gaining twice
£100 to outweigh an equal chance of losing £100. That shows how
strongly they dislike losing money.

In fact people dislike parting with almost anything. Kahneman has another experiment.[3] He separates students randomly into two groups. The first group is shown a particular type of mug and asked how much they would be willing to pay for it. They reply $3.50, on average. Members of the second group are each given the same type of mug and then shortly afterwards they are asked how much they would need to be paid to give it back. The answers are remarkable: $7 on average. This is totally at variance with standard economic theory, which predicts that the two numbers would be the same.

But it is clear what is happening. The members of the second group have a mug, and parting with it hurts. They have become attached to the status quo, as we always do. So parting with the mug hurts twice as much (in money terms) as gaining the mug helps. This is the same ratio as emerged from the first study I mentioned. In that case losing £100 hurt twice as much as gaining £100 helped (so that you needed £200 to level the bet). Once again, the ratio is two to one.

In fact many studies have found that a loss hurts roughly twice as much as an equal gain helps.[4] That is why people are so keen to avoid loss, and so unwilling to incur the risk of loss. This explanation of aversion to risk is much more coherent than the standard economic explanation, which generally ignores the risky element in any project where the risk is small enough.[5]

It is precisely because people hate loss that we have a social safety net, and in Europe a welfare state. People want the security that these entities provide. But that desire for security is what Ronald Reagan, Margaret Thatcher and George W. Bush have challenged. They have stressed that security can be dangerous. Of course it can be. But if security is what most of us desperately want, it should be a major goal for society. The rich have quite a lot of it and the poor less. A happy society requires a lot of it all round.

The Fallacy of Competitiveness

However, many people think we can no longer afford so much security. The reason they give is globalisation, which confronts us with competition we never experienced before. In this situation, it is said, we can no longer afford the luxury of our former lifestyle: life is bound to be tougher for everyone.

That is complete nonsense. For a country as a whole, new opportunities to trade are always an advantage. Consumers are able to import more, and at lower prices than before. Firms and workers also benefit, from improved opportunities to sell abroad. There are of course some casualties—the firms and workers who used to produce things we now import (like shirts, cars or steel) or whose exports have been undermined by new foreign competition. But the average Western citizen has gained enormously from the growth of world trade over the last half century and will continue to do so.[6]

Moreover, there has been no increase in the fraction of workers exposed to foreign competition. Manufacturing has become more exposed, but it now employs a smaller fraction of workers, owing to the growth of the service sector. So the share of trade in overall economic activity has not in fact risen that much.[7]

Contrary to common belief, there has been no increase in the rate of job destruction over the last twenty-five years in the United States or in Europe.[8] And workers' real wages have increased on average by at least 1% a year.[9] Firms have done even better, especially in Europe where the ratio of profits and rents to wages has risen from 33% in the 1970s to nearly 50% now. No sign of a profits squeeze from foreign competition!

In fact much talk of competitive challenge is talk to frighten the children—or in this case the workers. A firm must of course remain competitive in order to survive. But countries always survive through automatic processes of adjustment.[10] Thus no Western nation has to reject its former lifestyle because it can no longer afford it. We can choose any degree of security we like, but our level of pay will then inevitably reflect our choice.

That is in fact the chief lesson economics teaches here. A nation can always compete, because people will get paid according to their productivity. If we want to make people more secure, we may have to accept lower pay than otherwise. That is our choice. But in a context where living standards are rising steadily, it is no great hardship.

Nor does globalisation pose any new limits on government expenditure or labour market policies. It is of course difficult for one country to attract capital if corporate taxes are higher than those elsewhere, but most taxes come from labour, which is much less mobile. That is why many of the smallest and most open countries in Europe (the Scandinavians) have been able to continue with the highest tax rates. The European welfare state certainly needs reforming, as I shall show, but not because of globalisation. And in many cases these reforms would make people more, not less secure.

That is what they want. They want security in all the first five of our Big Seven sources of happiness: income, work, family, community and health.

Income

The two big threats to a stable income are fluctuations in employment and the coming of old age. And two of the key achievements of the modern state have been greater economic stability and better old age pensions.

Since the Second World War, fluctuations in employment

have been much smaller than in the previous hundred years. This has been partly due to state intervention—or at the very least the expectation that the state would intervene if necessary. Because of this, households and firms have had the confidence to spend.

Yet if faced with the choice between economic stability and long-run growth, some economists give great weight to long-run growth, on the grounds that a small difference in the growth rate has in due course a huge impact on living standards. On this line of thought, little harm is done by an occasional bust bringing "creative destruction" in its wake, because the long-run gain outweighs a small immediate cost. That is the view of the Nobel Prize winner Robert Lucas of the University of Chicago.[11] But modern psychology leads to a different emphasis. The short-run psychological cost of fluctuations in employment is great, while the long-run gain from growth is relatively small because the value of each extra dollar becomes smaller and smaller as people become ever richer. Fortunately, fewer politicians than economists question the value of economic stability, for it benefits both workers and employers.

However, in recent years there has begun a new debate about income in old age. Currently this income comes in most countries mainly from a state pension (or social security payment), based on previous earnings. This promise is underwritten by the ability of the state to collect contributions from existing earners.

But now some people say, "Shouldn't more income in old age come from a private pension, paid out from money invested in the stock market?" In many countries there was increasing support for this idea, until the stock market crashed in 2001. The idea now appears less attractive, and in Britain, where private pensions already provide roughly half of all income in old age, the system has proved a disaster for many investors. Both experience and happiness research confirm the wisdom of an earnings-related state pension, based on the state's capacity to collect current contributions. Those who so desire should be able to opt out of some of the contributions and related benefits. But surely everyone should be offered a chance to participate, without thinking, in an arrangement that is free of anxiety.

Work

Another key element of most people's well-being is work. Indeed, we saw in chapter 5 that unemployment is one of the worst things that can happen to anyone. In impact it is similar to marriage break-up—you cease to be needed. This psychic effect comes on top of the effect of reduced income.

Thus a key priority for any civilised society is a low level of unemployment. But how can this be achieved? In the last twenty-five years many European countries have allowed unemployment to rise to levels unknown since the 1930s and to remain there. To find out how to reduce unemployment, we have to explain the inter-country differences shown in the table opposite. After much disagreement about this in the 1980s, a consensus has emerged among mainstream economists. This says that you cannot permanently reduce unemployment by increasing the aggregate demand for a country's output, because this will only produce rising inflation. Instead, you have to alter the structure of the labour market.

Two main factors matter.[12] The first is how people are treated if they are unemployed. If they are paid unemployment benefits for an indefinite period and not required to fill the vacancies that exist, there will be many long-term unemployed people, even when vacancies abound. In the European boom around the year 2000, that was the situation in both France and western Germany.[13] So inflation rose, and the European Central Bank raised interest rates, bringing the boom to an end.

Unemployment rate, 2000–2004	
Spain	11.3
Italy	9.3
France	9.0
Germany	8.3
United States	5.3
Sweden	5.2
Britain	5.1
Denmark	4.6
Netherlands	3.4

By contrast, there are other European countries—like Denmark, the Netherlands and Britain—in which you can only get benefits if you look really hard for work. In return you get more help with looking. This is the welfare-to-work approach, a policy of stick and carrot. In these countries there is much lower unemployment. For example, in Denmark you have the right to offers of work or useful activity by the end of your first year of unemployment. At that point the state ensures that you are provided with work to do. But you have to take advantage of what you are offered. Thus there are rights and responsibilities. The worker has the right to get offers, but also the obligation to accept one of the offers.

That is the best approach—midway between the indulgence of the old Franco-German approach and the severity of the United States, where unemployment insurance ends after six months and people can get driven into very unproductive and low-paid jobs.

If people are so unhappy when they are unemployed, you might ask why they don't always take just any job. The answer is that the rational calculus does not apply. After a period of unemployment, benefit-recipients enter a phase of grey resignation, where any change can appear dangerous. Their "tastes" change. It is the role of the employment office to push people out of that state and into meaningful activity. If we could mobilise more of Europe's unemployed, these extra employees could find jobs like those that already exist, and at existing rates of pay.

In 1997 Europe's prime ministers pledged to guarantee to every worker an opportunity of work or training within a year of becoming unemployed. Only Denmark and the Netherlands have so far implemented that pledge. In most parts of Europe it could be done within five years, provided the workers had to accept one of the opportunities offered. To implement that strategy is a major priority.

However, there are some regions of Europe where unemployment is intractably high for a different reason: because pay is excessive relative to the productivity in the region. That is true in eastern Germany, southern Italy and southern Spain. In those regions there has been strong political and trade union pressure to link local pay levels to pay in other parts of the country, where productivity is higher. If this linking continues, employers will never provide enough jobs in those regions. Regional pay must be linked to regional productivity, through more decentralised or flexible wage-setting. That is a second key requirement for full employment.

So in Europe reforms of benefits and of pay are essential. What about the freedom of employers to hire and fire? In Europe this is already restricted. Is this a good idea? In terms of happiness at work it sounds good—we have already seen how much people value job security. But if it is difficult to fire workers, employers will be less likely to take people on. So isn't it bad for employment?

Probably not. The consensus view is that rules about firing do discourage the hiring of workers, but they also, obviously, discourage the firing of workers. On balance the two cancel out, leaving the level of unemployment unaffected. Because employers hire fewer workers, there is more long-term unemployment. But because they fire fewer workers, there is less short-term unemployment. The overall level of unemployment remains roughly the same.[14] Given this, Americans and Britons should surely stop telling their European colleagues to move radically in the direction of hire-and-fire. If Europeans value their security, let them have it. North of the Alps they have after all achieved U.S. levels of productivity per hour despite their job security.[15]

One could of course argue that job security should be left to negotiation between an employer and his workers. But if an individual worker asks his employer for more security in return for a lower wage, it casts doubt on his willingness to work. So collective action (including legislation) to provide reasonable job security is an important element of a civilised society. Of course workers should be sacked for bad behaviour, which is currently quite difficult in countries like Italy. But workers also should be entitled to proper notice and compensation for redundancy, and redress if wrongfully dismissed.

So "flexibility" is not a sensible mantra, if we want full employment and a decent quality of working life. Instead, we should be stressing welfare-to-work and reasonable job security as well as flexible wages.

There is one other thing: skills. People without skills are much more likely to be out of work and, if in work, low paid. In Britain and the United States roughly one in five of the population is functionally illiterate: for example, they cannot read a simple instruction on a medicine bottle. This contrasts with roughly one in ten in Germany, Sweden and the Netherlands.[16]

In Britain and the United States fewer people also have job-specific skills than in continental Europe: over a third have no form of job-relevant qualification.[17] Thus it is not surprising that the lowest-paid tenth of workers in Britain and the United States are paid roughly half the hourly wage of their counterparts in western Germany. The most tested method of acquiring manual skills is through apprenticeship, and the countries that practise it have the fewest young people who are disengaged—neither studying nor working.[18] It is vital for our youth that we expand this apprenticeship route to a skill.

Opponents of the idea argue that in a changing world the skills people need change so often that heavy investment in one skill is pointless. However, people change jobs much less often than most people think: the average person is in a job lasting about seven and a half years in the United States and ten years in Britain.[19] Even if people do eventually change occupations, the best possible start in life is to be introduced properly to what it is to be "professional." And if people are displaced from an occupation in which job prospects have become poor, they should be offered retraining of real quality. A compassionate state protects those who lose from economic change.

Family Life

Of all the factors that affect happiness, your family life or other close relationship comes first. Yet the role of the state in family life has always been a matter of dispute. Increasingly, people feel that in adult relationships the state has little role—except when there arc children. Thus I will concentrate on policies that bear on the welfare of children.

As we have seen, it can do serious damage to children if they grow up with a single parent, or have two parents who fall out. What can be done about this?

The first step is to be clear about the principles involved. Children are not, as some laissez-faire economists believe, consumer items that parents are free to consume like houses or cars. They are sentient beings whom society has a duty to protect. Producing a child is therefore an act that carries immense responsibility, even more responsibility than adopting a child, since by that stage the child already exists. Society takes enormous trouble over who is allowed to adopt a child, but none about who is allowed to produce one. This has led the psychologist David Lykken to suggest that parents should have to get a licence before child-bearing, or otherwise risk the danger that their child will be taken away for adoption.[20] His proposal goes much too far, but it focuses the mind on the serious nature of what is at stake — that the interests of the child are as important as those of the parents. So what to do?

The first step should be compulsory parenting classes in school, which would explain what a huge task and responsibility it is to rear a child.

Next, a couple should only produce a child when they are committed to each other and ready to look after the child. There should be no expectation that, once married, people should immediately have children. People need time before or after marriage to enjoy each other, and to get to know each other. There is little worse for children than to be born when neither parent wants them. Such children, often born to single mothers, have a high risk of criminal behaviour. That is why laws to permit abortion have greatly reduced the level of crime. On one estimate these laws are the biggest single cause of declining crime in America.[21] This effect can be traced out because abortion was legalised in different

U.S. states in different years. Crime in each state fell on average fifteen to twenty years after abortion was legalised, and the higher the abortion rate, the greater the decline in crime.

Once a woman is pregnant, both parents should be encouraged to attend free parenting classes, alongside the prenatal classes. The classes should cover relationships between the two parents, as well as between parents and child, since the child's welfare will be damaged by family break-up.

Family break-up can occur because of internal strains or external assault. Shortage of time is a major source of internal strain. For the happiness of our children we need more family-friendly practices at work, and high-quality child care, priced in relation to income. Flexible working practices are an essential investment in a happy society, as are entitlements to parental leave. The Scandinavian countries are a model for the rest of the world, and this may be one reason why they are among the happiest.

However, there should be no social pressure on parents to work, unless they are living on benefits at other people's expense.[22] The issue is of course one of extreme delicacy. But the general finding of social science research is that once children are over one year old, they will flourish equally well whether both parents work or only one.[23] So each family should feel free to make its own choice. An exception is bound to arise when parents wish to claim state benefits, paid at other people's expense. In this case they should be willing to seek work, at least part time, once the children are of school age.

If families run into trouble, they should seek early help. If they find their children difficult, there are now excellent programmes such as Australia's Positive Parenting Programme (Triple P), which has been shown to cut disruptive behaviour by two-thirds while reducing parental stress and improving the parents' marriage.[24]

But if anything is going to roll back the upward trend in family break-up, it is most likely to be a change in attitudes. Our society has become more tolerant in many ways that increase happiness, but should it be okay when an outside person disrupts a stable parenting couple? We surely need more inner warning signals against certain types of behaviour. Romantic love is one of life's finest and most generous feelings, but it is not always noble. The saying that "all's fair in love and war" is probably the most fatuous saying ever—about love *and* war.

Community

Close relationships do not operate in a vacuum. The context is your community—your friends and neighbours and the places where you live and shop and work. As you interact with this environment, do you feel that the world around you is friendly or threatening?

As we have seen, key aspects of social capital, like trust and membership in voluntary associations, contribute greatly to happiness. What in turn affects these? Culture and values are important, but so are mundane facts like the degree of geographical mobility.

A high-turnover community is rarely friendly. Yet economists are generally in favour of geographical mobility since it moves people from places where they are less productive to ones where they are more productive. But geographical mobility increases family break-up and criminality.

If people live near where they grew up, close to parents and old friends, they are probably less likely to break up: they have a network of social support, which is less available in more mobile communities.[25] Similarly, if people are highly mobile, they feel less bonded to the people among whom they live, and crime is more common.[26] A good predictor of low crime rates is how many friends people have within fifteen minutes' walk.[27] Crime is lower when people trust each other,[28] and people trust each other more if fewer people are moving house and the community is more homogeneous.[29] So violence tends to be high where residential mobility is high, and where there are concentrations of people who are new to the area.[30]

These are important findings, for if we look at the failures of modern societies, high crime is surely the most obvious one. It is linked to low trust, as is the level of mental illness: mental illness is more likely if you live in an area where your group is in the minority than if you live where your group is in the majority.[31]

If mobility has these costs, they should be taken into account before Europeans are urged to match U.S. levels of geographical mobility, or indeed immigration.[32] The main argument in favour of immigration is of course the gain to the migrants. Native residents may also gain from cultural exchange, especially if the immigrants are skilled. Yet many of the arguments used in favour of immigration are fallacious. By increasing our population we will of course increase our total national income, but broadly speaking, the income of people who are already here will be unaffected.[33] When business says it needs more immigration, it often means that it will otherwise have to pay higher wages.

At the local level, good physical planning can reduce the costs of mobility. On the Eastlake estate in one of Britain's new towns, ground-floor residents had high rates of mental illness. They were anxious because all and sundry could walk around the space in front of their apartments. As an experiment the planners closed off most of the paths going through the estate, so that anyone outside a window was now likely to be a neighbour. Mental illness fell by a quarter.[34]

Health of Mind

The final key element of security is health. People want to be healthy, and if they are not, they want good treatment, free of anxiety. So a good health-care system is a key feature of the good life.

But which illnesses are the worst? In an interesting study Alex Michalos asked people how satisfied they were with their overall health.[35] Their objective health was then analysed, using the standard test known as SF-36. This records eight main types of poor functioning: poor mobility, physical pain, mental disturbance and so on. Of these, mental disturbance caused much the greatest dissatisfaction with overall health.

Clearly, mental health is a key part of health, but it is more than that. It is central to our overall happiness. For example, we might ask, Which causes much more misery: depression or poverty? The answer is depression. It explains more of the variation in happiness than income does, even after we allow for the interrelation between poverty and depression.[36] So mental illness is probably the largest single cause of misery in Western societies. According to the World Health Organization, mental illness or addiction causes nearly half of all the disability that people are experiencing, as the chart below shows.[37]

Yet until recently, it was difficult to talk about mental illness (outside New York, of course). So people pretended it was really uncommon, when in fact most people had relatives or colleagues who had suffered.

Altogether about a third of us experience serious mental illness during our lives, including about 15% who experience an episode of severe, disabling depression. Episodes of illness do not last forever, but they often recur. So in any one year about 20% of us have

Causes of disability (United States and European Union)

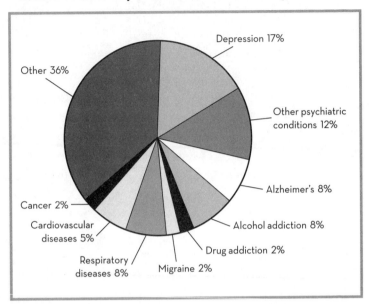

serious mental problems and 6% of us have a severe depression. These are U.S. figures, and those for Britain are similar.[38]

Until fifty years ago there was no effective treatment for mental illness. Since then the treatment of mental illness has been transformed. First came the breakthroughs in drug therapy in the 1950s, which have done more to reduce extreme misery than any other change over the last half century. Then from the 1970s onwards came major developments in psychotherapy—especially cognitive-behavioural therapy (CBT).

Both drugs and therapy have been tested in double-blind clinical trials, in which neither the patient nor the researcher knows whether real treatment is being given. For patients who become depressed, either drugs or weekly therapy will lift about 60% of sufferers out of their depression within four months. After successful treatment the risk of relapse is greater for those treated with drugs, unless they keep on taking them. But if people have had sixteen weeks of therapy, or drug treatment that continues, three-quarters of them will avoid further depression over the next two years.[39]

The cost of these treatments is not large relative to the huge improvement in well-being.[40] Yet the majority of people who are mentally ill get no treatment.[41] Not all seek help, and not all of them get diagnosed correctly and agree to be treated. Thus under a half of all those who experience a major depression get treated, and most of these are not treated by a specialist. In Britain only one in five patients in major depression sees a psychiatrist, and most are put on drugs by a general practitioner.[42] Under one in ten patients sees a psychologist. There are simply too few psychiatrists and too few psychologists. The situation is similar in the United States.

That is not the way to treat a major human problem. We spend too little on mental illness, compared with other diseases. If we take the entire toll of disease, which includes both disability *and* premature death, mental illness accounts for a quarter of the total.[43] Yet in the United States only 7% of health expenditures are targeted at mental illness, and in Britain only 13%.[44] The share of public research expenditures is even less, at 5%.[45]

Our priorities need a radical change. It is a scandal how little we spend on mental illness compared with, say, poverty. In the fight against misery, psychiatry is in the front line. Along the barricades of the twenty-first century it is a key place where idealists should rally.

· · ·

We have reached a whole new set of issues, which are personal, not social, and comprise the final stage of our enquiry. As was said earlier, happiness comes from without *and* from within. The inner life and the inner being determine how we react to life and what we give to it. In the words of William Cowper,

> *Happiness depends, as nature shows,*
> *Less on exterior things than most suppose.*[46]

So how can we gain control over our inner life? There are well-tried mental disciplines that work for many people. But, for others, psychiatric drugs are also needed. In the next two chapters we look at each of these mechanisms for achieving the calm of mind that we desire.

"I don't sing because I am happy. I am happy because I sing."

CHAPTER

Can mind control mood?

*Most folks are as happy as
they make up their minds to be.*
ABRAHAM LINCOLN

No one can make you feel inferior without your consent.
ELEANOR ROOSEVELT

In a recent experiment the psychologist Jon Kabat-Zinn offered a course of meditation to workers in a corporation. He divided the applicants randomly in two. He put one group on a waiting list in order to have a control group. The other group he taught in a weekly session of meditation for eight weeks. They were also expected to practise on their own each day. The happiness of both groups was measured before and after the course, both by questionnaire and by EEG tests on the brain.

The results were remarkable. Four months after the course had ended, the people who had taken it were strikingly happier than those who had not. If you imagine ranking one hundred people from the most miserable to the most happy, the course lifted those who had taken it by at least twenty places in this ranking—an astonishing effect.[1]

So meditation is good for the spirit. It is also good for the body. At the end of the course everybody was given a flu jab, whether they had taken the course or not. Those who had done the course developed a much stronger immunity to flu as a result of the injection.

Jon Kabat-Zinn was not surprised by these results. Earlier experiments had shown how during meditation there are changes in heart rate and hormonal balance, and indeed in EEG happiness readings.[2] What was striking about the new experiment was that the effects lasted so long.

The fact is that we can train our feelings. We are not simply victims of our situation, or indeed of our past—exaggerated ideas often associated with Karl Marx and Sigmund Freud, respectively. Instead, we can directly address our bad feelings and replace them by positive feelings, building on the positive force that is in each of us, our better self.

It is impossible to be happy without developing a positive outlook, and the inner feeling of a positive space that is ultimately impervious to outside events. Easy words to say, but extremely difficult for most people, unless they have some kind of discipline to help.

Fortunately, such disciplines exist, as they do for playing the violin. If you want to be a top-class violinist, you have to practise for about ten thousand hours before the age of eighteen. You also have to study with a competent teacher. When you have done this, you have radically altered your brain, increasing the number of neuronal connections between the relevant neurons.[3]

Likewise, we can train ourselves in the skills of being happy. We all have our own strategies for doing this, whether we're conscious of them or not, culled through unknown channels from the wisdom of the past. But it is worth looking at some of the best-known strategies, from Buddhism to modern positive psychology. Though seemingly different, all the strategies offer one basic message—that we can liberate the positive force within us by dropping our negative self-perceptions and our inappropriate goals. We can learn that the glass is, after all, half-full and not half-empty.

Buddhism

Buddhists like the Dalai Lama believe that the aim of life is happiness and the avoidance of suffering.[4] They also believe, correctly, that you cannot have positive and negative feelings at the same time.[5] So the mind has to eliminate its negative thoughts and replace them with positive ones.

On the negative side, Buddhism tells us to address the "poisons" that are disturbing our peace of mind: our unrealistic cravings and our tempestuous anger and resentment. But not by frontal assault. We are to do it by calmly observing what is happening to us. If we feel anger, we do not simply suppress it; we note it from a detached point of view so that it can no longer consume us. As Thich Nhat Hanh puts it in his book on anger, we shall always have anger inside us, but we can manage it by making friends with it, treating it like a little baby.[6] Then we can see how childish our cravings and our anger are: Buddhists call them "delusions," because we think they can consume us, when they cannot.

In psychological jargon the problem is one of "framing"—by focusing on one particular desire or feeling we give it excessive salience. Instead of thinking that what we want is 100% good and what we hate is 100% bad, we need to get them both into perspective. As we shall see, this programme for countering negative thoughts is not unlike the processes of modern cognitive therapy.

At the same time as he dethrones his negative thoughts, the Buddhist develops his positive capacity for compassion—colonising, as it were, the empty space. The basic idea of compassion is the understanding that everyone suffers, including the person you are most angry with. There are many routines for developing compassion, but a good Buddhist will spend thousands of hours in the silent practice of compassion for all, self and other, friend and foe, great and small. Compassion towards others can be practised in two ways: either by thinking about them with the deepest possible empathy from outside, or by imagining that you are actually the other person. But compassion can go wider than people. Some Buddhists say nice things in their head to the objects they encounter as they go about their business; they find this has a good effect on their general outlook. Physiologically, we know that simply smiling improves people's hormones.[7] By contrast, malicious gossip, much practised in the West but condemned by Buddhists, gives only short-run pleasure.

If you feel better towards other people, you feel better towards yourself. As the Dalai Lama has put it,

> I feel from my own experience that when I practise compassion, there is an immediate direct benefit to myself. . . .
> I get 100% benefit, while the benefit to others may be 50%.[8]

There are surely some critical situations where that does not hold and where good actions can bring massive internal stress.[9] But, in general, compassionate feelings do bring their own reward. You get more from life if you try to "do good" than if you try to "do well."

A good test of your state of mind is to compare your number of positive and negative thoughts. That is a recommendation both of the ancient Buddhist Abhidharma and of modern cognitive therapy. It can be extremely helpful in relationships. For example, the psychologist John Gottman has analysed how married couples discuss their problems. In stable marriages, people utter five positive thoughts for every negative one, while in failing marriages the ratio is less than one to one.[10]

But how to develop the positive thinking? In Buddhism the technique for developing your emotional strength is meditation. The supreme value of this is that it makes you calm. You cannot really address your emotions unless you are calm.

In meditation a person focuses his mind on an object of contemplation, without becoming attached to it. He savours it in a spirit of mindfulness, while sitting completely still. For novices the first object of attention is generally the breath. When the mind is disturbed, the breath is generally tense and often disturbed. But when the breath is calmly observed, it soon comes to a sweet regularity. Disturbing thoughts or physical discomforts must of course be ignored. With this technique a person regains control of his inner being and can go on to contemplate a whole range of objects, all observed with compassion and detachment. The first step is to achieve compassion towards yourself—or self-acceptance. Then you can practise compassion for others.

Thomas Carlyle, the nineteenth-century British writer, would have liked that. A woman said, "Sir, I accept the universe"; and he replied, "Gad, you'd better."

A central aspect of Buddhist philosophy is the concept of flux. All feelings of joy and even physical pain are observed to fluctuate, and we see ourselves as like a wave of the sea—where the sea is eternal and the wave is just its present form. To many Buddhists this reality makes them feel part of a greater whole, which gives meaning to life.

Indeed, the very concept of self is brought into question. Buddhists believe that our troubles generally come from attempting to defend or promote our "self," not realising that our life can run in many different channels and that we are not the centre of the universe. Things may not be exactly as we would want them, but we can survive and experience great happiness, provided we do not insist on having life continuously on our own terms. The goal is not self-realisation but a harmonious relation to the world about us, and above all inner strength and equanimity. In the last resort, as the Buddha said, you should "take refuge in yourself and not in anything else."[11]

The Mystical Tradition

Buddhism is essentially a psychological practice, and Buddhists do not rely on a belief in God. By contrast, Christians, Muslims and Jews believe in a God who either made the universe or at least sustains it. So these religions involve the individual's relationship to God, but to a God who is as much within us as outside—that positive force which, once accessed, gives us the feeling of being free.

Most religions are less explicit than Buddhism about the management of one's feelings. They have many don'ts, but less detailed help on how to reach a state of serenity and loving-kindness. However, in all religions there is also a mystical tradition that does focus on those issues.[12]

For Catholics the *Spiritual Exercises* of Saint Ignatius provide an example. The first words of the book are striking: "Man was made to praise, revere and serve God, and by this means to experience salvation." Going on, Saint Ignatius explains that "praise" means being grateful—an essential condition for happiness and easier if you have some idea of who or what you are grateful to. "Serving God" includes serving your fellows. And salvation involves being "indifferent" to what happens to you, so long as you are fulfilling the purpose for which you were created. Everyone, Ignatius says, experiences desolation, but he tells you how to handle it, noting like the Buddhists that everything changes, including pain.[13] A key tool is thankfulness, and many people deliberately think of five things each day to be thankful for. Some even carry a pebble to remind them.

Protestantism too has its mystical movements. For example, Quakers believe centrally that there is "something of God in everyone" and that we should respond to it—in ourselves and in others. One has to start with oneself. George Fox, the founder of Quakerism, wrote this about it:

> The pearl is hid in the field and the field is in your hearts and there you must dig to find it, and when you have digged deep and found it, you must sell all to purchase and redeem this field.[14]

When you have found the treasure within, you will have something precious to give to others. When Quakers hold their weekly meeting, it is a mainly silent event, in which together the people experience the deeper parts of their nature. Again pain is not ignored but observed in a spirit of peace.[15]

Nearly all religions agree that we are sometimes unable to help ourselves by conscious effort. At that point we do best to hand ourselves over to help from the deep inner positive force within us, which some people identify as divine. That is, for example, the basic approach of Alcoholics Anonymous (AA), which is the most successful organisation in the world for treating alcoholism. People attending AA meet, like the Quakers, in a reverential atmosphere and listen to one another in a spirit of respect and peace. Each member is working through the Twelve Steps, which every member is expected to follow:

1. We admitted we were powerless over our emotions—that our lives had become unmanageable.

2. We came to believe that a Power greater than ourselves could restore us to sanity.

3. We made a decision to turn our will and our lives over to the care of God *as we understood Him.*

4. We made a searching and fearless moral inventory of ourselves.

5. We admitted to God, to ourselves and to another human being the exact nature of our wrongs.

6. We were entirely ready to have God remove all these defects of character.[16]

And so on. By giving people a sense of purpose and hope, AA has been able to transform lives.

As we saw in earlier chapters, belief in God seems to be good for happiness. It certainly helps if you believe there is a purpose in the universe. But if you cannot believe that, you can still believe in purposes created by man. And if the purpose is human happiness, psychology can tell you a lot about how to bring it about. Like Buddhism and the mystical tradition, modern psychology can help us learn to be happy.

Cognitive Therapy

In the last thirty years practical psychology has been through a revolution. Before that, it was focused heavily on what had gone wrong with people. The dominant idea, from Freud, was that people are victims of their childhood experiences and can only become all right if they can relive and understand their past. Fortunately, this turned out not to be true. In many cases excessive focusing on the past had the framing effect of giving it excessive salience, making it more difficult to make progress. This was true of much psychoanalysis but also, for example, of "debriefing" after accidents.[17]

So in the 1960s psychologists began to develop more forward-looking techniques for helping people. Cognitive therapy was invented by Aaron Beck. According to him, depression involves a vicious circle of automatic thoughts that are self-destructive and self-reinforcing. In many cases the patient concludes that almost anything he tries will end in catastrophe. Here is an example from the psychologist Paul Gilbert of a patient who was perpetually anxious.[18] Gilbert asked him to describe a typical situation of fear, and the patient said, "A train journey."

THERAPIST: Okay, so here you are on the train and you feel it start to move. What is going through your mind?

PATIENT: I might get anxious.

T: Okay you get anxious. What would happen then?

P: I start to sweat.

T: And that bothers you because?

P: Other people might see this.

T: I see. So you are worried that you may become anxious, and this might lead you to start sweating. If this happened, other people might see it. Is that how it seems to you?

P: Yes.

T: Okay, can we explore the meaning of sweating and other people being able to see this? Let's just focus on that for a moment and see what is the most worrying thing about that.

P: Well, they may think there is something wrong with me, like I'm ill or something.

T: Like you are ill or something?

P: Yes, they may feel I'm contagious and be repelled by me.

T: Repelled by you?

P: Yes, repelled by the way I look. Later I think if I can't control this I will always be alone.

Aaron Beck believed that depression can be cured by getting you to challenge each negative thought as it arises—to imagine you are a third party interrogating your own beliefs. This may involve putting the negative belief to some kind of systematic test—including conducting quasi-scientific experiments to see if the forecast disaster actually happens. This technique of mental self-discipline proves remarkably effective in treating major and minor depression, as well as anxiety and panic attacks.[19]

It often includes significant elements of "behavioural therapy," in which, for example, the patient commits to a programme of physical exercise or of helping other people. Behavioural sequences are particularly important in treating phobias and obsessive-compulsive disorder: through them a person may be progressively desensitised to the experience that terrifies him. These cognitive-behavioural therapies stand in marked contrast to therapies that advocate the venting of emotion, which have been found to be ineffective.[20]

If happiness depends on the gap between your perceived reality and your prior aspiration, cognitive therapy deals mainly with the perception of reality.[21] But it is also important to have sensible aspirations. Many people are driven to depression by unrealistic goals.[22] Spouses who want to change the character of their partner are unlikely to achieve happiness, nor are people who wish they themselves were better looking. In every walk of life the Serenity Prayer has the right approach to things that distress us:

> Give me the serenity to accept the things I cannot change,
> the courage to change the things I can, and the wisdom to
> know the difference.

So increasingly cognitive therapy also seeks to curb unrealistic goals, as well as negative thoughts.

Positive Psychology

Everyone needs meaningful goals. From this perception has emerged a new movement that calls itself "positive psychology" and is led by Martin Seligman. Its concepts apply to people at all points in the spectrum of happiness. The central idea is to focus on the true sources of authentic happiness—which include some sense of meaning in one's life. Positive psychology suggests that we should focus on those areas of life where we can really flourish— that is, our strengths. To make progress, it is more important to develop our strengths than to wrestle with our weaknesses.[23]

Another key insight relates to our basic attitudes. Increasingly today, people feel that they *must* make the most of everything. In other words, rather than being happy with what is good enough, they must have the best. This puts them under enormous strain, for there is always the risk of missing an opportunity. Continuous reoptimisation (sometimes dignified by the name "flexibility") is the real enemy of happiness, as can be observed among young people who spend the day reorganising their evening arrangements each time a better opportunity arises.

One gets some idea of the strain of optimising by comparing the happiness of "maximisers" (who seek the best) and "satisficers" (who are content with what is good enough). Barry Schwartz of Swarthmore College and his colleagues have devised good scales that enable us to sort people into these two categories, and we do indeed find that the maximisers are less happy than the satisficers.[24] Maximisers may indeed get some better "objective" outcome through all their searching, but even so, they are less happy. Why?

One reason is that they have more regrets. When they have made a decision and implemented it, they continue to analyse what would have happened if they had taken a different decision. Another reason is that they are more prone to make social comparisons. If they are given a task that is also given to a peer, their happiness at the end of the task is greatly affected by whether they did better or worse than their peer; this is not true of those who are simply satisficers.

These findings suggest two important conclusions. First, our increasing tendency to do the best for ourselves is doing us no good. In particular we spend too much time living in the future rather than the present. Some planning is essential, but too many people are mainly focused on tomorrow. When tomorrow comes, they will be planning for the day after.

Yet life is not a dress rehearsal. So the Buddhist concept of mindfulness has a message for all of us. It says: cultivate the sense of awe and wonder; savour the things of today; and look about you with the same interest as if you were watching a movie or taking a photo. Engage with the world and with the people around you. In one sense, as Leo Tolstoy said, the most important person in the world is the one in front of you now.[25]

A second conclusion is that we have to control our tendency to compare ourselves with others. We should try to make the happiness of others our goal, and to enjoy the success of others. We should also have confidence in our own judgements rather than the judgements of others. In the end the only person's opinion of you that matters is your own.

So we should praise, not scorn, the self-help movement, especially when it aims at the inner self, and we should always treasure the old aphorisms: count your blessings; don't cry over spilt milk; and avoid false gods.

There is ultimately one common strand in what can make us happy: it is love. It is remarkable how we use this word. We love our spouses; we love our pets; we love doughnuts; we love playing tennis; we love Mozart; we love Venice. Towards all of these we have positive feelings that take us out of ourselves. As Ezra Pound wrote, "What thou lovest well remains, the rest is dross."[26]

Education of the Spirit

So how can public policy help? As we have seen, our happiness depends profoundly on our attitudes, and these can be learned and practised. Unless you acquire good attitudes early, you get into situations where it is ever more difficult to learn them. Poverty of spirit is contagious. That is why education of the spirit is a public good.

People have never been indifferent to the attitudes that other people's children acquire — because they affect us all. But in recent decades it has become increasingly difficult for teachers to teach moral values as established truths, rather than as interesting topics for discussion. We have to pull back from this situation and teach the wisdom of the ages as well-established principles.[27]

Controlled trials have shown that well-designed courses in emotional intelligence have significant effects on children's mood and on their consideration for others; these effects are still evident two years later.[28] Since all children benefit from acquiring inner strength, some of these courses have been aimed at all children. What is needed now is a school subject running through years one to twelve that would include the following topics:

- Understanding and managing your feelings (including anger and rivalry)

- Loving and serving others (including practical exercises and learning about role models)

- The appreciation of beauty

- Causes and cures of illness, including mental illness, drugs and alcohol

- Love, family and parenting

- Work and money

- Understanding the media and preserving your own values

- Understanding others and how to socialise

- Political participation

- Philosophical and religious ideas

This list is not that different from the one prepared by Daniel Goleman in his bestseller *Emotional Intelligence*.[29] The curriculum should also include physical exercise, which is good for mental health, and music and art, which give us treasured skills we can fall back on throughout our lives.

In Britain there is a subject called "social, personal and health education," which gets roughly an hour a week in most schools from age five to sixteen.[30] Regrettably, it is often taught by non-specialist teachers even in secondary schools, and its purpose is not radical enough — it should aim to produce a happier generation of adults than the current generation.

It will be hard to do this without changing the values of the whole youth culture. So what is needed now is a real controlled experiment. Since attitudes are influenced by the wider society, it is no use testing such a curriculum on a random selection of children in one particular school, or indeed on one particular school in one city: the youth culture is too strong. Only if all the schools and cultural organisations in one city or state joined in could we really see what might be achieved in a generation. We should still have to contend with the overall effect of national TV, but we could surely give it a try. The aim would be to encourage more wholesome attitudes and more robust and virtuous characters: no less. From the searchings discussed in this chapter will surely be found some of the central strands in twenty-first-century culture.

The Placebo Effect

Yet, unfortunately, some people believe we are as we are, and no mental practices can change us. So how do these people account for the placebo effect? All doctors know that a dummy pill, with nothing in it, will cure a substantial proportion of their patients.[31] Yet, if there is nothing in the pill, what is curing them? Their beliefs are curing them. They improve because they believe they can. If beliefs can cure our body, they can surely help our spirit.

So education and therapy can help us develop our positive feelings—above all a generous and forgiving spirit that seeks to achieve harmony. But no one finds this easy all the time. For some people who are mentally ill, more is needed. Fortunately, there is a second possibility, to which we now turn: psychiatric drugs.

"Discouraging data on the antidepressant."

Do drugs help?

Cocaine isn't habit forming.
I should know—I've been using it for years.
TALLULAH BANKHEAD[1]

For many people, psychiatric drugs had a bad name until recently—largely because of the influence of Sigmund Freud. Yet, until he was nearly forty, Freud tried to understand and cure mental disease by physical methods.[2] Apart from his main work on neurology, he became interested in whether cocaine could be a cure for nervous exhaustion of the kind he himself experienced. So he took the drug himself. He was not disappointed. He wrote to his fiancée, "Woe to you my princess when I come. I will kiss you quite red, and feed you until you are plump. And if you are forward, you shall see who is the stronger, a gentle little girl who doesn't eat enough or a big wild man who has cocaine in his body."

In 1884 he wrote an article, "On Cocaine," for a medical journal, in which he described how the Incas chewed coca leaves for centuries to increase the physical capacity of their bodies for hard labour (a property later exploited by their Spanish conquerors to increase the output of gold). Freud went on to praise the mental benefits of cocaine. "It brings almost an exhilaration and lasting euphoria.... You perceive an increase of self-control and possess more vitality and capacity for work.... The result is enjoyed without any of the unpleasant after-effects that follow exhilaration brought about by alcohol." He also pointed to the properties of cocaine as a local anaesthetic—which enabled his colleague Karl Koller to found the modern science of eye surgery.

Freud's article had a big impact around Europe, and doctors everywhere were prescribing cocaine for anxiety and depression. Its use became as common as that of Valium today. At the same time, cocaine became (in small doses) a regular item of consumption in tonic wines, and from 1886 in Coca-Cola. (It was not until the twentieth century that the coca in Coke was replaced by caffeine.)

But nemesis was to come. Freud's friend Ernst Fleischl had developed excruciating pain following the amputation of his thumb. He took morphine but became addicted to it. Freud advised replacing the morphine with cocaine. But Fleischl became addicted to this too. He was now injecting himself with cocaine, and every high was followed by a worse crash into depression. In the end he became psychotic.

Fairly soon the medical community turned against the repeated use of cocaine. At the same time, Freud was changing his general approach to mental disease. Increasingly he despaired of understanding how the biology of the brain affects the mind. More and more he focused on how the mind itself affects mental experience. The clinical practice that this made possible, away from the laboratory, also made it much easier for him to support his wife and six children.

At that time Freud's decision about the brain made sense. The tools with which neuroscientists would one day bring relief to minds in torment did not exist. The instruments of science were not powerful enough; the chemical understanding, deficient. Even so, Freud always retained his belief in the underlying molecular nature of mental processes, and in *Beyond the Pleasure Principle*, published in 1920, he insists that "the deficiencies in our description would probably vanish if we were already in a position to replace the psychological terms by physiological or chemical ones." It was not till the 1950s that scientists began to justify Freud's early belief in the power of medical science to relieve a mind in torment.

Traditional Drugs

Of course there is nothing new about the use of drugs. For thousands of years we have used them to lift our spirits and to numb our pain. The most common drug is alcohol, which has always been made worldwide. Other drugs include opium, cocaine, tobacco and cannabis. Opium came from Asia, until derivatives like morphine and heroin could be manufactured in the lab. Cocaine, tobacco and cannabis originated in Latin America.

Most of these drugs have two distinct uses. They can control pain and they can elevate your spirits. In Europe alcohol was the surgeon's main anaesthetic until 150 years ago. Morphine is still the main controller of searing pain, while cocaine is the basis for many local anaesthetics.

But the widest use of all these drugs is "recreational"—to liberate the spirit and enhance the experience of life. Most drugs can do this if taken in moderation. And most people do practise moderation. But unfortunately most of these drugs are (in some degree) addictive. In other words, if you want to continue experiencing the same effect, you have to take more and more of the drug. In some cases that can kill you. But it is also extremely painful, and often agonising, to stop.

Thus recreational drugs can only lift the spirits for a part of the time. By contrast modern psychiatric drugs increasingly have the power to alter people's lives.

Disorders of the Mind

What drug you need depends on what kind of problem you have. If we consider only serious mental problems, about a third of us will experience one of them some time in our life. They include schizophrenia (1% of us), depression (15%), manic-depression (1%), and intense anxiety, including panic attacks, phobias, obsessions and general anxiety.[3]

These are terrible states, not only for those who experience them but for their relatives as well. Most people with *schizophrenia* who are untreated are in torment, and all have lost contact with important aspects of reality. They suffer from devastating delusions about themselves or about others who are "persecuting" them. Many hear voices giving them messages or issuing orders. Some have visual hallucinations. Others believe themselves to be someone quite different, like the pope. These delusions can occasionally lead to violent behaviour; before modern drugs existed, many people with schizophrenia were put into straitjackets and padded cells. Anyone who has seen a person with schizophrenia screaming in pain, banging his head with his fists, can never forget it. But most sufferers go in the opposite direction, into a form of painful withdrawal accompanied by some form of delusion. Schizophrenia generally appears in the late teens or early twenties, though somewhat later in women than in men. Until modern drugs, the majority of people with schizophrenia spent much of their life in hospital.

Schizophrenia causes major misperceptions of reality. *Depression* by contrast is a disorder of feeling. We all become what we would call depressed at some time in our lives. But a major depression is something quite different.[4] Here is how the composer Hector Berlioz expressed it:

> It is difficult to put into words what I suffered—the longing that seemed to be tearing my heart out by the roots, the dreadful sense of being alone in an empty universe, the agonies that thrilled through me as if the blood were running ice-cold in my veins, the disgust with living, the impossibility of dying.
>
> I had stopped composing; my mind seemed to become feebler as my feelings grew more intense. I did nothing. One power was left me—to suffer.

He described a typical experience:

> The fit fell upon me with appalling force. I suffered agonies and lay groaning on the ground, stretching out abandoned arms, convulsively tearing up handfuls of grass and wide-eyed innocent daisies, struggling against the crushing sense of *absence*, against a mortal isolation. Yet such an attack is not to be compared with the tortures that I have known since then in ever-increasing measure.[5]

Gerald Manley Hopkins expressed his experiences in his powerful Dublin sonnets. In "No Worst, There Is None," he wrote:

O the mind, mind has mountains; cliffs of fall
Frightful, sheer, no-man-fathomed. Hold them cheap
May who ne'er hung there.

Unlike most schizophrenia, depression comes and goes; sometimes it disappears forever. *Manic-depression*, however, usually recurs. Manic-depressives alternate between periods of depression and shorter periods of mania, with normal periods in between.[6] When they are manic, they are highly excited and often sleep little. They initiate grandiose schemes—and then everything crashes. One in ten commits suicide. Some famous manic-depressives, like Vincent van Gogh, have left great monuments behind them. William Pitt the Elder was a manic-depressive, and as Britain's prime minister he organised the conquest of Canada. Then, when his ministers proposed disastrous taxes on the American colonies, he was too depressed to object, and so eventually the American colonies were provoked to fight for their independence.[7] Such is the influence of mental illness in history.

Finally, there are those who suffer from extreme *anxiety*. This includes extreme fearfulness, or panic attacks (when people often feel they are going to die) or phobias (of going out, or meeting people, or meeting insects). Somewhat similar are those with obsessive-compulsive disorders, who may spend hours each day washing their hands or checking that the back door is locked. These can be crippling conditions.

Schizophrenia and manic depression are roughly as common in every country, whether rich or poor, Communist or capitalist, hot or cold. Depression varies more between countries. But all these conditions, including extreme anxiety disorders, have a genetic element. That does not mean they are caused exclusively by the genes, nor are they generally caused by experience alone.

Quite simply, if your particular mix of genes and experience is bad enough, you are at risk.

We can see this clearly in the following chart. Among people whose identical twin is schizophrenic, 48% are schizophrenic also. This is the result of common genes and a similar environment. To isolate the effect of the genes we can look at non-identical twins who have the similar environment but less similar genes. When the twin is not identical, the proportion falls to 17%. So having the same genes as someone with schizophrenia makes a person much more likely to be schizophrenic. This is a hard truth and difficult for some people to accept, although it is a welcome truth for those parents who have been told a child's illness was entirely due to the

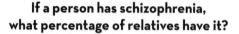

If a person has schizophrenia, what percentage of relatives have it?

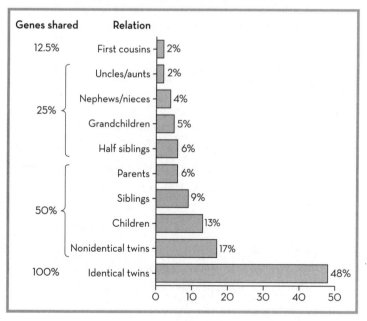

way they treated the child in infancy. It is difficult to forgive the unhappiness caused to parents by psychoanalysts like R. D. Laing who insisted that schizophrenia was caused solely by experience.[8]

The genetic factor is even more powerful in manic depression than in schizophrenia, while it is slightly less powerful in straight depression and anxiety states. There is only one reason for belabouring the genetic factor: to emphasise that there is in part a physical origin of mental problems. This makes it unsurprising that they can be helped by physical methods, and have been.

Since the Second World War, the progress in psychiatric drugs has been remarkable. Even though many drugs still produce unpleasant and sometimes dangerous side effects, they have transformed the lives of millions and largely emptied our mental hospitals. In some cases this may have gone too far, in order to cut costs. But in the United States the number of beds for mental patients has fallen from over half a million in 1950 to under 100,000. In Britain inpatient numbers have fallen from around 200,000 to 30,000.[9]

Drugs for the Mind

So what were the chief pharmaceutical discoveries? There were four main breakthroughs, all in the 1950s and all with drugs that are used to this day. For schizophrenia, the drug is an antihistamine called chlorpromazine. Two French psychiatrists first tried this on schizophrenia in 1952. As one of them wrote twenty years later,

> Psychiatric wards twenty years ago still included agitated patients who did not respond to common therapeutic procedures. Existing treatments could not abolish straitjackets and cells. If we were to recreate now the atmosphere of an agitated ward for our students' instruction, they would

laugh or become sceptical. Nevertheless, anti-schizophrenic drugs originated in that atmosphere. We had scarcely treated 10 patients—with all due respect to the fervent adherents of statistics—when our conviction proved correct. It was supported by the sudden, great interest of the nursing personnel, who had always been reserved about innovations.[10]

Chlorpromazine not only reduces the delusions that afflict most schizophrenics, but it can sometimes (but not always) activate people who have withdrawn into themselves.

Soon after this discovery, a Swiss psychiatrist discovered the power of the drug imipramine to lift depression. Imipramine is one in a family of drugs known as tricyclics.

Perhaps the most remarkable and accidental of all the findings was the discovery by an Australian psychiatrist of lithium as a help for manic-depression. Lithium has the remarkable property that it can help in both directions: it can pull you up when you are down and down when you are high. In other words, while the first two drugs pull you in one direction only, lithium acts as a stabiliser in both directions—as is needed to control alternating moods of mania and depression.

All these drugs are profoundly different from "recreational" drugs, which give a temporary lift in spirits or control pain. The new drugs are specific to particular types of mental problem. Also, if taken regularly they can produce a permanent change in the way a person functions and experiences life. They are not addictive.

This cannot be said for the fourth major drug discovery of the 1950s, diazepam, better known by the trade name Valium, and sometimes called "mother's little friend." Valium reduces anxiety. Until Valium was discovered, the main drugs used to control worry were barbiturates, but these were killers if taken in an overdose.

Valium was safer and was so successful that in 1975 15% of Americans were taking it or something similar.[11] But its addictive properties brought it into disrepute, and now it is only used for crisis periods of a few weeks. For treating anxiety on a long-term basis, doctors now use antidepressants, or beta blockers that reduce the stress response.

Unfortunately, none of the drugs we have been looking at are perfect. None of them works in every case, and even when they control the mental illness, they can have nasty side effects. For example, the tricyclics can give you a dry mouth, an irregular heartbeat and difficulty in urinating; lithium can cause constipation. These side effects vary depending on the drug in question and an individual's response. This means that the drugs are "dirty"—they are not specific enough to focus exclusively on the area of the brain that is disturbed. Instead, they invade many other parts of the brain that are working quite well.

To reduce the side effects of these drugs therefore became one of the main objectives of researchers. And there have been some breakthroughs. The most famous of these is Prozac (fluoxetine), which has been taken by millions who suffer from depression, including Princess Diana. Unlike the earlier drugs, Prozac is a purpose-built drug resulting from a long development process in a drug company (Eli Lilly), using pioneering brain science. To understand such an effort, and indeed to understand the nature of the human animal, we have to trace out some of the basic processes going on in our brains.

How Drugs Work

The human brain consists of neurons, which pass messages to each other. There are some 100 billion neurons, and each neuron is connected to 1,000 or more other neurons. Thus each one of us has in his head a network as large as the whole telephone system of New York or London.[12]

Sensations come into the brain through nerves from the rest of the body and interact with the vivid internal life of the brain to produce our feelings and our responses, conscious and unconscious. The messages travel within each neuron by a method of electrical transmission. When they get to the end of the neuron, they release a chemical "neurotransmitter," which flows across the "synapse," the gap between that neuron and the next. This then sets off the electrical impulse that travels down the next neuron. Thus to influence the flow of messages in the brain, you can increase or decrease the action of these neurotransmitters.

There are at least fifty of these neurotransmitters, and each pathway from one neuron to another uses only a few of them. Thus there are circuits in the brain associated with different neurotransmitters. Since different circuits perform different functions and generate different feelings and behaviour, we can affect both feeling and functioning by operating on the relevant neurotransmitter. That is precisely what drugs do.

The principal neurotransmitters that affect mental well-being are dopamine and serotonin. Schizophrenia is associated with too much dopamine. So chlorpromazine "works" by blocking the passage of dopamine into the receiving neuron. By reducing activity in the dopamine circuits, it lessens the experience of schizophrenia. There is however a limit to the dosage, for unfortunately a person with too little dopamine gets Parkinson's disease, that terrible condition of uncontrollable shaking. People who die with Parkinson's have only 20% of the normal level of dopamine.

Depression, by contrast, is associated with too little serotonin: serotonin is typically low among people who commit suicide. Thus depression can be helped by an increased supply of serotonin, and the main task in developing Prozac was to find a drug that did just that and nothing else.[13]

What about recreational drugs? Most of the drugs that are stimulants work by increasing dopamine. This is true of cocaine, which is why too much of it can make you psychotic. Another (man-made) stimulant is amphetamine—the pep pill of the 1950s. It too increases the supply of dopamine.[14] Nicotine is more gentle—it kills the body, not the soul.

When we turn from stimulants to sedatives and soothing drugs like Valium, the key neurotransmitter involved is GABA (gamma-aminobutyric acid). GABA reduces the rate of firing of neurons and thus the degree of mental activity. Both Valium and barbiturate sedatives reinforce the action of GABA in slowing the rate of firing. Alcohol does exactly the same.

Finally, there is the control of searing pain.[15] When soldiers are seriously wounded in battle, about half of them feel little pain in the first few hours. This flies in the face of the simple neural model first put forward by the philosopher Descartes in the seventeenth century, according to which the nerves automatically transmit to the brain what the body is experiencing. The reason is the synapses. To get to the brain, the pain signal has to be carried across the synapses by a neurotransmitter. But the passage of the signal can be blocked by natural neurotransmitters called endorphins, and these are manufactured and released during trauma. They also appear after twenty minutes' jogging to kill the pain and give you your second wind. That is why exercise can also be so good for mental pain.

It turns out that morphine is essentially the same chemical as the endorphins except that it comes from the poppy and is also the active ingredient in opium and heroin (a morphine derivative). It obstructs pain by fitting into the same blocking sites as those that accept the endorphins on the receiving neuron. The tragedy is that while the euphoria produced by the endorphins is non-addictive because of their speed of natural decay, the external opiates are addictive. No one has yet been able to produce an "external" non-addictive opiate that can penetrate into the brain.

Prozac Nation?

What a life we could have if such a thing were possible. We would not of course choose euphoria all the time because part of the time we should need our minds to be sharp enough to organise our existence. But for the millions in mental torment it would be an unbelievable relief to have something better than what they have now. So how far should drugs be used to alter people?

There are some good reasons to be cautious, and some bad ones. Many of the most attractive drugs like Prozac are fairly new, and we cannot yet be quite certain about their side effects. Many people are still quite reasonably influenced by the thalidomide tragedy in the late 1950s, when over ten thousand pregnant mothers who took the drug produced deformed babies.

Yet time will pass, and these anxieties will probably abate. A deeper issue will then become dominant: are we willing to change our natures permanently by the use of drugs? If things become bad enough, most of us are. Most schizophrenics and manic-depressives take their medication, though in many cases it requires a massive struggle involving the support of doctors, relatives and social workers. But what about the person whose temperament is generally depressive or hyperanxious?

The psychiatrist Peter Kramer wrestles with this question and describes the evolution of his own thinking in *Listening to Prozac*.[16]

He practises psychotherapy, and he believes in the importance of understanding yourself. But year after year he has seen patients, stuck in some grey, quasi-existence, who are raised by Prozac to a new level of ongoing fulfilment. They do not become vegetables, but more vital and courageous in their engagement with life. As one patient put it, "You stop thinking about yourself all the time." You may even care less about social comparisons.

Not all patients who try Prozac are so positive, but what should we think about its use for those who are? Is this personality change by pill? Those who have the good experience say something different. They observe the change, but they describe it as "feeling more myself." Before Prozac the positive part of themselves had felt pulled down by the negative part, but now no longer.

To some critics this is just too easy. The most puritanical of them argue that misery is a part of human experience. We should therefore accept misery rather than fight it. This view is simply immoral.

A different puritanism says we *should* fight mental disorder, but only by mental, not by physical, means. To treat ourselves with drugs is considered unnatural, while to struggle with ourselves is to continue as we have struggled for millennia. But if we thought we should never tamper with nature, we would never treat cancer, heart disease, rheumatic hips or any of the thousand ailments from which we suffer. Such an approach to mental problems reveals a body/mind dualism: a view that doctors should stick to physical illness and leave the mind to psychology and religion. But we know too much since Darwin to think like that. It is almost inevitable that as medical drugs improve, more people will use them to lift their state of mind.

Killing Creativity?

In that process will we diminish the creative spark that is so often linked to the experience of misery? It is a valid question. People have always recognised a link between artistic creativity and extreme emotional experience. As King Theseus says in *A Midsummer Night's Dream*,

> *The lunatic, the lover and the poet*
> *Are of imagination all compact;*

They

> *. . . apprehend*
> *More than cool reason ever comprehends.*

Modern research has confirmed a link between creativity and mental instability. One study of 291 world-famous men now dead shows that great artists and creative writers were more likely to have suffered from depression than the population at large.[17] During their depressions of course they mostly produced nothing.[18] The creativity came in between and was sometimes accentuated by the mania that goes with manic depression.[19] Studies of contemporary writers and artists tell the same story.

So if artists are treated for mental problems, do they become less creative? Edvard Munch, who painted the famous picture of *The Scream* and was hospitalised a number of times, had a clear view on this problem. He remarked, "A German once said to me: 'But you could rid yourself of many of your troubles.' To which I replied, 'They are part of me and my art. They are indistinguishable from me, and it would destroy my art. I want to keep those sufferings.'"

However, what does the evidence show? In particular what happens when manic-depressives are put on lithium, which cuts down both the depression *and* the mania? When samples of artists and writers who have taken lithium were asked about its effects, the majority reported that under lithium their creativity increased or was unaffected.[20] They were also happier.

Thus it is not clear that the creativity of these unbalanced people came from their experience of suffering. It may have come largely from their genes. Here is the evidence. We can take manic-depressive people and their relatives and compare their creativity. It turns out that the relatives are *more* creative than the manic-depressives themselves—they have many of the same genes but fewer of the bad experiences, which helped to produce the manic-depression.[21]

On this evidence little is lost if we relieve manic-depressives of the burden of their terrible experiences. It is of course up to every individual to decide whether to accept treatment. But we should remember that before lithium came in, one in five manic-depressives committed suicide. How many more van Gogh pictures might have been painted, and how much suffering reduced, with the aid of modern psychiatry?

If we really want to increase suffering, it is easy to arrange. Instead, we should use our expanding knowledge to control the misery that comes from awkward genes and destructive upbringings.

. . .

Ironically, what will in the end defeat the bad drugs, especially heroin and cocaine, will be new medical drugs that work better than they do. These new drugs will be safer and non-addictive. Side by side with cognitive therapies, they will enable many people whose natures are rough or whose lives have been tough to become happier people.

"*Sometimes having to have the happy childhood my parents
never had is just too much of a responsibility.*"

Conclusions for today's world

Nature, Mr. Allnut, is what we are
put into this world to rise above.

KATHARINE HEPBURN TO
HUMPHREY BOGART IN *THE AFRICAN QUEEN*

S o here we are as a society: no happier than fifty years ago.[1] Yet every group in society is richer, and most are healthier. In this new land of opportunity, what are we not doing that we could?

I have tried in this book to summarise the evidence.[2] We know enough now to see which social philosophies will increase happiness and which will reduce it. Here are some of the main things that we know, and their implications—twelve truths about happiness.

Happiness Matters

- **Happiness is an objective dimension of all our experience.**[3] And it can be measured. We can ask people how they feel. We can ask their friends or observers for an independent assessment. Also, remarkably, we can now take measurements of the electrical activity in the relevant parts of a person's brain. All of these different measurements give consistent answers about a person's happiness. With them we can trace the ups and downs of someone's experience, and we can also compare the happiness of different people. The measurements are still quite crude but improving rapidly.

  So happiness is a real, objective phenomenon. Moreover, good feelings drive out bad feelings and vice versa, so that happiness is a single dimension of all our waking experience, running from the utmost pain and misery at one extreme to sublime joy and contentment at the other.

- **We are programmed to seek happiness.**[4] One source of happiness often conflicts with another, and we choose our sources according to their comparative costs and how they benefit our happiness. Generally, what makes us happy is good for us, and has therefore helped to perpetuate the species. This applies not only to our love of food and sex, but also to our instinctive capacity for cooperation: most, but not all, moral behaviour makes a person feel better. If we are programmed to seek happiness, it is no wonder that happiness is so central an issue in our lives.

- **It is thus self-evident that the best society is the happiest.**[5] Or that is what I argue. The authors of the American Declaration of

Independence had the right idea. This means that public policy should be judged by how it increases human happiness and reduces human misery. Likewise, private behaviour should aim at producing the greatest overall happiness.

Many arguments have been brought against this philosophy, but none of them stand up. Indeed, many of them vanish in the light of our new psychological knowledge. And no one has proposed any other "ultimate" principle that could arbitrate when one moral rule (like truth-telling) conflicts with another (like kindness).

- **Our society is not likely to become happier unless people agree that this is what we want to happen.**[6] Hence the greatest happiness ideal has two functions. It can help us think dispassionately about how to organise society. And it can also inspire us with a passionate commitment to the common good. Modern society desperately needs a concept of the common good around which to unite the efforts of its members. Here is the right concept. We want to increase the general happiness and we commit ourselves to that end. No individual will ever completely reach that ideal. But if we acknowledge the ideal, we are likely to live closer to it.

Sources of Happiness

So what makes people happy?

- **Humans are deeply social beings.**[7] Most people prefer to be in company most of the time. Friendship and marriage make people happier. Unemployment causes misery that goes far beyond the effect of losing income, because it breaks a social tie. In fact to a large extent our social ties define our personal identity and give meaning to our life. So it is a deep fallacy of many economists to think of human interaction as mainly a means to an end, rather than also an end in itself. This applies also to the political process. Many economists complain that people care about processes and not simply about "outcomes." But if people are like that, who are we to say they should be different?

- **As social beings, we want to trust each other.**[8] The average happiness in one country compared with another can be largely explained by six key factors (and so can the suicide rate). These are: the proportion of people who say that other people can be trusted; the proportion who belong to social organisations; the divorce rate; the unemployment rate; the quality of government; and religious belief. Unhappily, over the last forty years levels of trust have fallen drastically in Britain and America, though not in continental Europe. In the United States and Britain today the percentage of adults who think that most people can be trusted is half that of the 1950s. Policies that encourage trust are thus extremely important. These include moral education in schools, and policies to build stable families, communities and work-places.

   We do not want high turnover in jobs, in housing or in marriages, except where clear advantages outweigh the human and other costs. Nor do we want our firms and public services to be repeatedly restructured, with massive loss of trust at every stage. Unfortunately, political leaders in the United States and Britain have elevated "flexibility" and "change" to the same level as motherhood and apple pie. But there are huge advantages to inflexibility and predictability, as continental Europeans appreciate. The evidence shows that continuous reoptimisation is not the best route to happiness: you are more likely to be happy if you settle for what is "good enough" than if you feel you must always have the most.

People also want to be trusted and respected themselves. This requires that they have some autonomy. Most of us like to feel we are working well or helping others because we could not expect to be respected otherwise. That is a key element in the motivation to work—the satisfaction of the professional norm. Yet in recent years employers have used more and more financial incentives to motivate people; performance-related pay has been creeping in everywhere, including the public services.

Those who favour it believe that if they add an extra incentive, people are bound to work harder. They assume that all other incentives will retain their existing force. Yet that is not how people are. If you pay people for something, they stop feeling that you automatically expect it of them. In consequence they may even work less. So introducing targets and paying people to achieve them may not be the best way to revolutionise the public services.

- **People are also deeply attached to the status quo.**[9] They hate loss of any kind, and they care less about gains than about losses. Researchers typically find that an income loss of £100 hurts twice as much as an income gain of £100 helps. This is not an inconvenience to be ignored, but a fact to be respected. Yet rationalisers happily reorganise things without weighing properly the cost to happiness from breaking up a settled order.

  More generally, people like what is familiar to them. Crime and mental illness are higher in transient or mixed communities, other things being equal. This is an important cost of high mobility. Anglo-American economists may preach to Europeans that they should move house more often. This would surely increase productivity, but it is not desirable unless the gains from higher productivity would outweigh the costs of greater crime and family instability. Happiness, not dynamism, should be the goal of public policy.

- **Human beings are also status conscious.**[10] Natural selection has planted in us the desire to do better than other people, or at least to keep up with them. This is what causes the rat race. In any race there is a fixed number of winners. For every winner there is a loser: it is a zero-sum game. This is equally true of the race for status, since the total amount of status in a society is fixed. That is one major reason why as a society we have not grown happier.

  So what can be done? If a person works harder and earns more, he may himself gain by increasing his income compared with other people. But the other people lose because their income now falls relative to his. He does not care that he is polluting other people in this way, so we must provide him with an automatic incentive to do so. Taxation provides exactly this incentive. If we make taxes commensurate to the damage that an individual does to others when he earns more, then he will only work harder if there is a true net benefit to society as a whole. It is efficient to discourage work effort that makes society worse off. Thus taxation is a way of containing the rat race, and we should stop apologising for its "dreadful" disincentive effects. If tax-cutters think people should work still harder, they need to explain why.

  There is also another tactic for limiting the rat race: education. We are past the period of evolution when only the fittest can survive. So we should teach our young to give less value to status and more value to helping other people. This idea is not new, but it is taking a real beating in the current era of unrestrained individualism. It can only win with the backing of solid intellectual argument.

- **Human beings are also very adaptable.**[11] Like other animals, our feelings adapt to our experience, so that when things change, our initial reactions eventually diminish and we revert towards our initial state of feeling. If things get better, we after a while take them for granted. If they get worse, we also eventually largely accept them. This is another reason why economic growth has not increased welfare as much as we expected. The number of people who are dissatisfied with their financial position is still as high as it was thirty years ago, although people are many times richer. How depressing!

In other words, income is addictive. Suppose my income and spending rise this year: next year I will need more income still in order to achieve a given level of happiness. In fact to a large extent it is the change in income rather than income itself that affects happiness — unless you are very poor. In this respect income is very different from, say, friendship, because if I make more friends this year, that has permanent effects on my happiness — I do not take them for granted and need still more friends in the year that follows. We habituate more rapidly to things that money can buy than to things it cannot buy — more to goods than to relationships.

Since most people do not foresee the addictive effects of income and spending, taxation has again a useful role, just as it has with other forms of addiction like smoking. Taxes discourage us from overwork, from running on a treadmill that brings less advance in happiness than we expected.

If we combine this habituation argument with the one about

status-seeking, we can argue strongly that up to some level taxes are not inefficient, as is so often alleged. Rather, we need the tax on income from work in order to maintain a tolerable work-life balance. By contrast, tax cuts would of course increase production, but would they improve the quality of our lives?

- **In any case extra income increases happiness less and less as people get richer.**[12] This was the traditional argument for redistributive taxation, and modern happiness research confirms it. The argument applies both within countries and across countries. In poor countries extra income increases happiness much more than in rich countries, and that is why helping the Third World should be one of the major ethical goals for Western society. Moreover, policies that will certainly increase misery, like easier laws on gambling, can never be justified by the income they would generate. Income is not everything.

- **In fact happiness depends on your inner life as much as on your outer circumstances.**[13] Through education and practice, it is possible to improve your inner life — to accept yourself better and to feel more for others. In most of us there is a deep positive force, which can be liberated if we can overcome our negative thoughts. To develop this inner strength of character should be a major goal of education. For adults there is a range of spiritual practices that help to bring peace of mind, from Buddhist meditation to positive psychology. For those who are struggling, cognitive therapy has a good record of success. For those in the extremes of misery, psychiatric drugs and cognitive therapy have probably helped more than any other changes in the last fifty years, and we can expect further major advances.

- **Public policy can more easily remove misery than augment happiness.**[14] This is because the causes of misery are the more obvious, especially when we look beyond the family circle. It is also morally right to give extra weight to removing misery. So that should be a major focus for public policy. In the West the most miserable group of people are the mentally ill. We know how to help most of them, but only about a quarter are currently in treatment. We owe them better.

Verdict on Economics

Given all this, are mainstream economists right or wrong in how they approach our problems?[15] Partly right, partly wrong. Here is the good part. Each individual knows more about himself than anyone else does. So there are huge gains all round if we can freely exchange goods and services with each other—including our labour. This is especially so where markets are large and well-informed and no one affects anyone else except through the process of voluntary exchange. Indeed, economists have correctly shown that if these conditions exist and contracts can be enforced and tastes are given, the outcome will be fully "efficient." In other words, everyone will be as happy as is possible without someone else being less happy. This important claim helps to explain the extraordinary success of post-war capitalism in producing material advance.

Yet why did this advance not guarantee a rise in personal happiness? The reason is that many of the most important things that touch us do not reach us through voluntary exchange. Nor have our tastes, expectations and norms remained unchanged—and these too affect our happiness.

Other people affect us through so many channels that voluntary exchange is only a limited part of the story. For example, we are directly affected by our experience of how other people live. Our children are affected even more. Advertising too affects our perceptions. We are also affected in a quite involuntary way by crime on the streets, the friendliness of our neighbours and, perhaps, the seductive tendencies of our spouse's colleague. That is why we have laws and codes that regulate all kinds of institutions and behaviour, going far beyond the simple enforcement of voluntary contracts.

Moreover, our values can change. In the last forty years we have become increasingly individualistic, especially in Britain and the United States. We are ever more influenced by exaggerated versions of the "survival of the fittest" (Charles Darwin) and "the invisible hand" (Adam Smith).[16] A result has been the well-documented decline in trust.

Our leaders use increasingly tough language to describe the world we live in. They talk much less of security and community, and more of the competitive struggle. They argue that we can no longer afford to provide security. As most economists would agree, this is nonsense. As we become ever richer, we can freely choose how much of our extra wealth we devote to higher living standards and how much to security in employment, in old age and in our community. The aim of politics is to make the world a more friendly place and not an assault course.

A Better World: Taking Happiness Seriously

So what is my picture of a better society in which people feel under less threat and less pressure, and can really exploit the end of scarcity that science makes possible? What should we do differently if we shifted our goal towards achieving a happier way of life?[17]

- We should monitor the development of happiness in our countries as closely as we monitor the development of income.

- We should rethink our attitude on many standard issues. On taxes, we should recognise the role they play in preserving the work-life balance. On performance-related pay, we should worry about its tendency to encourage the rat race. On mobility, we should consider its tendency to increase crime and weaken families and communities.

- We should spend more on helping the poor, especially in the Third World. The United States at present spends 0.13% of its income on overseas aid, Britain 0.31%.[18] We now understand better how to spend this money.[19] If you want to relieve hunger and misery, here is a ready-made route. We should be proud to make this a goal of our affluent societies.

- We should spend more on tackling the problem of mental illness. This is the greatest source of misery in the West, and the fortunate should ensure a better deal for those who suffer. Psychiatry should be a top branch of medicine, not one of the least prestigious.

- To improve family life, we should introduce more family-friendly practices at work—more flexible hours, more parental leave and easier access to child care.

- We should subsidise activities that promote community life.

- We should eliminate high unemployment. Here tough-and-tender works best. After a time everyone should be given a chance to work, but should have to take advantage of the opportunity in order to continue receiving support.

233

- To fight the constant escalation of wants, we should prohibit commercial advertising to children, as in Sweden. We should also cut tax allowances for pictorial advertising to adults by business.

- Finally, and perhaps most importantly, we need better education, including, for want of a better word, moral education. We should teach the principles of morality not as interesting points for discussion but as established truths to hold on to, essential for a meaningful life. We should teach the systematic practice of empathy, and the desire to serve others. This needs a proper curriculum from the beginning of school life to the end, including detailed study of role models. The curriculum should also cover control of one's own emotions, parenting, mental illness and of course citizenship. But the basic aim should be the sense of an overall purpose wider than oneself.

Conclusion

A society cannot flourish without some sense of shared purpose. The current pursuit of self-realisation will not work. If your sole duty is to achieve the best for yourself, life becomes just too stressful, too lonely—you are set up to fail. Instead, you need to feel you exist for something larger, and that very thought takes off some of the pressure.

We desperately need a concept of the common good. I can think of no nobler goal than to pursue the greatest happiness of all—each person counting. This goal puts us on an equal footing with our neighbours, which is where we should be, while it also gives a proper weight to our own interest, since we know more about ourselves than anyone else does.

Some people say you should not think about your own happiness, because you can only be happy as a by-product of something else.[20] That is a dismal philosophy, a formula for keeping oneself occupied at all costs. Of course you cannot be happy without a wider goal than yourself, but you cannot be happy either without self-knowledge and self-acceptance. If you feel low, there are centuries-old philosophies to help. Better to seek the beauty within than to have an affair.

So happiness comes from outside and from within. The two are not in contradiction. The true pilgrim fights the evils in the world out there and cultivates the spirit within.

The secret is compassion towards oneself and others, and the principle of the Greatest Happiness is essentially the expression of that ideal. Perhaps these two ideas could be the cornerstones of our future culture.

Mankind has come a long way since the Stone Age, and we in the West are probably happier than any previous society.[21] But the anxieties that were useful in the Stone Age ought to be unnecessary today. So we should rededicate our society to the pursuit of happiness rather than the goal of dynamic efficiency. Life is for living. Through science, absolute material scarcity has been conquered in the West, and we need to think hard about what would now constitute progress. I believe passionately that progress is possible.

We cannot end better than with Jeremy Bentham. Shortly before his death he sent a birthday letter to a friend's young daughter, in which he wrote,

Create all the happiness you are able to create: remove all the misery you are able to remove. Every day will allow you to add something to the pleasure of others, or to diminish something of their pains. And for every grain of enjoyment you sow in the bosom of another, you shall find a harvest in your own bosom; while every sorrow which you pluck out from the thoughts and feelings of a fellow creature shall be replaced by beautiful peace and joy in the sanctuary of your soul.[22]

I call that pretty good advice.

My thanks

This book is almost a joint production—so many people have helped. The book would never have happened without Daniel Kahneman. In 1998 he gave the Robbins Lectures at the London School of Economics and fired me with the evidence that happiness can be measured and explained. I had been waiting to hear this news since I first wrote about happiness in 1980, and I soon decided to write this book.

I have been extremely fortunate at every step. Daniel Kahneman invited me for two substantial visits to the Center for Health and Well-Being at Princeton, for which I am extremely grateful. From this emerged two two-day conferences at the London School of Economics, one general and one on the first draft of this book, which led to massive rewriting. At the same time Nicholas Humphrey, Michael Marmot and I were leading a small happiness forum, which met monthly for a year.

I was also invited to give the 2003 Robbins Lectures on the subject "Happiness: has social science a clue?" These lectures, available on the web, seemed to strike a chord. The web site received fifty thousand hits and provoked one thousand emails. I am extremely grateful to all who wrote in.

It is impossible to thank adequately all thirty-five people who have generously commented on the book. Many of them also provided other vital advice. The people who have helped me most include

> *Psychology*: Sarah Blakemore, Avshalom Caspi, David Clark, Helena Cronin, Richard Davidson, Ed Diener, Dylan Evans, Jeffrey Gray (tragically dead), David Halpern, Nicholas Humphrey, Felicia Huppert, Oliver James, Daniel Kahneman and Tim Shallice.

> *Medicine/Psychiatry*: Michael Marmot, Randolph Nesse, Steven Rose, Michael Rutter, Burton Singer, Leslie Turnberg, Simon Wessely and Lewis Wolpert.

> *Sociology/Anthropology*: Mary Douglas, Kate Gavron, Tony Giddens, Christopher Jencks, Sara McLanahan, Robert Putnam and Garry Runciman.

> *Philosophy*: Roger Crisp, Keith Dowding, Bhikhu Parekh, Amartya Sen and Peter Singer.

> *Economics*: Tim Besley, Andrew Clark, Gavyn Davies, Mike Elsby, Stanley Fischer, Richard Freeman, Bruno Frey, John Helliwell, Will Hutton, Richard Jackman, Hamish McRae, Alan Manning, Stephen Nickell, Andrew Oswald, Matthew Rabin and Robert Skidelsky.

> *General*: Colin Ash, Jane Atkinson, William Barnes, Chris Beauman, Bob Gavron, Molly Meacher, Julia Neuberger, Hetan Shah and Nigel Wentworth.

Needless to say, they do not always agree with me.

Five people have been particularly crucial. Andrew Oswald has been the pathfinder of happiness studies in Britain, first at the London School of Economics and then at Warwick. Richard Davidson is the leading neuropsychologist in this field and has generously initiated me both here and at his laboratory. Nicholas Humphrey and Randolph Nesse are leading evolutionary thinkers, and Michael Marmot is a pioneer on the social aspects of health. All have provided a wealth of wisdom and encouragement.

The whole project has depended on the support of the London School of Economics, which has been my happy home for forty years, and of the Economic and Social Research Council, which has generously financed the Centre for Economic Performance for the last twenty-five years.

At the Centre I have been incredibly lucky in my team: Linda Cleavely has been a quite brilliant producer of manuscripts; Niall Flynn a thoughtful and committed research assistant; and Marion O'Brien, as always, a perfect organiser of my life. I have been privileged to have a wonderful agent, Caroline Dawnay of PFD, and at Penguin two great editors—Scott Moyers in New York and Stuart Proffitt in London—who have enormously improved the book.

Molly, my wife, by her faith in the project, her clarity of mind and her support, has made it all possible.

Thank you all.

Richard

Sources of tables, charts and diagrams

P. 14 How happy are we?
World Values Survey (1981, 1990, 1995–97). An up-to-date analysis based on the General Social Survey and Eurobarometer also shows both countries are very similar.

Pp. 15, 16 Happiness ... activities/Happiness ... people
Kahneman et al. (2004), table 1. Average happiness is measured by positive affect minus negative affect.

P. 16 Average happiness at different times of day
Kahneman et al. (2004), figure 1. The data are for negative affect but with the sign reversed.

P. 18 The brain's response to two pictures
Sutton, S. K., Ward, R. T., Larson, C. L., Holden, J. E., Perlman, S. B. and Davidson, R. J. "Asymmetry in pre-frontal glucose metabolism during appetitive and aversive emotional states: An FDG-PET study," *Psychophysiology* 34, S89. Diagram kindly provided by Richard Davidson.

P. 30 Income and happiness in the United States
Income per head (adjusted for prices)
Bureau of Economic Analysis, U.S. Department of Commerce, National Income and Product Accounts, table 7.1 Real GDP per person per year.

Happiness
1946–71: American Institute of Public Opinion (AIPO) (Gallup), reported in T. W. Smith, "Happiness: Time trends, seasonal variations. In-

tersurvey differences and other mysteries," *Social Psychology Quarterly* 42(1), Mar. 1979, 18–30.

1972–2000: General Social Survey (GSS).

The survey questions were comparable but not identical:

AIPO: In general, how happy would you say that you are—very happy, fairly happy or not happy?

GSS: Taking things all together, how would you say you are these days—would you say that you are very happy, pretty happy or not too happy?

The GSS got fewer replies in the top category than the AIPO for obvious reasons (the difference between "pretty happy" and "fairly happy"). My approach is to accept the GSS replies and adjust all the AIPO ones to give the same AIPO reply in 1971 as the GSS reply in 1972. See R. G. Niemi et al., *Trends in Public Opinion*, 1989; New York: Greenwood Press, Table 15.1.

Note also that fewer people in the GSS are "very happy" compared with WVS data in the table on p. 14. This is because of the difference in the adjacent category: "pretty happy" in the GSS and "quite happy" in the WVS.

P. 31 Happiness according to income position

World Values Survey. For the U.S., 1981, 1990 and 1995–97; for the UK, 1981 and 1990.

P. 32 Income and happiness: Comparing countries

Income per head

World Bank, *World Development Report*. Real GDP per person per year in 1999, measured at purchasing power parity in U.S. dollars.

Happiness

World Values Survey, fourth wave, around 1999. Where not available, an earlier wave.

The questions were:

i) Taking all things together, would you say you are very happy, quite happy, not very happy, not at all happy?

ii) All things considered, how satisfied are you with your life as a whole these days? Please use this card to help with your answer.

1	2	3	4	5	6	7	8	9	10

Dissatisfied   Satisfied

The value shown in the graph is the average of per cent "quite" or "very happy" and per cent "satisfied" to level 6 or above.

P. 43 Required real income and actual average real income
Rainwater (1990), table 1. The question has not been asked since 1986, when Gallup moved from face-to-face to telephone interviewing.

P. 50 Hours worked in the year
Annual hours of all workers are taken from OECD *Employment Outlook* 2003, p. 322. They are then multiplied by the ratio of weekly hours worked by full-time workers to weekly hours worked by all workers (from European Labour Force Survey and U.S. Current Population Survey).

P. 57 If one twin has the problem, ...
McGue and Bouchard (1998), table 1.

P. 63 The Big Seven factors affecting happiness
Annex 5.2. at http://cep.lse.ac.uk/layard/annex.pdf.

P. 64 Effects on happiness
All rows except 8 and 9: Helliwell (2003a), table 3, based on World Values Survey. To find the effect of a 33% decrease in family income, I assume that we move from the sixth decile group to the fourth decile group (correct for the UK, see Office of National Statistics *Economic Trends*, April 2000, p. 62).
Row 8: Blanchflower and Oswald (1999), table 7. Very approximate.
Row 9: Di Tella et al. (2003), tables 8 and 10.

P. 79 Family problems
1960: McLanahan and Sandefur (1994), p. 138.

2000: Column 1   U.S.: *Statistical Abstract of the USA* (data for 1997). UK: *Social Trends*, No. 31, 2001 edition (data for 1999).

Columns 2 and 3   G. Martin and V. Kats, "Families and work in transition in 12 countries, 1980–2001," *Monthly Labor Review*, September 2003, tables 4 and 6.

P. 81 Percentage saying . . .
Putnam (2000), p. 139.

P. 85 Percentage of married people . . .
General Social Survey.

P. 106 Percentage of male deaths caused by warfare
Pinker (2002) as adapted from Keeley (1996), p. 90. The figures are based on the records of twentieth-century anthropologists. Archaeological findings confirm the story they tell.

P. 163 Percentage of children . . .
World Health Organization, *Young People's Health in Context. Health Behaviour in School-aged Children (HBSC) Study: International report from the 2001/2 survey*, edited by Candace Currie et al., fig. 2.18.

P. 173 Unemployment rate, 2000–2004
EU, *European Economy*, 2003, No. 4, pp. 108–9.

P. 182 Causes of disability (United States and European Union)
www.who.org. The data relate to the incidence of disability. The degree of disability for each disease is evaluated by a panel of medical experts (with a measure that lies between 0 and 1). The WHO then add up the disability scores and analyse which diseases are contributing how much to the overall incidence of disability. The results are very similar for the United States and the European Union.

P. 211 If a person has schizophrenia, . . .
Gottesman (1991). Having schizophrenia refers to having it at any time of your life.

List of annexes

Available at http://cep.lse.ac.uk/layard/annex.pdf

These annexes contain a variety of supporting technical analyses. Some contain more statistical tables, some give detailed research evidence and some are speculative analyses.

3.1—Trends in happiness

4.1—Role of income comparisons and habituation

4.2—Productivity and growth in Europe and the USA

4.3—Is happiness cardinal and comparable?

5.1—Heritability

5.2—Domain satisfaction and overall happiness

5.3—Causes of national life-satisfaction and suicide rates

6.1—Effect of TV on happiness

8.1—How caring about others could make people happier

8.2—The value of creating or extending life

11.1—Rates of mental illness and the proportion of sufferers being treated

14.1—Topics needing further research

14.2—Selected reading (by chapter)

Notes

Chapter 1: What's the problem?

1. For continental Europe we have no data before 1975. But the data since then show a slight upwards trend in happiness—unlike in the United States, Britain and Japan (see chapter 3). In Third World countries happiness has increased. But this book deals only with the richer countries of the world.
2. Strictly, to a situation where no one can become happier without someone else becoming less happy.
3. Hobbes (1642).
4. Frankl (1985).

Chapter 2: What is happiness?

1. *The Code of the Woosters.*
2. Robinson and Downhill (1995), figures 23.1 and 23.6.
3. See Davidson (1992, 2000) and, more technical, Davidson et al. (2000). The area concerned is the dorsolateral prefrontal cortex. The left side is especially active in the types of happiness experienced when approaching a goal (though also after meditation). The right side is especially active in self-criticism and self-monitoring. The correlations between the brain measures and self-reported feelings are naturally less than 100%.
4. For an excellent survey of the concept of objective happiness see Kahneman's chapter 1 in Kahneman et al. (1999).
5. Diener and Suh (1999). Note that people answer similarly about themselves whether they are replying to an interviewer or filling in a form: there is thus little bias due to the interview situation. One can also analyse facial expression, especially the frequency of "Duchenne smiles," when the eye smiles as well as the mouth. These measurements also correlate with self-reported happiness, but less well.
6. See Kahneman et al. (2004).
7. On this section see Davidson (1992 and 2000, pp.1202–4). Also Davidson et al. (2000). All remarks in this section relate to right-handed people. EEG means electroencephalogram; MRI means magnetic resonance imaging; PET means positron emission tomography, where radioactive isotopes are put in the bloodstream and then traced.
8. The brain sections are taken at right angles to the spine and at varying distances from the top of the head.

9. Lisanby (2003).
10. Clow et al. (2003).
11. Fox and Davidson (1986).
12. I am using the word "feelings" to denote conscious experience, and "emotion" to refer to the total process of affective response, see for example, Damasio (1994).
13. Coghill et al. (2003). Interestingly, the brain response in the thalamus, a more primitive part of the brain, is virtually the same for all subjects. But this is not where conscious experience occurs.
14. In an interesting experiment a British team took sixteen couples and gave a series of random electric shocks to either the man or the woman. When the man was being shocked, the woman received a signal of what was happening. Her brain was monitored both when she was shocked (physical pain) and when her partner was shocked (mental pain). The brain response in two brain areas was similar in both situations (Singer et al., 2004). On the more general interaction of physical and mental pain see Romano and Turner (1985) and Turk and Okifuji (1994).
15. To investigate this requires data within the same individual over time. For example if a person's mood is stimulated by positive and negative film clips and observed a number of times using EEG, there is a strong negative correlation of left and right activation.

    A quite different issue is to compare different individuals. When the reporting period is not instantaneous, we naturally find the same person reporting both positive and negative feelings. Indeed, some people report many of both and some report few of both, which tends to introduce a positive statistical correlation between positive and negative feelings, when measured across people. But these results are not relevant because
    (i) the feelings are not instantaneous
    (ii) they involve more measurement error than readings on the same person over time, and
    (iii) the researchers test for a linear relationship between positive and negative feelings, while the true relationship is in fact L-shaped (where positive feelings are measured on one axis and negative feelings on the other).

    The study of Texas women highlights the difference between correlations over time and across people. The correlation of positive and negative feeling across situations for the same person was –.83, while the correlation across individuals was only –.42 (see an earlier draft of Kahneman et al., 2004).

    On these issues see also Green et al. (1999), and Russell and Carroll (1999a and b), who give further evidence in favour of the existence of a single dimension of happiness/unhappiness.
16. They are discussed at length by Csikszentmihalyi (1990). He describes, for example, a chess-player reporting afterwards on how he feels during a game: "I have a general feeling of well-being and that I am in complete control of my world." However Seligman (2002, p.116) argues that during flow you have no positive feeling: that feeling only comes in retrospect. Seligman distinguishes altogether three different types of happiness – the pleasant life (of the senses), the good life (flow) and the meaningful life (commitment to some other). Clearly all these factors interact to influence the overall stream of happiness that we experience.

17. See Keyes et al. (2002), model 4, and the forthcoming paper by Ryff in F. Huppert et al. (2005), *The Science of Well-being*, Oxford: Oxford University Press. Their work also shows that refined measures of purposeful enjoyment, positive self-regard, positive relationships, environmental mastery, and personal growth can often predict physical markers such as cortisol levels, immune function, heart function, bone-mineral density, sleep quality, and left-right frontal asymmetry of brain activity. And they can do this better than single-question responses on life satisfaction.

18. Ryff would not agree with my conclusion, and she is right to argue against facile and mechanical views of happiness. But in the wide spectrum of opinion on these matters, the gap between "Benthamite" and "neo-Aristotelian" thinkers is very small compared to the gap between those two positions and the rest.

19. On these ethical issues see chapter 8.

20. Danner et al. (2001), table 3, rows 5 and 8.

21. See, for example, Ryff and Singer (2003), Goleman (1996, chapter 11), and Rosenkranz et al. (2003).

22. Ryff and Singer (2003) and Davidson et al. (2000). These relationships have been found using both self-reported happiness and brain measurements of happiness. Ryff and Singer also show the good effect of loving relationships on a weighted average of stress-related physical indicators that they refer to as "allostatic load."

23. Redelmeier and Singh (2001).

24. Some aspects of moral behaviour fall outside this statement—see chapter 8.

25. For example Clark (1997) stresses models of the organism in which there is relatively little coordination between activities (see pp. 219–27).

26. On humans see, for example, Deaton and Muellbauer (1980). On animals see Shizgal and Conover (1996) and Cabanac (1992). In humans we also have direct examples of how measured happiness influences behaviour. For example, workers who are least satisfied with a job are most likely to quit it (Clark, 2001), and the unemployed people who most dislike unemployment are the most likely to find work (Clark, 2003a).

27. See, for example, Bargh and Chartrand (1999), which summarises the experiments reported in the next paragraph.

28. See chapter 9. Darwin believed this model applied to all sentient animals (Badcock, 2000, pp. 125–26).

29. Nesse and Williams (1996, chapter 14). Two other key psychological mechanisms are loss-aversion and the neglect of duration in the recall of past pain (people tend to focus instead on the peak and end levels of pain). The value of these mechanisms for survival is obvious: loss-aversion encourages resistance to loss, and the memory of peak pain helps us to avoid extreme future danger. Note also that most people who cannot feel pain are dead before they are thirty (Nesse and Williams, 1996, p. 35).

CHAPTER 3: ARE WE GETTING HAPPIER?

1. Neither has it diminished; see annex 3.1 at http://cep.lse.ac.uk/layard/annex.pdf. I do not discuss in this book the specific experience of blacks in the United States, which is a whole subject in itself. Blacks have certainly become happier, though they are still less happy than whites (General Social Survey).

2. The source is Gallup, which gives the following percentages "very happy" as opposed to "fairly happy" or worse: 1948, 40; 1952, 42; 1957, 52. These compare with the

World Values Survey, which gives the following percentages "very happy" as opposed to "quite happy" or worse: 1981, 38; 1990, 35; 1998, 33.

3. See World Database of Happiness, available on the web.

4. Interestingly, self-reported health *has* risen over time in the United States (General Social Survey), reflecting accurately the increase in objective absolute healthiness.

5. It would be sufficient to examine how in a sample the relationship between self-reported happiness and brain measurements had changed. Note of course that none of our figures include the 0.3% of the population in hospital, where physical pain and mental suffering have been significantly reduced since World War II.

6. Easterlin (2001). In Europe we have separate trends for life satisfaction and happiness. Not surprisingly life satisfaction, which is a more relative concept, has grown less than happiness; see annex 3.1 at http://cep.lse.ac.uk/layard/annex.pdf. Interestingly, Clark (2002a) suggests that in Britain in recent years successive cohorts are less satisfied.

7. Nor across those countries is additional income associated with additional life expectancy. Yet in any one country life expectancy, like happiness, rises with (relative) income. See Marmot (2004).

8. If your eye suggests the difference is not great, notice that the percentage *not* happy/satisfied is nearly four times as high in India as in the United States.

9. Diener and Oishi (2000), p. 204.

10. Helliwell (2003a), table 6. However, this finding is heavily influenced by Eastern Europe and the Soviet republics, where the correlation of income and happiness is especially high. In annex 4.3 at http://cep.lse.ac.uk/layard/annex.pdf we explain how it is possible to compare the changes in happiness that occur at different points in the income scale.

11. Inglehart and Klingemann (2000, p. 176) give data for one Russian region in 1981. They also give data for Hungary in 1981 that place Hungary level with Bangladesh.

12. Veenhoven (2000).

13. Shao (1993). Indeed, the answers in the two languages were as consistent as the answers found in another group of Chinese students who were asked the same questions three weeks apart, using the Chinese language both times.

14. See, for example, Di Tella et al. (2003), table 10.

15. For this paragraph see Fombonne (1995).

16. See chapter 13.

17. See chapter 11, note 39.

18. The main source for the United States is the 1982 Epidemiological Catchment Area (ECA) study of 18,000 adults in their homes; see Fombonne (1995), p. 555. In the ECA data there has been a roughly equiproportional increase in depression, schizophrenia and panic disorder (Fombonne, 1995, p. 564). More recently for the United States and five other countries we have the retrospective evidence of the WHO International Consortium in Psychiatric Epidemiology (2000), p. 420; for the United States this uses the 1992 National Co-Morbidity Survey.

19. Wells and Horwood (2004).

20. For a general survey see Fombonne (1995), pp. 554–55. For example, in one Swedish district, Lundby, a careful study of the whole population showed significant increases in depression (severe or medium) between 1947–57 and 1957–72 (Hagnell et al.,

1990, pp. 81–82, tables 48c and d). In Britain the Office of National Statistics (2001) (hereafter abbreviated ONS; 2001), table 3.3 showed that mental illness increased in men by around 14% between 1993 and 2000; there was no change for women. For longer term changes in Britain see Ferri et al. (2003), p. 230. Notice that none of the findings in this section relate to how doctors diagnosed individual patients, which has surely changed over time.

21. On this and the following paragraph see Silbereisen et al. (1995). In the United Kingdom, 26% of people undertook hazardous drinking in the last year (ONS, 2001, table 2.14). The proportion of people experiencing "alcohol dependence" in the last six months was 8% and "drug dependence" 4% (over half on cannabis only). Both figures are for the year 2000 and are at least 75% higher than seven years earlier (table 3.5). The UK government estimates that the cost of alcohol-related crime, illness, work absence and family break-up is around £20 billion a year (Cabinet Office, 2004). On possible measures to counter alcohol abuse, see Academy of Medical Sciences (2004). For relevant U.S. data see diagram on page 182.

22. Diekstra et al. (1995). For youths, Germany is an exception—perhaps their apprenticeship system is a good prophylactic.

23. Smith (1995a).

24. Today a high proportion of criminals are on drugs, and many crimes are committed to pay for drugs. This may be a partial explanation of current crime rates. But it is unlikely that criminals who are dependent on drugs are happy. Nor are the ½% who are dependent on gambling (Orford et al., 2003).

25. Wilson and Herrnstein (1985).

CHAPTER 4: IF YOU'RE SO RICH, WHY AREN'T YOU HAPPY?

1. Quoted in Frank (1999), p. 10.

2. Solnick and Hemenway (1998), table 2. The students were in the School of Public Health.

3. See pp. 43–47 below and annex 4.1 at http://cep.lse.ac.uk/layard/annex.pdf.

4. See pp. 48–49 below.

5. For general discussion see Layard (1980) and Frank (1985, 1999).

6. General Social Survey data. See Lane (2000), p. 25.

7. Bewley (1999).

8. Ashenfelter and Layard (1983).

9. Medvec et al. (1995).

10. Clark (1996b). Also unemployment hurts you less if more "other people" are unemployed, and if you have been unemployed previously (Clark, 2003a).

11. Postlethwaite et al. (1998).

12. Blanchflower and Oswald (2004). The study relates to the United States, and other people's income was measured by the average income in the state where the respondent lived.

13. See annex 4.1 at http://cep.lse.ac.uk/layard/annex.pdf. At this stage our knowledge does not enable us to distinguish between externalities working through income and externalities working through consumption.

14. See Stutzer (2003), summarised in annex 4.1 at http://cep.lse.ac.uk/layard/annex.pdf.

In that study a person's income affects happiness roughly eight times more than others' income does. By contrast a study of British job satisfaction finds that only relative wages matter (Clark and Oswald, 1996).

15. Lyubomirsky and Ross (1997).

16. See Frederick and Loewenstein (1999) and Clark et al. (2003). We discuss marriage more fully in the next chapter.

17. Van Praag and Frijters (1999).

18. Van Praag and Frijters (1999) give estimates for nine countries, all between 35 and 65 cents. The "required income" also varies with family size in a way that produces sensible equivalence scales for family income requirements. Stutzer (2003) gets an esitimate of 40 cents (see annex 4.1 at http://cep.lse.ac.uk/layard/annex.pdf).

19. There are varying degrees of addiction. Suppose $H_t = f(c_t - \lambda c_{t-1})$ where H is happiness and c is the logarithm of consumption. We start from a steady state and increase consumption by $x\%$ in period T. If $\lambda = 1$ we have "complete addiction" and consumption must continue rising by $x\%$ in every period in order to preserve happiness at the level in period T. If λ is less than 1, we have "partial addiction" and consumption growth could eventually level off while keeping happiness at its level in period T.

20. Frank (1999) and Frey and Stutzer (2003a).

21. See Loewenstein and Schkade (1999), Loewenstein et al. (2003), Frey and Stutzer (2003b) and Gilbert and Watson (2001). However, employers seem to understand that employees' morale is helped if, as they age, they experience regular increases in income, even when this is not fully matched by increased productivity. That is one reason why a person's earnings in a firm rise more with age than his productivity does (Frank and Hutchens, 1993).

22. This is the main distortion, rather than the distortion in favour of spending as against saving (Layard, 2005). The argument assumes there are corrective taxes.

23. OECD *Employment Outlook* 2003, p. 322. Australia works slightly longer.

24. See annex 4.2 at http://cep.lse.ac.uk/layard/annex.pdf.

25. Freeman and Schettkat (2001).

26. See annex 4.2 at http://cep.lse.ac.uk/layard/annex.pdf.

27. In U.S. purchasing power (World Bank, *World Development Report*, 2000–1, foreword).

28. See *Economist*, April 24, 2004, p. 30.

29. This is so, holding constant the average income in the country. For example, in the U.S. General Social Survey one can regress happiness on income and income squared. The latter term is always significant, which is why the single term $\log Y$ is used in annex 4.1. See also Helliwell (2003a), but his findings relate to income rankings and leave open the issue of whether it is income or income rank that matters.

Throughout this book we assume that happiness is measurable and comparable between people. On the concept of measurability see annex 4.3 at http://cep.lse.ac.uk/layard/annex.pdf.

30. If only income rank matters, then the dispersion of income has no effect on average happiness, since average rank is fixed. But there is as yet no clear evidence about the importance of rank as compared with relative income.

31. Health experts likewise pursue both approaches. For example Wilkinson (1996) believes that relative income affects health *and* that inequality has wider "environmental" effects on society. By contrast Deaton (2003) questions both these effects, arguing

that the social gradient in health can be explained by different absolute levels of income. The evidence on p. 150 below suggests that more than absolute income is involved, as Marmot (2004) argues.

32. Graham and Pettinato (2002), Clark (2003b), Senik (2003). See also Alesina et al. (2001, 2003).

33. Helliwell (2003a).

CHAPTER 5: SO WHAT DOES MAKE US HAPPY?

1. From "Empedocles on Etna."

2. Floud (1998). Two inches equals one standard deviation of male height. For a parallel analysis of IQ see the work of the psychologist James R. Flynn.

3. At each gene locus I have two representations of the gene (two "alleles"). One came from my father and one from my mother. For the same reason my father also had two alleles at that locus. But I only got one of my father's two alleles, randomly selected. So the chance I got one particular allele of my father's is one half. Similarly with my mother's alleles. The same set of chances applies to my sibling. So one time in two I will get the same allele as my sibling. Thus ordinary siblings "have roughly half their genes in common." But identical twins come from the same egg and have all their genes in common. (This analysis applies to those genes that differ between people, the so-called polymorphic genes. These genes comprise about a quarter of all our genes; the other three-quarters are the same for all humans.)

4. Lykken (1999), p. 56. The study uses the Tellegen Multi-dimensional Personality Questionnaire to measure well-being. The correlation coefficient between the happiness of the first-born and second-born twin is .44 for identical twins and .08 for non-identical twins. (The correlation coefficient between two variables x and y, each measured from their average, is the total, across all observations, of xy divided by the standard deviation of x times the standard deviation of y.)

5. Lykken (1999), p. 56. The same is true of non-identical twins reared apart, compared with those raised together. See also Plomin et al. (2001), p. 236.

6. Suppose $H = G + E + I (G,E) + e$
where H is measured happiness, G the genes, E experience, I an interaction effect $(G \times E)$ and e a measurement error. Then
Var (H)–Var (E)–Var (e) = Var (G) + Var (I) + 2 Cov (G,E) + 2 Cov (G,I) + 2 Cov (E,I).
The standard measure of "heritability" includes in the effect of genes all of the right-hand side of this equation. See Rutter (2001) and Plomin et al. (2001). For further detail on the measurement of heritability see annex 5.1 at http://cep.lse.ac.uk/layard/annex.pdf.

7. Great credit goes to Judith Rich Harris for insisting that these issues be taken seriously (see Harris, 1998, and Pinker, 2002). But her conclusion that upbringing has small effects is inconsistent with much of the recent evidence—see pp. 59–60 below.

8. Tienari et al. (1994), p. 23. The results are from the Finnish adoption study.

9. Bohman (1995), table 1. The results are from the Stockholm adoption study.

10. Cadoret et al. (1995), table 4. This is a U.S. study, based on four adoption agencies.

11. This is especially well documented for IQ, where the correlation between pairs of adoptive siblings is around .25 in childhood but fades towards zero in adulthood (Plomin et al., 2001, p. 177).

12. Caspi et al. (2004).

13. Caspi et al. (2003), figure 2. The gene is the 5-HTT gene. Caspi et al. (2002, figure 2) show a similar result for adult violence, which depends on both mistreatment as a child *and* the gene encoding monoamine oxidase A (MAOA), which metabolises various neurotransmitters.

14. To control for the full set of genes, one still needs to use twin studies. Jaffee et al. (2004) do this for seven-year-old British twins and show how physical maltreatment affects their behaviour, controlling for the genes. On the effects of child abuse on brain development see Teicher (2002).

15. Anisman et al. (1998). They also become better mothers.

16. Suomi (1997).

17. Collins et al. (2000), pp. 225–26.

18. An exception is O'Connor et al. (2000), who use the Colorado Adoption Project to show how parental separation affects the behaviour of twelve-year-olds.

19. Furstenberg and Kiernan (2001), table 1. The same is true for effects on school drop-out and teenage pregnancy, see McLanahan and Sandefur (1994), p. 70. For further evidence on parenting and depression see Cherlin et al. (1998), Glenn and Kramer (1985) and Ermisch and Francesconi (2001), who rely on sibling differences.

20. Amato et al. (1995). They interviewed parents over a period of twelve years, and in the last year they interviewed their children aged nineteen and over.

21. Neither studying nor working. All results control for mother's and father's education, race, number of siblings and area. See McLanahan and Sandefur (1994). In their appendix B they claim that the measured effect of being a single-parent child is not due to some feature of the parents that also precipitated the break-up of the marriage. Further evidence on the independent effect of losing a parent comes from the serious effect of parental death. On the effects of single parenthood on crime see Sigle-Rushton and McLanahan (2002). See also Lykken (2001).

22. Amato et al. (1995). If both spouses' parents are divorced, a couple is much more likely to divorce than if neither's parents are divorced. But McGue and Lykken (1992) show that much of the intergenerational transmission of divorce is due to genetic likeness of children and parents — identical twins have much higher concordance than non-identical twins.

23. McLanahan and Sandefur (1994), p. 67. In the United States roughly half of all children with a single mother never lived with their father.

24. Focusing on the behaviour of a sample of British five-year-olds, Jaffee et al. (2003) find that absence of the father has no negative effect, once the father's own level of antisocial behaviour has been allowed for. However, it is risky to extrapolate this to the effect of parental absence when a child is older.

25. See Easterlin (2001). The data compare different random samples of people in the same birth cohort taken at different ages. They relate to happiness uncorrected for other influences. Controlling for other influences, happiness falls somewhat up to about age forty and then rises.

26. The distribution of happiness is similar for men and women in most countries. However, in a regression where factors like income, age and employment status are controlled for, women are somewhat happier than men. The pattern of mental illness is

of course different for men and women: women are more prone to depression, and men to alcoholism.

27. See Keltner and Harker (2001), table 6. Diener et al. (1995) show some relation, but it becomes small when hair, jewellery and clothing are covered up (see their table 3).

28. Lykken (1999), p. 73.

29. Using the World Values Survey, Helliwell (2003a) finds no direct effect of education. Most studies using the Eurobarometer or U.S. General Social Survey data find some direct effect within each country (e.g., Di Tella et al., 2003), though one cannot tell whether this is an effect of the absolute level of education or the relative level.

30. See annex 5.2 at http://cep.lse.ac.uk/layard/annex.pdf. Other surveys give similar results. The last two factors cannot be ranked, but their relevance is shown in the table on p. 64. See also endnote 34.

31. To control for the social aspects of religion, we hold church attendance constant.

32. See Helliwell (2003a). His results are very similar to those from other surveys like the General Social Survey in the United States and the Eurobarometer Survey. For Eurobarometer and the U.S. General Social Survey results see Di Tella et al. (2003).

33. The scale is actually 1 to 10, but it is easier to explain if all units are multiplied by 10. The mean is then 68 and the standard deviation is 24. The question Helliwell uses relates to life satisfaction, but this is highly correlated with happiness. Di Tella et al. (2003) get very similar results when happiness is the dependent variable.

34. The Helliwell study also controls for age, education and seven area "fixed effects" (Western Europe and the United States, Scandinavia, former Soviet Union, Central and Eastern Europe, Latin America, Asia, Other). But dropping these area fixed effects makes little difference to the results.

35. Happiness is influenced much less by income than by "satisfaction with your financial situation," since the latter also reflects "perceived" relative income and financial commitments (see annex 4.1, section 1).

36. Frey and Stutzer (2003a).

37. Clark et al. (2003). See also Easterlin (2003).

38. The effect is about one-third of the change shown in the table; see Lucas et al. (2003), p. 532.

39. For further discussion see p. 71 below.

40. Clark et al. (2003).

41. Waite (1995).

42. Gardner and Oswald (2002).

43. Clarke and Berrington (1999), p. 7.

44. Ryff and Singer (2003), figure 57.4 and references there to other work by the same authors.

45. For a scientific analysis see Lewis et al. (2000).

46. Winkelmann and Winkelmann (1998), table 4.

47. Winkelmann and Winkelmann (1998), table 2; Layard (2003a).

48. Clark (2002b). I give low weight to his British Household Panel Survey results since the happiness question is inadequate.

49. Clark (2003a), table 4.

50. Clark et al. (2001).

51. Di Tella et al. (2001).
52. As we explain in chapter 11, lower unemployment cannot in the long run be achieved at the expense of higher inflation. In this context it is interesting to note that if inflation rises by 10 percentage points, happiness only falls by 1 point (using the index of happiness used in the table on p. 64). This is much less than the effect of a 10 percentage point rise in unemployment.
53. Marmot (2004).
54. Putnam (2000); Halpern (2004).
55. Knack (2001). The correlation coefficient was .65. The wallet experiment had been conducted by the *Reader's Digest*.
56. Michalos (2003) and annex 5.2 at http://cep.lse.ac.uk/layard/annex.pdf.
57. See, for example, Riis et al. (2002) on renal dialysis. However, a famous article by Brickman et al. (1978) clearly exaggerated the case for this, as even a look at their own figures shows.
58. Loewenstein and Schkade (1999).
59. See, for example, Frederick and Loewenstein (1999).
60. Frey and Stutzer (2000a, 2002).
61. On European deaths see Davies (1997), pp. 1328–29.
62. See Helliwell (2003b) for this and the next two paragraphs. See annex 5.3 at http://cep.lse.ac.uk/layard/annex.pdf for details of his findings.
63. The main such organisations are: those helping the young, old, sick or in trouble; political/lobby organisations; leisure organisations (arts, sports); and ethnic organisations. The classic study of membership is Putnam (2000).
64. Of the six factors discussed under personal freedom this variable uses only four: the rule of law, the effectiveness of government services, the absence of corruption, and the efficiency of the system of regulation.
65. See annex 5.3 at http://cep.lse.ac.uk/layard/annex.pdf.
66. Goleman (1996).
67. From "The Character of a Happy Life."
68. Across nations the relation cannot arise because people with a genetic predisposition to happiness are more inclined to believe in God. Countries where belief is higher also have lower suicide rates, other things being equal. Religious people are also more inclined to trust others (Soroka et al., 2003).
69. Lyubomirsky et al. (2003). See also Lyubomirsky et al. (2004, forthcoming), who stress the importance of what you give (do) compared with what you get (in terms of circumstances).
70. For example, Campbell et al. (1976) popularised this view, though their own thinking was more sophisticated. William James had a similar model.
71. Happiness can be viewed as depending positively on *both* (a) Achievement ÷ Goals *and* (b) Goals ÷ Potential.
72. Nesse (1999, 2000).
73. Scitovsky (1976).
74. Keynes (1930), Russell (1930). They both advocated more attention to the arts. Unfortunately, high culture has totally failed to satisfy this need in the last fifty years (Pinker 2002, chapter 20).

75. Csikszentmihalyi (1990). "Ecstasy" is derived from a Greek word meaning standing outside yourself.

CHAPTER 6: WHAT'S GOING WRONG?

1. See Scott-Clark and Levy (2003) and articles in the *Journal of Bhutan Studies*.
2. Popenoe (1996), p. 19. Not all their parents ever married. Of the children of married parents one-third experience a divorce before they are sixteen.
3. Ellwood and Jencks (2004).
4. Lord Chancellor's Department (1999), p. 3.
5. For the United States see Popenoe (1996), p. 34, and for Britain see ONS *Population Trends*, No. 114, table 1.
6. British data (Kiernan, 2003, p. 12); Lord Chancellor's Department (1999).
7. Cutler et al. (2000). This is based on cross-country analysis of youth suicide rates but is consistent with the fact that when divorce peaked around 1980, youth suicide stopped rising.
8. Interestingly, in the U.S. General Social Survey, average happiness in each marital state has been increasing, but the changing weights have kept average overall happiness from rising.
9. Home Office (2003).
10. Blomquist et al. (1988) estimate that individuals in the best (lowest) crime areas sacrifice money through higher rents and lower wages in order to purchase greater safety. They sacrifice 11% of mean income in wage and rent differentials, as compared with individuals in the worst (highest) crime areas. This is a proxy measure of the "cost" of crime. But Michalos and Zumbo (2000) query the size of the effect of crime on happiness.
11. United States: FBI, *Uniform Crime Reports*; Britain: *Recorded Crime Statistics* 1898–2002. There was of course some unknown increase in the fraction of crimes which were recorded.
12. The main reasons for the fall in crime in the United States since 1991 appear to be increased numbers in prison, increased police, and fewer unwanted births due to legalised abortion (Levitt, 2004).
13. Home Office (2003).
14. Hall (1999), p. 432, and World Values Survey 1995. In 1981 the figure was 43%.
15. Putnam (2000), p. 140. Using the World Values Survey the figures are: 1981, 40%; 1990, 51%; 1995, 36%; 2000, 36%. Using the GSS the figures are: 1972, 46%; 1980, 46%; 2000, 34%.
16. Putnam (2000).
17. Within birth cohorts there is no decline over the lifetime (Putnam, 2000, p. 141).
18. *Historical Statistics of the USA* and *Statistical Abstract of the USA*.
19. http://www.chipubliv.org/004chicago/disasters/infant_mortality.html.
20. There were a few exceptions, like the Lancashire mill towns in Britain, where women arranged complicated rosters of child care.
21. Schreiner (1911).
22. See Mincer and Layard (1985).
23. See also Ellwood and Jencks (2004).

24. Ellwood and Jencks (2004).
25. In Britain we have data on the percentage of married people who consider theirs a "happy relationship." For those aged thirty-three in 1991 it was 81%, and for those aged thirty in 2000 it was 64%. Men and women gave virtually the same answers. See Ferri et al. (2003), table 4.1.
26. Gallup, 2004 data.
27. Smith (1995b). The figure given is the median.
28. Nielsen Media Research.
29. Williams (1986). The study controlled for changes in other comparable towns that already had TV.
30. Children's reading was also reduced, especially for people with lower IQ.
31. See, for example, Huesman and Eron (1986), chapter 1.
32. Phillips (1983). The two days are the third and fourth after the fight. There is no off-set on other days.
33. Gould (2001) summarises the evidence. In one notorious period after the showing of a young man's suicide in a German TV drama, youth suicide was dramatically higher, with no subsequent low to offset this. The main additional deaths were under trains, as in the television drama (Schmidtke and Häfner, 1988).
34. Williams (1986). The study also showed that television increased children's perception of the difference in roles between men and women. Another place where television arrived late was St. Helena; research there on changes in child behaviour showed mixed results, but television viewing was in any case light—about one hour a day (Charlton et al., 2002).
35. Television was introduced in different U.S. states in different years. Using this data Hennigan et al. (1982) show no effect on violence. Larceny however increased by 5% in the first year, when half the population had sets.
36. Gerbner et al. (1980) and Signorielli and Morgan (2001), p. 348.
37. Belk and Pollay (1985).
38. Schudson (1984).
39. O'Guinn and Shrum (1997). This holds constant the income and education of the respondent.
40. See annex 6.1 at http://cep.lse.ac.uk/layard/annex.pdf. If we explain happiness directly by television watching, there is the obvious problem of reverse causality. But if we show a mechanism like that uncovered in annex 6.1, a causal link becomes much more plausible.
41. Estimate in Schor (1999).
42. It also has bad effects by encouraging physical sloth and thus obesity, and low self-respect.
43. Kenrick et al. (1993).
44. Kenrick et al. (1989). See also James (1998). Women have always worried about their looks (see Jane Austen's novels), but they are probably now more likely to underestimate how they look.

Chapter 7: Can we pursue a common good?
1. Wright (1994), Ridley (1996).
2. Hobbes (1651), chapter 13.
3. The dilemma with this name is as follows. There are two prisoners who cannot com-

municate with each other. If each confesses, they will get 2 years each. If one confesses and the other doesn't, the confessor will go free and the other will get 5 years. If neither confesses, they will each get a ½ year. Each will have an incentive to confess. But both would be better off if neither confessed.

4. O'Neill (2002).

5. Robinson and Darley (1997).

6. See, for example, Wolpin (1979).

7. This is so whatever strategy the other party is following (or nearly so). See Axelrod (1984). The number of plays must be unpredictable, otherwise no cooperation occurs in the last game, or the one before that, etc.

8. See, for example, Fehr and Fischbacher (2003). They contrast, for example, the behaviour of the "proposer" in the Ultimatum Game with his behaviour in the Dictator Game. In both games the proposer decides how ten dollars shall be divided between himself and a responder. In the Dictator Game the responder has no say, but in the Ultimatum Game the responder can refuse to accept, in which case the proposer gets nothing either. This leads the proposer to offer more in the Ultimatum Game. However, as Fehr also points out, to reject an offer is an altruistic act intended to punish bad behaviour. He shows that such "altruistic punishment" is necessary for the survival of cooperation in large societies.

9. Zahn-Wexler et al. (1992).

10. If those around you are immoral, it can of course lead to dreadful behaviour (Milgram, 1963).

11. Wilson (1993).

12. Hare (1999).

13. Brown (1991).

14. Loehlin (1992).

15. Rilling et al. (2002), table 6. When the game was against a computer, there was no such brain reaction in the otherwise identical situation.

16. Skyrms (1996). Capuchin monkeys also recognise the principle of fairness and thus reject unfair offers (Brosnan and de Waal, 2003).

17. For some evidence see Schwartz (1970) and Lyubomirsky et al. (2004). However, some cheats do also survive in the competitive struggle. Frank (1988) has a nice explanation of how in equilibrium both cheats and non-cheats can survive—by consorting with people like themselves. See also Fehr and Fischbacher (2003), who show how multiple equilibria are possible: if there are enough selfish people, even unselfish people will behave selfishly.

18. See, for example, Rabin (1998).

19. Pigeons, faced with a small meal now and a big one in four seconds, choose the small meal that is immediately available. But faced with a small meal in ten seconds and a big one in fourteen seconds, they choose the big one that comes with a longer delay. See Ainslie and Herrnstein (1981). There is now a large economic literature which confirms that people have a stronger preference for consumption "today" relative to "tomorrow" than for "tomorrow" compared with the "day-after."

20. Damasio (1994).

21. Frank (1988), table 7.2.

22. It is not clear how far economics teaching has contributed to this, but the theory of

the principal-agent problem has surely encouraged short-run selfishness in business through its impact on systems of remuneration. On economics teaching see Frank et al. (1996) and Frey and Meier (2002).

23. Becker (1981).
24. Murstein et al. (1977).
25. Clark and Mills (1979).
26. Hornstein et al. (1968). I report only the result when the supposed finder was a native. (This is a different study from the one reported on page 69.)
27. They were not always cooperative within the group either; see, for example, Edgerton (1992).
28. Keely (1996).
29. Stone (1983), drawing mainly on the evidence of T. R. Gurr.
30. Sherif (1966). The Stanford Prison Experiment gave similar results.

CHAPTER 8: THE GREATEST HAPPINESS: IS THAT THE GOAL?

1. See page 271, last note.
2. See Bentham (1789). Bentham's forerunners included Hutcheson, Helvetius, Beccaria, Priestley and the Encyclopaedists. Confusingly, Bentham, like Hutcheson, occasionally used the phrase "the greatest happiness of the greatest number." But he explicitly corrected this, saying that he meant the greatest total sum of happiness (Parekh, 1974, p. 99). Unfortunately, the ambiguous phrase survived into common parlance.
3. In chapter 2 we gave an evolutionary explanation of why the search for happiness is so central to our nature. But this does not mean that the aim of policy should be the satisfaction of our ex ante desires, for in some cases this would reduce our happiness. Thus I am advocating the promotion of good feelings, not the satisfaction of desires.
4. He lists, for example, economic facilities, social opportunities, protective security, political freedom and transparency guarantees; see Sen (1999), p. 38 and Sen (1992). In his view conflicts between these objectives should be resolved through the political process. I am more hopeful that evidence can be brought to bear, evidence that tells us about how achieving these objectives affect people's feelings. Nussbaum (2000) offers a more detailed list of capabilities: life; bodily health; bodily freedom; senses, imagination and thought; emotions; practical reason; affiliation; relations with other species; and control of one's environment.
5. In the *Odyssey*, Odysseus and his men come ashore in the land of the lotus-eaters, and after eating lotuses they have no other wish than to stay and continue in that way. This story inspired the poem "The Lotos-Eaters" by Alfred, Lord Tennyson, in which the men express their preference for calm over toil.
6. Nozick (1974). For a good discussion see Crisp (2003), who also discusses the evolutionary reasons why we often think of accomplishment and honesty as ultimate values.
7. I should also consider my own feelings, if they differ markedly between the two possible actions.
8. In this approach I am not deriving an "ought" from an "is," because the "ought" is already there. I am accepting the idea of moral action (see chapter 7) and seeking to give it more precise content.

9. In the Bible the principle of loving your neighbour first appears in Leviticus 19:18, and the principle of do as you would be done by in Matthew 7:12.

10. This is illustrated in annex 8.1 at http://cep.lse.ac.uk/layard/annex.pdf. This starts with all income going to one person (A) and shows how he will behave and feel according to how much he cares about the welfare of the other person (B). The more A cares about B, the more he gives to B and the happier are B *and* A.

11. See Smart and Williams (1973) and Sen and Williams (1982).

12. Used in Mill (1861). Even if it *were* true that you could not be happy by directly trying to be so, you could quite well pursue happiness indirectly, by doing things and adopting activities that you knew were ultimately favourable to happiness.

13. Williams queries this. He gives the following example. Suppose I am shown twenty South American Indians who will be shot by an army officer. But I am assured that if I shoot one of these twenty myself, the rest will go free. Williams says it is not obvious what I should do, because I am less responsible for what others do (even if I can determine it) than for what I do myself (see Smart and Williams, 1973, pp. 98–99). The Greatest Happiness principle focuses instead on the whole stream of consequences (which includes the action), rather than simply the quality of the action.

14. See Sen (1999).

15. See pp. 51–52.

16. Fogel and Engerman (1974).

17. See Layard and Walters (1978), pp. 45–46. An even more difficult issue is the way to value new lives and extensions to existing lives. On this see annex 8.2 at http://cep.lse.ac.uk/layard/annex.pdf.

18. Rawls (1971) argues that the sole criterion should be the welfare of the least well-off person. No gain to anyone else could outweigh a loss to him. However, the concept of welfare that Rawls uses here is not the same as happiness. It is the external means to happiness — "primary goods" such as "rights, liberties and opportunities, income and wealth, the social bases of self-respect." If people differ in their tastes or capacity for happiness, that, in Rawls' view, is up to them.

19. This was shown in an interesting lecture by Barbara Maugham of the Institute of Psychiatry at a Royal Society Conference on "The Science of Well-being" held in London, November 19–20, 2003. She showed that if individuals are divided into three equal-sized groups called very happy, happy and unhappy, the measurable characteristics and situations of the unhappy and happy differ greatly, while those of the happy and very happy differ much less.

20. The welfare of animals also has to be given weight. However, our ability to measure their feelings is still very limited, see Dawkins (2003).

21. Hare (1981), chapters 2 and 3. Thus we use the Greatest Happiness principle to devise "rules" as well as to judge "acts."

22. Warnock (1998), chapter 3.

23. See, for example, Frey and Stutzer (2000a).

24. See, for example, Singer (1981).

25. Wolpert (2005).

26. Wright (2000) argues convincingly that the properties of the universe made probable the eventual emergence of conscious beings, capable of love.

27. A possible exception is some hunter-gatherer societies (Sahlins, 1972; Biswas-Diener et al., 2003). In the latter study the life-satisfaction score (from 1 to 7) for Maasai tribesmen averaged 5.4, which compares with 5.8 for the United States and 5.7 for Britain (World Database of Happiness). In hunter-gatherer societies one should not underestimate the fear associated with witchcraft, war and natural disaster, and the pain when loved ones die early. See Edgerton (1992).

28. Bentham was not always clear about the philosophical status of his ideas, but see Ayer (1948) for a sympathetic account. For a less sympathetic account see Parekh (1974). However, some of Parekh's psychological criticisms have been superseded by modern findings in psychology reported in chapter 2 (e.g., that happiness and unhappiness lie on a single continuum, and that the quest for good feeling is a general human motivator, with some exceptions of course).

CHAPTER 9: DOES ECONOMICS HAVE A CLUE?

1. Smith (1776), book 1, chapter 2.
2. A century ago Vilfredo Pareto defined a situation as efficient if it would be impossible by some change to make one person better off without making someone else worse off (Layard and Walters, 1978, p. 7).
3. See, for example, Layard and Glaister (1994).
4. This is the so-called Hicks-Kaldor test (Layard and Walters, 1978, p. 32).
5. See p. 122. On top of this we need to allow for changes in the length of life; see annex 8.2 at http://cep.lse.ac.uk/layard/annex.pdf.
6. See for example Marshall (1890).
7. In other words it was "cardinal," see annex 4.3 at http://cep.lse.ac.uk/layard/annex.pdf.
8. See, for example, Robbins (1932).
9. In this case happiness is "ordinal" not "cardinal." The discovery was Pareto's, and the related concept of revealed preference was developed by Samuelson (1948).
10. Nordhaus and Tobin (1973).
11. For clear presentations of the psychological approach to the last three features see Kahneman (2003a and b).
12. See, for example, Mirrlees (1971)—a very technical paper. Other key figures were Tony Atkinson and Joseph Stiglitz; see Atkinson and Stiglitz (1980). During the 1970s Amartya Sen became increasingly disenchanted with happiness as a social goal (see chapter 8).
13. If we start from an income distribution that is more unequal than is optimal, the speed at which we move towards the long-run optimum will be affected by the degree of loss-aversion in the short and long run. See Layard (1980).
14. See, for example, Layard and Walters (1978), p. 323.
15. Arrow and Hurwicz (1977) showed how piecemeal decision-making would lead to an overall optimum, provided there were no economies of scale.
16. For the most radical statement of this position see Becker and Stigler (1977). For standard welfare economics it is not necessary to assume that tastes are constant but only that they are unaffected by policy.
17. Note also that in standard economics, states of happiness can only be ranked, while psychology also measures the differences in intensity between states of happiness.
18. See chapter 10, pp. 156–58.

19. There is a huge literature on the so-called principal-agent problem. This addresses the question of how best to align the interests of the agent (e.g., the CEO) with those of the principal (e.g., the shareholders). However, the implementation of this idea has led to many abuses where CEOs have got underserved rewards, and to an excessive preoccupation with financial rewards.
20. O'Neill (2002).
21. Chapter 10, pp. 158–60.
22. Nickerson et al. (2003). However, the evidence used in that paper suggests that people who care about money also get more of it, and they end up neither less nor more happy than people who care less about money.
23. See annex 8.1 at http://cep.lse.ac.uk/layard/annex.pdf.
24. See chapter 7, note 22.
25. See the beginning of chapter 11.
26. See p. 256, note 5. The phenomenon of loss-aversion reflects a kink in the equation relating happiness to income. This means that cost-benefit analysis cannot be done satisfactorily in units of money for someone of a specified income level. It will in due course be more straightforward to do it in units of happiness.
27. Runciman (1966)
28. On this whole section see Kahneman and Tversky (2000, especially chapter 1) and Rabin (1998).
29. See chapter 4.
30. Their preferences between consuming in year $T+1$ and year $T+2$ are different when viewed from year T than from year $T+1$. On this so-called time-varying "hyperbolic" discounting see Rabin (1998, pp. 38–41) and Frederick et al. (2002).
31. Private conversation in April 2001. Ellsberg is an expert on decision theory.
32. Kahneman and Tversky (2000, p. 652).
33. Some governments already show signs of interest. For the United Kingdom see Cabinet Office (2002a and b).

CHAPTER 10: HOW CAN WE TAME THE RAT RACE?

1. From his poem "Leisure," written in 1911.
2. Brammer et al. (1994). On status see also Marmot (2004) and de Botton (2004).
3. The role of females is also important: they have to want the top monkey. This can happen both because he brings more bananas and because he is top. If it is the second reason, it seems natural that human females, once liberated from dependence on men, come to seek status directly through their own efforts rather than through the status of their menfolk.
4. On this paragraph see Marmot (2004). The difference in life expectancy quoted below compares administrative/executive grades with clerical/support grades and relates to life expectancy at age forty.
5. In Irvine, *Antipanegyric for Tom Driberg*, 1976.
6. Blanchflower and Oswald (2004). The happiness function quoted is
$H_i = \log Y_i - 0.3\log \bar{Y}$, where H_i is happiness, Y_i is income and $\bar{Y}$ is average income. This can also be written $H_i = .7 \log Y_i + 0.3 \log (Yi/\bar{Y})$, the formulation used here.
7. Taxes on income from work cut work, if the tax proceeds are spent sensibly. There is

then no "income effect" (which would tend to increase work), but there is a "substitution effect" (away from work).

8. The argument has been around now for at least fifty years; see Duesenberry (1949), chapter 6, which makes the same argument as here. It appeared again in various guises in Hirsch (1976), Layard (1980), Boskin and Sheshinski (1978) and numerous writings by Frank. But it does not appear to have made it into any standard textbook on public finance.

9. Another important problem is what economists call adverse selection. For example, in New York law firms, associates work excessive hours to prove that they are fit to be partners. Each has an incentive to work longer than anyone else to signal his commitment. But they would mostly prefer to work fewer hours (for less pay) if others did the same (Landers et al. 1996, table 7). In law and finance especially, this signalling issue fuels a macho culture of work.

10. See chapter 4, note 19, for definitions of addiction. Note that smoking is in this sense much less addictive than alcohol or drugs.

11. Frank (1999), chapter 6.

12. On this paragraph see Loewenstein and Schkade (1999), p. 90.

13. Using the happiness equation of chapter 4, note 19: $H_t = f(c_t - \lambda c_{t-1})$. The higher c_{t-1}, the higher c_t must be to yield a given H_t. "Required log consumption" is λc_{t-1}.

14. Gruber and Mullainathan (2002).

15. Even if the tax system is in overall terms distorting, it is less so than it would have been if it included no corrective element.

16. Suppose there are n people and I earn an extra dollar. According to note 6, my happiness rises by $1/Y_i$. The happiness of the average other person falls by $0.3/\bar{Y}n$, and the combined happiness of all others falls by $0.3/\bar{Y}$. If $\bar{Y}_i = \bar{Y}$, this external disbenefit is 30% of what I gain.

17. If we took the numbers seriously, they could justify on efficiency grounds a tax of, say, 60% on additional income (30% plus three-quarters of 40%). This is a typical marginal tax rate in Europe, after allowing for all the taxes and contributions levied on income and on expenditure. See Collier (2004), table 1, which shows a marginal tax rate of 60% in Europe (averaged across countries) and 40% in the United States. Average tax rates are lower: the share of GDP going to all taxes is 43% in the Euro area, 38% in Britain, 30% in Japan and 29% in the United States—the main single reason for low U.S. taxes being the private financing of much health care (OECD, *Economic Outlook*, No. 72, p. 207).

    In the text I present the discussion in terms of income taxes, which are familiar to all readers. But it is always more efficient to tax spending than income, because a tax on income means taxing saving twice: first when the saved income is received, and second when the saving produces further income. It thus distorts the choice between present and future spending. However, in spite of Frank (1999) and Loewenstein et al. (2003), addiction does not significantly add to the arguments in favour of taxing expenditure rather than income. The main problem with addiction is its effect on labour-leisure choice, rather than on decisions about saving (see Layard, 2005).

18. Sennett (2003).

19. Fernie and Metcalf (1999).

20. Locke et al. (1981).

21. Nickell (1995), pp .91–96.
22. Blanchflower and Oswald (2000), table 19. As their table 7 shows, job satisfaction in Britain fell between 1991 and 1997 in the public but not the private sector.
23. Titmuss (1970) showed that the supply of blood was more satisfactory and safe in Britain, where blood was freely given, than in the United States, where it was largely paid for.
24. Gneezy and Rustichini (2000).
25. Deci and Ryan (1985).
26. Frey and Oberholzer-Gee (1997).
27. Frey and Jegen (2001).
28. One could express the preceding argument as follows:
    Happiness$_i = f$ (Leisure$_i$, Valued consumption$_i$) + α Rank$_f$ + β Output$_f$
    At the level of the whole society Σ Rank$_i$ is constant, so we want α to be as small as possible, otherwise the quest for rank will lead to fruitless reduction of leisure. In contrast, we want β to be as large as possible, so that people will work to produce output (as well as to get paid) and will obtain direct happiness from doing so.
29. For the exact definition of the law see www.konsumentverket.se.
30. A view unfortunately popularised by Galbraith (1958).
31. Rayo and Becker (2004).
32. For example, in recent years the suicide rate in Sweden has been the same as in West Germany and lower than in France (Helliwell, 2003b, figure 2).
33. Gavron et al. (1998).
34. Keynes (1930).

CHAPTER 11: CAN WE AFFORD TO BE SECURE?

1. Quoted in the *Observer*, October 3, 1971.
2. Kahneman and Tversky (2000), p. 58.
3. Kahneman et al. (1990).
4. See annex 4.1 at http://cep.lse.ac.uk/layard/annex.pdf.
5. The most common economic approach to risk-aversion is internally inconsistent. It assumes (i) that an individual maximises the utility that he can expect, after taking into account the different probabilities of different external events and (ii) that he has a stable function relating utility to wealth, which exhibits diminishing marginal utility of wealth. But as Rabin (2000) has shown, such a function cannot explain why people can be both averse to small risks and willing to accept some large ones. These two sets of facts could, however, be explained in terms of expected utility if the function relating utility to wealth had a kink (or near kink) at current wealth, implying that the function changes when wealth changes.
6. See Krugman (1996). The same is true of the average Third World citizen, though Third World agricultural purchasers would have gained more if there had been less agricultural protection in Europe and the United States (i.e., *more* globalisation). In the West, unskilled workers have lost slightly from globalisation, but have been largely protected from it by the rise of untraded domestic services (Katz and Autor, 1999, pp. 1536–37).
7. For the European Union the share of GDP traded with other countries has not risen in the last twenty years. The same is true for Japan. For the United States the share of exports has been stable, but the share of imports has risen (EU, *European Economy*,

2003, No. 4, Annex). In general the output of tradeables has risen faster in volume terms than GDP, but their price relative to non-tradeables has fallen.

8. Davis and Haltiwanger (1999, pp. 2735–37).

9. EU, *European Economy*, 2003, No. 4, p. 163. For the next set of figures on the non-wage share of GDP see p. 167.

10. If the exchange rate is flexible, it is the prime adjustment mechanism that maintains competitiveness. If the exchange rate is fixed, the price level adjusts, though this may involve some extra unemployment for a while.

11. Lucas (2003). Remarkably, Lucas argues that the complete elimination of all economic fluctuations would only increase happiness as much as a 0.05% increase in personal consumption. In this assessment he does not consider the evidence on loss-aversion, or the work of any psychologist.

12. See, for example, Layard et al. (1991), Nickell and Layard (1999) and Layard (1999a, 2003a).

13. See Layard (2003a) and de Koning et al. (2004) on this and the following paragraphs.

14. Bentolila and Bertola (1990), Bertola (1994) and Nickell and Layard (1999).

15. See annex 4.2 at http://cep.lse.ac.uk/layard/annex.pdf.

16. Moser Working Group (1999). Data based on the International Adult Literacy Survey (IALS).

17. Steedman (2000).

18. Layard (2003b).

19. For the United States see Current Population Survey; for Britain see Gregg and Wadsworth (2002), table 1. The median uncompleted job spell is about 3.75 years in the United States and 5 years in Britain, and on average a spell is observed halfway through its duration.

20. Lykken (2001).

21. See Levitt (2004), table 5, allowing for the fact that property crime is the biggest category of crime. See also Donohue and Levitt (2001).

22. At Lisbon in 1999 the EU leaders adopted the target that at least 70% of men and women aged fifteen to sixty-four should be in work by 2010, compared with 63% in 1999. The main aim was to discourage people of working age from living on state benefits, but unfortunately the target did not specifically identify this group.

23. Waldfogel (2002).

24. Huppert (2003).

25. See Young and Wilmott (1957).

26. Glaeser and DiPasquale (1999), Sampson et al. (1997).

27. Sampson and Groves (1989).

28. Halpern (2001), table 5. See also Halpern (2005).

29. On interarea data for the United States, see Alesina and La Ferrara (2000). On Canadian data, Soroka et al. (2003) show that people trust each other less where mobility is higher and where population density is higher. On cross-country data see Knack and Keefer (1997, table VII), though La Porta et al. (1997, p. 337) show little bivariate relation between trust and ethno-linguistic diversity. At the experimental level Harvard students are less likely to behave in a trusting and trustworthy way towards members of other nationalities or ethnic groups (Glaeser et al., 2000).

30. Sampson et al. (1997). We can tell that the cause is running from mobility to vio-

lence, because residential stability also predicts types of community solidarity that are conducive to low violence.

31. Halpern and Nazroo (2000), Faris and Dunham (1939). Remarkably high rates of mental illness have been found among Afro-Caribbeans living in England, compared with Afro-Caribbeans living in the Caribbean (James, 1998).

32. In Canada it has been found that immigrants are less likely to trust others than natives are (Soroka et al., 2003), but their levels of trust are similar to those in the country from which they come. See also Rice and Feldman (1997) on immigrants to the United States.

33. See Layard et al. (1992). In general, immigration will leave the unemployment rate unchanged but will increase total employment and output. Unskilled immigration will hurt those existing citizens who are unskilled, and it will benefit the rest.

34. Halpern (1995), p. 207.

35. Michalos (2004).

36. UK National Child Development Study. This is a follow-up study of all children born in a week in March 1958. We analyse the data for 1991 when they were thirty-three. Happiness (H) is measured by converting the four possible answers into a 4-point scale (1–4). Income (Y) is measured by log family income per adult. Malaise (M) is measured by a caseness index based on 24 Yes/No indicators. If we do a multiple regression (with beta coefficients) to "explain" happiness, we get $H = -.28M + .08Y$ plus an ancillary equation $M = -.21Y$. Even if we substitute the ancillary equation into the main equation, this analysis suggests that "malaise" is much more important than income. This is not of course a truly causal model, for some of the malaise indicators are direct components of happiness. But given the huge difference in coefficients, the statement in the text seems correct.

37. World Health Organization (2002). Years lost to disability (YLD). Available on WHO web site. The figures are very similar in the United States and in Western Europe, and therefore there is no need to show them separately.

38. The U.S. annual prevalences are from Department of Health and Human Services (hereafter abbreviated DHHS; 1999), p. 47, and lifetime prevalences from WHO International Consortium (2000), table 3, suitably scaled down. The data exclude people suffering only from alcohol and drug dependence, or Alzheimer's disease. The data are based on the 1982 Epidemiologic Catchment Area Study and the 1990–92 National Co-Morbidity Study. The conditions comprise (with their annual prevalences) schizophrenia (1%), manic-depressive episode (1%), major depression (5%) and anxiety disorders (13%, including generalised anxiety, panic attacks, phobias and obsessive-compulsive disorder). The U.S. results are consistent with the recent WHO World Mental Health Survey Consortium (2004), which covers the United States and fourteen other countries.

For Britain, data on numbers suffering at a point in time are in ONS (2001), table 2.7. In Britain at any one moment the proportion suffering from any mental disorder is 16%, including 3% suffering from an episode of major depression and 9% from a somewhat less serious mixture of anxiety and depression.

For a summary of overall numbers in different countries see annex 11.1 at http://cep.lse.ac.uk/layard/annex.pdf, table A.

39. The sources for this paragraph are Craighead et al. (2002, tables 10.1 and 10.2), Hol-

lon and Beck (2004, figures 10.1 and 10.2), DHHS (1999, chapter 4) and Department of Health (2001). The proportion who recover within four months of diagnosis are roughly 60% of those who are "treated," 30% of those given a placebo and a smaller number who would recover spontaneously.

Even for severe depression, drugs and therapy appear to be equally effective. The combination can sometimes help but is not generally better than one or the other on its own. What does make sense is to try one, and if it fails, move to the other.

All this evidence comes from controlled trials, with well-trained workers. There is little good evidence on results in the "field."

40. Around $2000/£1000.

41. On this paragraph see annex 11.1 at http://cep.lse.ac.uk/layard/annex.pdf, table B. Only in the cases of schizophrenia and manic depression are the majority treated.

42. In 2000, 6% of all adults in Britain were being treated with medication for mental or emotional problems (ONS, 2001, table 5.2).

43. www.who.org; see also World Health Organization (2002).

44. For the United States see DHHS (1999), chapter 6; for Britain see Department of Health, Hospital and Community Health Services Programme Budget.

45. This relates to publicly funded research. In the United States the National Institute of Mental Health receives 5% of the budget of the National Institutes of Health. In the United Kingdom 5% of the UK Medical Research Council budget goes on mental health.

46. From "Table Talk."

Chapter 12: Can mind control mood?

1. See Davidson et al. (2003), for example, figure 2. The effect of the course is such as to raise someone who was initially at the fiftieth percentile of happiness to the seventieth percentile.

2. See references in Davidson et al. (2003).

3. Elbert et al. (1995). Similarly, taxi drivers strengthen the part of the brain connected to spatial navigation (Maguire et al., 2000).

4. See Dalai Lama and Cutler (1998), and for more detail on methods of mental discipline, Dalai Lama (2001).

5. See chapter 2.

6. Thich Nhat Hanh (2001).

7. Davidson et al. (1990).

8. Goleman (2003), p. 284.

9. It is also true that some people can be very happy while being rather selfish. Samuel Pepys records feeling pretty good during the Great Plague, when he was busy at work, rising rapidly and philandering (Tomalin, 2002).

10. Gottman (1994).

11. Said on his deathbed to his disciple Ananda (*Mahaparinibbana Sutta*).

12. In Islam the main mystical tradition is from the Sufis.

13. For a modern interpretation of Saint Ignatius' *Spiritual Exercises* see Hughes (1985).

14. Quoted in Farrow (1984).

15. See, for example, Gorman (1973).

16. The wording of step one is the modified one used by Emotions Anonymous. They

replace the word "alcohol" with "our emotions." For a good guide to the Twelve Steps see Phillip (1990).

17. For whatever reasons there has been no controlled trial of psychoanalysis (Roth and Fonagy, 1996). Controlled trials of debriefing after accidents show negative results, though of course accident victims who develop symptoms can be helped by cognitive therapy that includes well-focused reliving of the past (Clark and Ehlers, 2005).

18. Quoted by James (1998).

19. See chapter 11, note 39; see also Seligman (1994).

20. See Seligman (2002), pp. 69, 211.

21. It can be shown that depressive people may make more accurate forecasts than non-depressed people, who are overoptimistic. This is called "depressive realism." But (i) the depressive forecast is often a self-fulfilling prophecy, and (ii) overoptimism often raises the chance of success. On the value of optimism see Frederickson (1998) and Frederickson et al. (2000). However, in some fields excessive optimism is dysfunctional—in financial speculation for example.

22. Nesse (1999, 2000).

23. Seligman (2002). His book offers techniques for identifying your strengths.

24. See Schwartz et al. (2002) for this and the following paragraph. This does not mean that the Benthamite ideal of maximum collective happiness is wrong, but it does shed light on how to attain it.

25. See Thich Nhat Hanh (1975). Tolstoy's remark is in the short story "Three Questions."

26. *The Pisan Cantos.*

27. Wilson (1993).

28. See Greenberg et al. (2000) and the special issue of the *American Psychologist*, 2003, issue 6–7, June/July, pp. 452–90. See also chapter 11 in Goleman (2003), which describes in some detail Greenberg's PATHS programme (Promoting Alternative THinking Strategies) for six- and seven-year-olds.

29. Goleman (1996).

30. It is non-statutory, but "citizenship" has since 1999 become statutory for children aged eleven to sixteen.

31. Evans (2003) and Humphrey (2002), chapter 19.

Chapter 13: Do drugs help?

1. In *Pentimento* by Lillian Hellman.

2. The main sources for this chapter are Barondes (1999) and Snyder (1996).

3. For sources see chapter 11, note 38. There is some controversy over whether obsessive-compulsive disorder should be classified as an anxiety disorder.

4. The most common definition used today is that by the American Psychiatric Association in the classification system known as DSM IV (meaning the fourth edition of the *Diagnostic and Statistical Manual* of mental disorders): a major depressive episode occurs when over at least two weeks there is "depressed mood and loss of interest or pleasure in almost all activities." In addition at least five of the following must be present over the last two weeks:

   depressed mood most of the day
   diminished interest or pleasure
   significant gain or loss of weight

inability to sleep or sleeping too much
reduced control over bodily movements
fatigue
feelings of worthlessness or guilt
inability to think or concentrate
thoughts of death or suicide

A lesser depression occurs when for most days in the last two weeks, there has been depressed mood and at least two of the following:

poor appetite or overeating
too much or too little sleep
fatigue or low energy
low self-esteem
poor concentration or inability to make decisions
feelings of hopelessness

5. Quoted in Jamison (1993), p. 19, who also quotes many other famous depressives. For other descriptions of depression by people who have experienced it see Styron (1991), Solomon (2001) and Wolpert (1999). Wolpert's book is a good general introduction to depression and its treatment.

6. A study by the National Institute of Mental Health in 2002 found that over the previous thirteen years a sample of manic-depressives had spent about 40% of the time being depressed, about 5% being manic, and 10% a mixture of the two, and the rest normal.

7. Peters (1998). The key events were in 1767–68.

8. Laing (1960).

9. For the United States see DHHS (1999); for Britain see Department of Health, *Health and Personal Services Statistics*. These decreases were also due to progress in psychotherapy, to public hostility to asylums and to the desire to save money. Given the weakness of "care in the community," the reduction may have been overdone.

10. Quoted in Barondes (1999).

11. Barondes (1999).

12. The number of possible connections is in each case of the order of 10^{15}.

13. Prozac reduces the reuptake of serotonin into the presynaptic neuron, so it is a "selective serotonin reuptake inhibitor" (SSRI). Serotonin is also known as 5-HT.

14. Cocaine inhibits dopamine reuptake, while amphetamine displaces dopamine from the vesicles in the presynaptic neuron. Ecstasy (MDMA) also increases the supply of dopamine and serotonin.

15. Observant readers will note that I have not discussed how lithium works, nor the psychedelic drugs like mescaline and LSD. This is because their action is poorly understood.

16. Kramer (1993).

17. Post (1994). By contrast, scientists, statesmen, thinkers and composers were similar to the population at large. On this issue see also Storr (1972) and Jamison (1993).

18. There are some obvious exceptions, like Gerard Manley Hopkins.

19. See Jamison (1993), pp. 61–89 and 241–51, for this and the following two paragraphs.

20. Schou (1979) and Marshall et al. (1970). See also Frederickson (1998) and Frederickson et al. (2000).

21. See Richards et al. (1988). The relatives are first-degree relatives, like siblings. See also Nettle (2001, pp. 149–51 and 173–86), who argues that these genes survived because creativity is attractive to women.

CHAPTER 14: CONCLUSIONS FOR TODAY'S WORLD

1. See chapter 3.
2. I list some unsolved research questions in annex 14.1 and give selected reading (chapter by chapter) in annex 14.2 at http://cep.lse.ac.uk/layard/annex.pdf.
3. See chapter 2.
4. See chapter 2.
5. See chapter 8.
6. See chapter 8.
7. See chapter 5.
8. See chapters 5 and 10.
9. See chapter 11.
10. See chapters 4 and 10.
11. See chapters 4 and 10.
12. See chapters 4 and 10.
13. See chapter 12.
14. See chapters 11 and 13 and chapter 8, note 20.
15. See chapters 9, 10 and 11.
16. The popular versions of Darwinism (unlike Darwin himself) ignore the importance of human cooperation. The popular version of Smith ignores his parallel analysis of the importance of human sympathy (Smith, 1759).
17. See especially chapters 10, 11 and 12.
18. www.oecd.org. The figures are for overseas development assistance as a percentage of GNP in 2002.
19. To discuss the necessary policies is beyond the scope of this book, but see Tarp (2000).
20. See for example Mill (1861). But those on the other side include Socrates, who believed in the "examined life," Csikszentmihalyi (1990) and the Dalai Lama (2001).
21. But see chapter 8, note 27.
22. Written June 22, 1830, and found in the girl's birthday album. Quoted in B. Parekh (ed), *Jeremy Bentham, Critical Assessments*, vol. I, pp. xvii.

References

A list of selected readings appears as an annex at
http://cep.lse.ac.uk/layard/annex.pdf.

Academy of Medical Sciences (2004), *Calling Time. The Nation's Drinking as a Major Health Issue*, London.

Ainslie, G. and Herrnstein, R. (1981), "Preference reversal and delayed reinforcement," *Animal Learning and Behaviour*, 9, 476–82.

Alesina, A., Di Tella, R. and MacCulloch, R. (2003), "Inequality and happiness: Are Europeans and Americans different?," Harvard, Institute of Economic Research Discussion Paper No. 1938.

Alesina, A., Glaeser, E. and Sacerdote, B. (2001), "Why doesn't the United States have a European-style welfare state?," *Brookings Papers on Economic Activity*, Fall, 187–277.

Alesina, A. and La Ferrara, E. (2000), "Participation in heterogeneous communities," *Quarterly Journal of Economics*, 115, 847–904.

Amato, P., Loomis, L. and Booth, A. (1995), "Parental divorce, marital conflict, and offspring well-being during early adulthood," *Social Forces*, 73, 895–915.

Anisman, H., Zaharia, M., Meaney, M. and Merali, Z. (1998), "Do early-life events permanently alter behavioural and hormonal responses to stressors?," *International Journal of Developmental Neuroscience*, 16, 149–64.

Arrow, K. and Hurwicz, L. (1977), "Decentralization and computation in resource allocation," in K. Arrow and L. Hurwicz (eds), *Studies in Resource Allocation Processes*, Cambridge: Cambridge University Press.

Ashenfelter, O. and Layard, R. (1983), "Incomes policy and wage differentials," *Economica*, 198, 127–43.

Atkinson, A. and Stiglitz, J. (1980), *Lectures in Public Economics*, London: McGraw-Hill.

Axelrod, R. (1984), *The Evolution of Cooperation*, New York: Basic Books.

Ayer, A. (1948) "The principle of utility," in G. Keeton and G. Schwarzenberger (eds), *Jeremy Bentham and The Law: A Symposium*, London: Stephens and Sons.

Badcock, C. (2000), *Evolutionary Psychology*, London: Polity Press.

Bargh, J. and Chartrand, T. (1999), "The unbearable automaticity of being," *American Psychologist*, 54, 462–79.

Barondes, S. (1999), *Molecules and Mental Illness*, New York: Scientific American Library.

Becker, G. (1981), *A Treatise on the Family*, Cambridge, MA: Harvard University Press.

Becker, G. and Stigler, G. (1977), "De gustibus non est disputandum," *American Economic Review*, 67, 76–90.

Belk, R. and Pollay, R. (1985), "Images of ourselves: The good life in twentieth-century advertising," *Journal of Consumer Research*, 11, 887–97.

Bentham, J. (1789), *An Introduction to the Principles of Morals and Legislation*, 1996 edition, edited by J. H. Burns and H. L. A. Hart, Oxford: Clarendon Press.

Bentolila, S. and Bertola, G. (1990), "Firing costs and labour demand: How bad is eurosclerosis?," *Review of Economic Studies*, 57, 381–402.

Bertola, G. (1994) "Flexibility, investment and growth," *Journal of Monetary Economics*, 34, 215–38.

Bewley, T. (1999), *Why Wages Don't Fall in a Recession*, Cambridge, MA: Harvard University Press.

Biswas-Diener, R., Vitterso, J. and Diener, E. (2003), "Most people are pretty happy but there is cultural variation: The Inughuit, the Amish and the Maasai," University of Illinois, mimeo.

Blanchflower, D. and Oswald, A. (1999), "Well-being, insecurity and the decline of American job satisfaction," Natural Bureau of Economic Research.

——. (2000), "Is the UK moving up the international well-being rankings?," Warwick University, mimeo.

———. (2004), "Well-being over time in Britain and the U.S.A.," *Journal of Public Economics*, 88, 1359–86.

Blomquist, G., Berger, N. and Hoehn, J. (1988), "New estimates of quality of life in urban areas," *American Economic Review*, 78, 89–107.

Bohman, M. (1995), "Predisposition to criminality: Swedish adoption studies in retrospect," in G. Bock and J. Goode (eds), *Genetics of Criminal and Antisocial Behaviour*, CIBA Foundation Symposium 194, Chichester, UK: John Wiley.

Boskin, M. and Sheshinski, E. (1978), "Optimal redistributive taxation when individual welfare depends on relative income," *Quarterly Journal of Economics*, 92, 589–601.

Braithwaite, J. (1989), *Crime, Shame and Reintegration*, Cambridge: Cambridge University Press.

Brammer, G., Raleigh, M. and McGuire, M. (1994) "Neurotransmitters and social status," in L. Ellis (ed), *Social Stratification and Socioeconomic Inequality*, vol.2, Westport, CT: Greenwood.

Brickman, P., Coates, D. and Janoff-Bulman, R. (1978), "Lottery winners and accident victims: Is happiness relative?," *Journal of Personality and Social Psychology*, 36, 917–27.

Brief, A., Butcher, A., George, J. and Link, K. (1993), "Integrating bottom-up and top-down theories of subjective well-being: The case of health," *Journal of Personality and Social Psychology*, 64, 646–53.

Brosnan, S. and de Waal, F. (2003), "Monkeys reject unequal pay," *Nature*, 425, 297–99.

Brown, D. (1991), *Human Universals*, New York: McGraw Hill.

Cabanac, M. (1992), "Pleasure: The common currency," *Journal of Theoretical Biology*, 155, 173–200.

Cabinet Office, UK (2002a), *Social Capital. A Discussion Paper*, London.

———. (2002b), *Life Satisfaction. The State of Knowledge and Implications for Government*, London.

———. (2004), *Alcohol Harm Reduction Strategy for England*, London.

Cadoret, R., Yates, W., Troughton, E., Woodworth, G. and Stewart, M. (1995), "Genetic-environmental interaction in the genesis of aggressivity and conduct disorders," *Archives of General Psychiatry*, 52, 916–24.

Campbell, A., Converse, P. and Rodgers, W. (1976), *The Quality of American Life*, New York: Sage.

Caspi, A., McClay, J., Moffitt, T., Mill, J., Martin, J., Craig, I., Taylor, A. and Poulton, R. (2002), "Role of genotype in the cycle of violence in mal-treated children," *Science*, 297, 851–54.

Caspi, A., Moffitt, T., Morgan, J., Rutter, M., Taylor, A., Arseneault, L., Tully, L., Jacobs, C., Kim-Cohen, J. and Polo-Tomas, M. (2004), "Maternal expressed emotion predicts children's antisocial behavior problems: Using monozygotic-twin differences to identify environmental effects on behavioral development," *Developmental Psychology*, 40, 149–61.

Caspi, A., Sugden, K., Moffitt, T., Taylor, A., Craig, I., Harrington, H., McClay, J., Mill, J., Martin, J., Braithwaite, A. and Poulton, R. (2003), "Influence of life stress on depression: Moderation by a polymorphism in the 5-HTT gene," *Science*, 301, 386–89.

Charlton, T., Gunter, B. and Hannan, A. (2002), *Broadcast Television Effects in a Remote Community*, Mahwah, NJ: Lawrence Erlbaum Associates.

Cherlin, A., Chase-Lansdale, P. and McRae, C. (1998), "Effects of parental divorce on mental health throughout the life course," *American Sociological Review*, 63, 239–49.

Clark, A. E. (1996a) "Job satisfaction in Britain," *British Journal of Industrial Relations*, 34, 189–217.

——. (1996b), "L'utilité est-elle relative? Analyse a l'aide de données sur les menages," *Economie et Provision*, 121, 151–64.

——. (2001), "What really matters in a job? Hedonic measurement using quit data," *Labour Economics*, 8, 223–42.

——. (2002a), "Born to be mild: Cohort effects in subjective well-being," CNRS Working Paper.

——. (2002b), "A note on unhappiness and unemployment duration," CNRS and DELTA, mimeo.

——. (2003a), "Unemployment as a social norm: Psychological evidence from panel data," *Journal of Labor Economics*, 21, 323–51.

——. (2003b), "Inequality-aversion and income mobility: A direct test," CNRS and DELTA Working Paper No. 2003-11

Clark, A. E., Diener, E., Georgellis, Y. and Lucas, R. (2003), "Lags and leads in life satisfaction: A test of the baseline hypothesis," CNRS and DELTA-Fédération Jourdan.

Clark, A. E., Georgellis, Y. and Sanfey, P. (2001), "Scarring: The psychological impact of past unemployment," *Economica*, 68, 221–41.

Clark, A. E. and Oswald, A. (1996), "Satisfaction and comparison income," *Journal of Public Economics*, 61, 359–81.

Clark, Andy. (1997), *Being There: Putting Brain, Body and World Together Again*, Cambridge, MA: MIT Press.

Clark, D. and Ehlers, A. (2005), "Posttraumatic stress disorder: From cognitive theory to therapy," forthcoming in R. Leahy and D. Fazzari (eds), *New Advances in Cognitive Therapy*, New York: Guilford Press.

Clark, M. and Mills, J. (1979), "Interpersonal attraction in exchange and communal relationships," *Journal of Personality and Social Psychology* 37, 12–24.

Clarke, L. and Berrington, A. (1999), "Socio-demographic predictors of divorce," in J. Simons (ed), *High Divorce Rates: The State of the Evidence on Reasons and Remedies*, London: Lord Chancellor's Department.

Clow, A., Lambert, S., Evans, P., Hucklebridge, F. and Higuchi, K. (2003), "An investigation into asymmetrical cortical regulation of salivary S-IgA in conscious man using transcranial magnetic stimulation," *International Journal of Psychophysiology*, 47, 57–64.

Coghill, R., McHaffie, J. and Yen, Y-F (2003), "Neural correlates of interindividual differences in the subjective experience of pain," *PNAS*, 100, 8538–42.

Collier, I. (2004), "Can Gerhard Schroeder do it? Prospects for fundamental reform of the German economy and a return to high employment," IZA Discussion Paper No. 1059.

Collins, W., Maccoby, E., Steinberg, L., Hetherington, E. and Bornstein, M. (2000), "Contemporary research on parenting: The case for nature and nurture," *American Psychologist*, 55, 218–32.

Craighead, W., Hart, A., Craighead, L. and Ilardi, S. (2002), "Psychosocial treatments for major depressive disorder," in P. Nathan and J. Gorman (eds), *A Guide to Treatments That Work*, New York: Oxford University Press.

Crisp, R. (2003), "Hedonism reconsidered," University of Oxford, mimeo.

Csikszentmihalyi, M. (1990), *Flow: The Psychology of Optimal Experience*, New York: Harper and Row.

Cutler, D., Glaeser, E. and Norberg, K. (2000), "Explaining the rise in youth suicide," NBER Working Paper 7713.

Dalai Lama (2001), *An Open Heart: Practising Compassion in Everyday Life*, New York: Little, Brown.

Dalai Lama and Cutler, H. (1998), *The Art of Happiness. A Handbook for Living*, New York: Penguin Putnam.

Damasio, A. (1994) *Descartes' Error: Emotion, Reason and the Human Brain*, New York: HarperCollins.

Danner, D., Snowden, D. and Friesen, W. (2001), "Positive emotions in early life and longevity: Findings from the nun study," *Journal of Personality and Social Psychology*, 80, 804–13.

Davidson, R. (1992), "Emotion and affective style: Hemispheric substrates," *Psychological Science*, 3, 39–43.

——. (2000), "Affective style, psychopathology and resilience: Brain mechanisms and plasticity," *American Psychologist*, 55, 1196–1214.

Davidson, R., Ekman, P., Saron, C., Senulius, S. and Friesen, W. (1990), "Emotional expression and brain physiology I: Approach/withdrawal and cerebral asymmetry," *Journal of Personality and Social Psychology*, 58, 330–41.

Davidson, R., Jackson, D. and Kalin, N. (2000), "Emotion, plasticity, context and regulation: Perspectives from affective neuroscience," *Psychological Bulletin*, 126, 890–906.

Davidson, R., Kabat-Zinn, J., Schumacher, J., Rosenkranz, M., Muller, D., Santorelli, S., Urbanowski, F., Harrington. A., Bonus, K. and Sheridan, J. (2003), "Alterations in brain and immune function produced by mindfulness meditation," *Psychosomatic Medicine*, 65, 564–70.

Davies, N. (1997), *Europe: A History*, London: Pimlico.

Davis, S. and Haltiwanger, J. (1999), "Gross job flows," in O. Ashenfelter and D. Card (eds), *Handbook of Labor Economics*, vol 3B, Amsterdam: North-Holland Elsevier.

Dawkins, M. (2003), "Who needs consciousness?," Department of Zoology, Oxford University, mimeo.

de Botton, A. (2004), *Status Anxiety*, London: Penguin.

de Koning, J., Layard, R., Nickell, S. and Westergaard-Nielsen, N. (2004), "Policies for full employment," UK Department for Work and Pensions. Also available online at www.dwp.gov.uk.

Deaton, A. (2003), "Health, inequality and economic development," *Journal of Economic Literature*, 41, 113–58.

Deaton, A. and Muellbauer, J. (1980), *Economics and Consumer Behaviour*, Cambridge: Cambridge University Press.

Deci, E. L. and Ryan, R. M. (1985), *Intrinsic Motivation and Self-Determination in Human Behaviour*, New York: Plenum Press.

Department of Health, UK (2001), *Treatment Choice in Psychological Therapies and Counselling*, London.

Department of Health and Human Services, U.S. (DHHS) (1999), *Mental Health, A Report of the Surgeon General*, Rockville, MD: DHHS.

Diekstra, R., Kienhorst, C. and de Wilde, E. (1995), "Suicide and suicidal behaviour among adolescents," in Rutter and Smith (1995).

Diener, E. and Oishi, S. (2000), "Money and happiness: Income and subjective well-being across nations," in Diener and Suh (2000).

Diener, E. and Suh, E. (1999), "National differences in subjective well-being," in Kahneman et al. (1999).

———. (eds) (2000), *Culture and Subjective Well-being*, Cambridge, MA: MIT Press.

Diener, E., Wolsic, B. and Fujita, F. (1995), "Physical attractiveness and subjective well-being," *Journal of Personality and Social Psychology*, 69, 120–29.

Di Tella, R., MacCulloch, R. and Oswald, A. (2001), "Preferences over inflation and unemployment: Evidence from surveys of happiness," *American Economic Review*, 91, 335–41.

———. (2003), "The macroeconomics of happiness," *Review of Economics and Statistics*, 85, 809–27.

Donohue, J. and Levitt, S. (2001), "The impact of legalized abortion on crime," *The Quarterly Journal of Economics*, 116, 379–419.

———. (2003), "Further evidence that legalized abortion lowered crime: A reply to Joyce," NBER Working Paper 9532.

Duesenberry, J. S. (1949), *Income, Saving and the Theory of Consumer Behaviour*, Cambridge, MA: Harvard University Press.

Easterlin, R. (2001), "Income and happiness: Towards a unified theory," *Economic Journal*, 111, 465–84.

———. (ed) (2002), *Happiness in Economics*, Cheltenham, UK: Edward Elgar.

———. (2003), "Explaining happiness," *Proceedings of the National Academy of Sciences*, 100, 11176–83.

Edgerton, R. (1992), *Sick Societies*, New York: Free Press.

Elbert, T., Pantev, C., Wienbruch, C., Rockstroh, B. and Taub, E. (1995), "Increased cortical representation of the fingers of the left hand in string players," *Science*, 270, 305–7.

Ellwood, D. and Jencks, C. (2004), "The spread of single-parent families in the United States since 1960," in Moynihan, D., Reinwater, L., and Smeeding, T. (eds), *Public Policy and the Future of the Family*, New York: Russell Sage Foundation.

Ermisch, J. and Francesconi, M. (2001), "Family structure and children's achievements," *Journal of Population Economics*, 14, 249–70.

Evans, D. (2003), *Placebo: The Belief Effect*, London: HarperCollins.

Faris, R. and Dunham, H. (1939), *Mental Disorders in Urban Areas*, Chicago: University of Chicago Press.

Farrow, J. (1984), "Spirituality and self-awareness," *Friends' Quarterly*, July.

Fehr, E. and Fischbacher, U. (2003), "The nature of human altruism," *Nature*, 425, 785–91.

Fernie, S. and Metcalf, D. (1999), "It's not what you pay it's the way that you pay it and that's what gets results: Jockeys' pay and performance," *Labour*, 13, 385–411.

Ferri, E., Bynner, J. and Wadsworth, M. (eds) (2003), *Changing Britain, Changing Lives. Three Generations at the Turn of the Century*, London: Institute of Education.

Fields, J. (2003), "Children's living arrangements and characteristics," March 2002, Current Population Survey, U.S. Census Bureau.

Floud, R. (1998), "Height, weight and body mass of the British population since 1820," NBER Historical Paper 108.

Fogel, R. and Engerman, S. (1974), *Time on the Cross: The Economics of American Negro Slavery*, Boston: Little, Brown.

Fombonne, E. (1995), "Depressive disorders: Time trends and possible explanatory mechanisms," in Rutter and Smith (1995).

Fox, N. and Davidson, R. (1986), "Taste-elicited changes in facial signs of emotion and the asymmetry of brain electrical activity in human newborns," *Neuropsychologia*, 24, 417–22.

Frank, R. (1985), *Choosing the Right Pond: Human Behaviour and the Quest for Status*, New York and Oxford: Oxford University Press.

——. (1988), *Passions Within Reason: The Strategic Role of the Emotions*, New York and London: W. W. Norton.

——. (1999), *Luxury Fever: Money and Happiness in an Era of Excess*, New York: Free Press.

Frank, R., Gilovich, T. and Regan, D. (1996), "Do economists make bad citizens?," *Journal of Economic Perspectives*, 10, 187–92.

Frank, R. and Hutchens, R. (1993), "Wages, seniority and the demand for rising consumption profiles," *Journal of Economic Behavior and Organization*, 21, 251–76.

Frankl, V. (1985), *Man's Search for Meaning*, New York: Basic Books.

Frederick, S. and Loewenstein, G. (1999), "Hedonic adaptation," in Kahneman et al. (1999).

Frederick, S., Loewenstein, G. and O'Donoghue, T. (2002), "Time discounting and time preference: A critical review," *Journal of Economic Literature*, 40, 351–401.

Frederickson, B. (1998), "What good are positive emotions?," *Review of General Psychology*, 2, 300–319.

Frederickson, B., Mancuso, R., Branigan, C. and Tugade, M. (2000) "The undoing effect of positive emotions," *Motivation and Emotion*, 24, 237–58.

Freeman, R. (1999), "The economics of crime," in O. Ashenfelter and D. Card (eds), *Handbook of Labor Economics*, vol. 3C, New York: Elsevier.

Freeman, R. and Schettkat, R. (2001), "Marketization of production and the US-Europe employment gap," *Oxford Bulletin of Economics and Statistics*, 63, 647–70.

Frey, B. and Jegen, R. (2001), "Motivation crowding theory," *Journal of Economic Surveys*, 15, 589–611.

Frey, B. and Meier, S. (2002), "Two concerns about rational choice: indoctrination and imperialism," Working Paper, Institute for Empirical Research in Economics, University of Zurich.

——. (2003), "Are political economists selfish and indoctrinated? Evidence from a natural experiment," *Economic Inquiry*, 41, 448–62.

Frey, B. and Oberholzer-Gee, F. (1997), "The cost of price incentives: An empirical analysis of motivation crowding-out," *American Economic Review*, 87, 746–55.

Frey, B. and Stutzer, A. (2000a), "Happiness, economy and institutions," *Economic Journal*, 110 (October), 918–38. Also in Easterlin (2002).

——. (2000b), "Maximising happiness?," *German Economic Review* 1, 145–67.

——. (2002), *Happiness and Economics: How the Economy and Institutions Affect Well-Being*, Princeton: Princeton University Press.

——. (2003a), "Testing theories of happiness," Working Paper, Institute for Empirical Research in Economics, University of Zurich.

———. (2003b), "Economic consequences of mispredicting utility," Working Paper, Institute for Empirical Research in Economics, University of Zurich.

Furstenberg, F. and Kiernan, K. (2001), "Delayed parental divorce: How much do children benefit?," *Journal of Marriage and the Family*, 63, 446–57.

Galbraith, J. K. (1958), *The Affluent Society*, London: Hamish Hamilton.

Gardner, J. and Oswald, A. (2002), "Is it money or marriage that keeps people alive?," University of Warwick, mimeo.

Gavron, R., Cowling, M., Holtham, G. and Westall, A. (1998), *The Entrepreneurial Society*, London: Institute for Public Policy Research.

Gerbner, G., Gross, L., Morgan, M. and Signorielli, N. (1980), "The 'mainstreaming' of America: Violence profile No. 11," *Journal of Communications*, Summer, 10–29.

Gilbert, D. and Watson, T. (2001), "Miswanting: Some problems in the forecasting of future affective states," in J. Forgas (ed), *Feeling and Thinking*, Cambridge: Cambridge University Press.

Gilbert, P. (1992), *Depression: The Evolution of Powerlessness*, New York: Guilford Press.

Glaeser, E. and DiPasquale, D. (1999), "Incentives and social capital: Are homeowners better citizens?," *Journal of Urban Economics*, 45, 354–84.

Glaeser, E., Laibson, D., Scheinkman, J. and Soutter, C. (2000), "Measuring trust," *Quarterly Journal of Economics*, 115, 811–46.

Glenn, N. and Kramer, K. (1985), "The psychological well-being of adult children of divorce," *Journal of Marriage and the Family*, 47, 905–12.

Gneezy, U. and Rustichini, A. (2000), "A fine is a price," *Journal of Legal Studies*, 29, 1–18.

Goleman, D. (1996), *Emotional Intelligence: Why It Can Matter More Than IQ*, London: Bloomsbury.

———. (2003), *Destructive Emotions: How Can We Overcome Them? A scientific dialogue with the Dalai Lama*, New York: Bantam Books.

Gorman, G. (1973), *The Amazing Fact of Quaker Worship*, London: Quaker Home Service.

Gottesman, I. (1991), *Schizophrenia Genesis*, New York: W. H. Freeman.

Gottman, J. M. (1994), *What Predicts Divorce? The Relationship Between*

Marital Processes and Marital Outcomes, Hillsdale, NJ: Lawrence Erlbaum Associates.

Gould, M. (2001), "Suicide and the media," *Awards of the New York Academy of Sciences*, 932, 200–221, April.

Graham, C. and Pettinato, S. (2002), *Happiness and Hardship: Opportunity and Insecurity in New Market Economies*, Washington, DC: Brookings Institution Press.

Green, D., Salovey, P. and Truax, K. (1999), "Static, dynamic and causative bipolarity of affect," *Journal of Personality and Social Psychology*, 76, 856–67.

Green, L., Fisher, E., Perlow, S. and Sherman, L. (1981), "Preference reversal and self-control: Choice as a function of reward amount and delay," *Behaviour Analysis Letters*, 1, 43–51.

Greenberg, M., Domitrovich, C. and Bumbarger, B. (2000), "Preventing mental disorders in school-age children," Prevention Research Center for the Promotion of Human Development, College of Health and Human Development, Pennsylvania State University.

Gregg, P. and Wadsworth, J. (2002), "Job tenure in Britain 1975-2000: Is a job for life or just for Christmas?," *Oxford Bulletin of Economics and Statistics*, 64, 111–34.

Gruber, J. and Mullainathan, S. (2002), "Do cigarette taxes make smokers happier?," NBER Working Paper 8872.

Hagnell, O., Essen-Möller, E., Lanke, J., Öjesjö, L. and Rorsman, B. (1990), *The Incidence of Mental Illness Over a Quarter of a Century*, Stockholm: Almqvist and Wiksell International.

Hall, P. (1999), "Social capital in Britain," *British Journal of Political Science*, 29, 417–61.

Halpern, D. (1995), *Mental Health and the Built Environment*, London: Taylor and Francis.

——. (2001), "Moral values, social trust and inequality: Can values explain crime?," *British Journal of Criminology*, 41, 236–51.

——. (2004), *Social Capital*, Cambridge: Polity Press.

Halpern, D. and Nazroo, J. (2000), "The ethnic density effect: Results from a national community survey of England and Wales," *International Journal of Social Psychiatry*, 46, 34–46.

Hare, R. (1981), *Moral Thinking: Its Levels, Method and Point*, Oxford: Oxford University Press.

———. (1999), *Without Conscience*, New York: Guilford Press.

Harris, J. (1998), *The Nurture Assumption*, New York: Free Press.

Helliwell, J. (2003a), "How's life? Combining individual and national variables to explain subjective well-being," *Economic Modelling*, 20, 331–60.

———. (2003b), "Well-being and social capital: Does suicide pose a puzzle?," University of British Columbia, mimeo.

Hennigan, K., Heath, L., Wharton, J., Del Rosario, M., Cook, T. and Calder, B. (1982), "Impact of the introduction of television on crime in the United States: Empirical findings and theoretical implications," *Journal of Personality and Social Psychology*, 42, 461–77.

Hirsch, F. (1976), *Social Limits to Growth*, London: Routledge and Kegan Paul.

Hobbes, T. (1642), *De Cive or The Citizen*, 1949 edition, edited by S. Lamprecht, New York: Appleton-Century-Crofts.

———. (1651), *Leviathan*, 1996 edition, edited by R. Tuck, Cambridge: Cambridge University Press.

Hollon, S. and Beck, A. (2004), "Cognitive and cognitive behavioral therapies," in M. Lambert (ed), *Handbook of Psychotherapy and Behavior Change*, 5th edition, New York: John Wiley.

Home Office, UK (2003), "Crime in England and Wales 2002/2003," London.

Hornstein, H., Fisch, E. and Holmes, M. (1968), "Influence of a model's feelings about his behavior and his relevance as a comparison other on observers' helping behavior," *Journal of Personality and Social Psychology*, 10, 220–26.

Huesman, L. and Eron, L. (1986), *Television and the Aggressive Child: A Cross-National Comparison*, Hillsdale, NJ: Lawrence Erlbaum Associates.

Hughes, G. (1985), *God of Surprises*, London: Darton, Longman and Todd.

Humphrey, N. (2002), *The Mind Made Flesh: Essays from the Frontiers of Psychology and Evolution*, Oxford: Oxford University Press.

Huppert, F. (2003), "A population approach to positive psychology: The potential for population interventions to promote well-being and prevent disorder," forthcoming in P. Linley and S. Joseph (eds), *Positive Psychology in Practice*, Hoboken, NJ: John Wiley.

Inglehart, R. and Klingemann, H-D. (2000), "Genes, culture, democracy and happiness," in Diener and Suh (2000).

Jaffee, S., Caspi, A., Moffitt, T. and Taylor, A. (2004), "Physical maltreatment victim to antisocial child: Evidence of an environmentally mediated process," *Journal of Abnormal Psychology*, 113, 44–55.

Jaffee, S., Moffitt, T., Caspi, A. and Taylor, A. (2003), "Life with (or without) father: The benefits of living with two biological parents depend on the father's antisocial behavior," *Child Development*, 74, 109–26.

James, O. (1998), *Britain on the Couch*, London: Arrow Books.

Jamison, K. (1993), *Touched With Fire: Manic-Depressive Illness and the Artistic Temperament*, New York: Free Press.

Kahneman, D. (1999), "Objective happiness," in Kahneman et al. (1999).

——. (2003a), "A psychological perspective on economics," *American Economic Review*, 93, 162–68.

——. (2003b), "Maps of bounded rationality: Psychology for behavioural economics," *American Economic Review*, 93, 1449–75.

Kahneman, D., Diener, E. and Schwarz, N. (eds) (1999), *Well-Being: The Foundations of Hedonic Psychology*, New York: Russell Sage Foundation.

Kahneman, D., Knetsch, J. and Thaler, R. (1990), "Experimental tests of the endowment effect and the Coase theorem," *Journal of Political Economy*, 98, 1325–48.

Kahneman, D., Krueger, A., Schkade, D., Schwarz, N. and Stone, A. (2004), "A survey method for characterizing daily life experience: The day reconstruction method (DRM)," *Science*, forthcoming.

Kahneman, D. and Tversky, A. (eds) (2000), *Choices, Values and Frames*, New York: Cambridge University Press.

Katz, L. and Autor, D. (1999), "Changes in the wage structure and earnings inequality," in O. Ashenfelter and D. Card (eds), *Handbook of Labor Economics*, vol 3A, New York: Elsevier.

Keely, L. (1996), *War Before Civilization: The Myth of the Peaceful Savage*, New York and Oxford: Oxford University Press.

Keltner, D. and Harker, L. (2001), "Expressions of positive emotion in women's college yearbook pictures and their relationship to personality and life outcomes across adulthood," *Journal of Personality and Social Psychology*, 80, 112–24.

Kenrick, D., Gutierres, S. and Goldberg, L. (1989), "Influence of popular erotica on judgments of strangers and mates," *Journal of Experimental Social Psychology*, 25, 159–67.

Kenrick, D., Montello, D., Gutierres, S. and Trost, M. (1993), "Effects of physical attractiveness on affect and perceptual judgments: When social comparison overrides social reinforcement," *Personality and Social Psychology Bulletin*, 19, 195–99.

Keyes, C., Shmotkin, D. and Ryff, C. (2002), "Optimizing well-being: The empirical encounter of two traditions," *Journal of Personality and Social Psychology*, 82, 1007–22.

Keynes, J. M. (1930), "Economic possibilities for our grandchildren," in *Essays in Persuasion*, 1963 edition, New York: W. W. Norton.

Kiernan, K. (2003), "Cohabitation and divorce across nations and generations," CASE paper No. 65, London School of Economics.

Knack, S. (2001), "Trust, associational life and economic performance," in J. Helliwell and A. Bonikowska (eds), *The Contribution of Human and Social Capital to Sustained Economic Growth and Well-Being*, Ottawa: HRDC and OECD.

Knack, S. and Keefer, P. (1997), "Does social capital have an economic payoff? A cross-country investigation," *Quarterly Journal of Economics*, 112, 1251–88.

Kramer, P. (1993), *Listening to Prozac*, New York: Viking.

Krugman, P. (1996), *Pop Internationalism*, Cambridge, MA: MIT Press.

La Porta, R., Lopez-De-Silanes, F., Shleifer, A. and Vishny, R. W. (1997), "Trust in large organizations," *American Economic Review*, 87, 333–38.

Laing, R. D. (1960), *The Divided Self*, London: Penguin.

Landers, R. M., Rebitzer, J. B. and Taylor, L. J. (1996), "Rat race redux: Adverse selection in the determination of work hours in law firms," *American Economic Review*, 86, 329–48.

Lane, R. (2000), *The Loss of Happiness in Market Democracies*, New Haven and London: Yale University Press.

Layard, R. (1980), "Human satisfactions and public policy," *Economic Journal*, 90, 737–50. Also in Layard (1999b) and Easterlin (2002).

——. (1997), *What Labour Can Do*, London: Warner Books.

——. (1999a), *Tackling Unemployment*, London: Macmillan.

——. (1999b), *Tackling Inequality*, London: Macmillan.

——. (2003a), "Good jobs and bad jobs," London School of Economics, Centre for Economic Performance, Occasional Paper No. 19.

——. (2003b), "Apprenticeship and the skills gap," in *Learning to Succeed. The Next Decade*, University of Brighton Education Research Centre, Occasional Paper, December.

——. (2003c), "Happiness: Has social science a clue?," The Robbins Lectures available at http://cep.lse.ac.uk/layard.

——. (2005), "Rethinking public economics: The implications of rivalry and habit," in L. Bruni and P. L. Porta (eds), *Economics and Happiness: Reality and Paradoxes*, Oxford: Oxford University Press.

Layard, R., Blanchard, O., Dornbusch, R. and Krugman, P. (1992), *East-West Migration: The Alternatives*, Cambridge, MA: MIT Press.

Layard, R. and Glaister, S. (eds) (1994), *Cost-Benefit Analysis*, Cambridge: Cambridge University Press.

Layard, R., Nickell, S. and Jackman, R. (1991), *Unemployment. Macroeconomic Performance and the Labour Market*, Oxford: Oxford University Press.

Layard, R. and Walters, A. (1978), *Microeconomic Theory*, New York: McGraw-Hill.

Lepine, J., Gastpar, M., Mendlewicz, J. and Tylee, A. (1997), "Depression in the community: The first pan-European study DEPRES (Depression Research in European Society)," *International Clinical Psychopharmacology*, 12, 19–29.

Levitt, S. (2004), "Understanding why crime fell in the 1990s: Four factors that explain the decline and six that do not," *Journal of Economic Perspectives*, 18, 163–90.

Lewis, T., Amini, F. and Lannon, R. (2000), *A General Theory of Love*, New York: Random House.

Lipset, S. (1960), *Political Man: The Social Bases of Politics*, New York: Doubleday.

Lisanby, S. (2003), "Focal brain stimulation with repetitive transcranial magnetic stimulation (rTMS): Implications for the neural circuitry of depression," *Psychological Medicine*, 33, 7–13.

Locke, E., Shaw, L., Saari, L. and Latham, G. (1981), "Goal-setting and task performance," *Psychological Bulletin*, 90, 125–52.

Loehlin, J. (1992), *Genes and Environment in Personality Development*, Newberry Park, CA: Sage.

Loewenstein, G., O'Donoghue, T. and Rabin, M. (2003), "Projection bias in predicting future utility," *Quarterly Journal of Economics*, 118, 1209–48.

Loewenstein, G. and Schkade, D. (1999), "Wouldn't it be nice? Predicting future feelings," in Kahneman et al. (1999).

Lord Chancellor's Department, UK (1999), "High divorce rates: The state of the evidence on reasons and remedies," LCD Research Series No. 2/99 (vol 1), London.

Lucas, R. (2003), "Macroeconomic priorities," *American Economic Review*, 93, 1–14.

Lucas, R., Clark, A., Georgellis, Y. and Diener, E. (2003), "Reexamining adaptation and the set-point model of happiness: Reactions to changes in marital status," *Journal of Personality and Social Psychology*, 84, 527–39.

———. (2004), "Unemployment alters the set-point for life satisfaction," *Psychological Science*, 15, 8–13.

Lykken, D. (1999), *Happiness*, New York: St. Martin's Griffin.

———. (2001), "Parental licensure," *American Psychologist*, 56, 885–94.

Lyubomirsky, S., King, L. and Diener, E. (2003), "Happiness as a strength: A theory of the benefits of positive affect," University of California, Riverside, mimeo.

Lyubomirsky, S. and Ross, L. (1997), "Hedonic consequences of social comparison: a contrast of happy and unhappy people," *Journal of Personality and Social Psychology*, 73, 1141–57.

Lyubomirsky, S., Sheldon, K. and Schkade, D. (2004), "Pursuing happiness: The architecture of sustainable change," forthcoming in *Review of General Psychology*.

McGue, M. and Bouchard, T. (1998), "Genetic and environmental influences on human behavioral differences," *American Review of Neuroscience*, 21, 1–24.

McGue, M. and Lykken, D. (1992), "Genetic influence on risk of divorce," *Psychological Science*, 3, 368–73.

McLanahan, S. and Sandefur, G. (1994), *Growing Up With a Single Parent*, Cambridge, MA: Harvard University Press.

Maguire, E., Gadian, D., Johnsrude, I., Good, C., Ashburner, J., Frackowiak, R. and Frith, C. (2000), "Navigation-related structural change in the hippocampi of taxi drivers," *Proceedings of the National Academy of Science of the United States of America*, 97, 4398–4403.

Marmot, M. (2004), *Status Syndrome*, London: Bloomsbury.

Marshall, A. (1890), *Principles of Economics*, London: Macmillan.

Marshall, M., Neumann, C. and Robinson, M. (1970), "Lithium, creativity and manic-depressive illness: Review and prospectus," *Psychosomatics*, 11, 406–88.

Medvec, V., Madey, S. and Gilovich, T. (1995), "When less is more: Counterfactual thinking and satisfaction among Olympic medalists," *Journal of Personality and Social Psychology*, 69, 603–10.

Meltzer, H., Gill, B., Petticrew, M. and Hinds, K. (1995), "Physical complaints, service use and treatment of adults with psychiatric disorders," OPCS Surveys of Psychiatric Morbidity in Great Britain, London: Her Majesty's Stationery Office.

Michalos, A. (2003), *Essays on the Quality of Life*, Dordrecht, Neth.: Kluwer Academic Publishers.

———. (2004), "Social indicators research and health-related quality of life research," *Social Indicators Research*, 65, 27–72.

Michalos, A. and Zumbo, B. (2000), "Criminal victimization and the quality of life," *Social Indicators Research*, 50, 245–95.

Milgram, S. (1963), "Behavioural study of obedience," *Journal of Abnormal and Social Psychology*, 67, 371–78.

Mill, J. S. (1861), *Utilitarianism*, 1993 edition, edited by G. Williams, London: Everyman.

Mincer J. and Layard, R. (eds) (1985), "Trends in women's work, education and family building," *Journal of Labor Economics*, 351–96.

Mirrlees, J. (1971), "An exploration in the theory of optimum income taxation," *Review of Economic Studies*, 38, 175–208.

Moser Working Group (1999), *A Fresh Start. Improving Literacy and Numeracy*, London: Department for Education and Employment.

Murstein, B., Cerreto, M. and MacDonald, M. (1977), "A theory and investigation of the effect of exchange-orientation on marriage and friendship," *Journal of Marriage and the Family*, 39, 543–48.

Nesse, R. (1999), "The evolution of hope and despair," *Social Research*, 66, 429–69.

———. (2000), "Is depression an adaptation?," *Archives of General Psychiatry*, 57, 14–20.

———. (ed) (2001), *Evolution and the Capacity for Commitment*, New York: Russell Sage Foundation.

Nesse, R. and Williams, G. (1996), *Why We Get Sick: The New Science of Darwinian Medicine*, New York: Vintage Books.

Nettle, D. (2001), *Strong Imagination: Madness, Creativity and Human Nature*, Oxford: Oxford University Press.

Nickell, S. (1995), *The Performance of Companies*, Oxford: Blackwell.

Nickell, S. and Layard, R. (1999), "Labor market institutions and economic performance," in O. Ashenfelter and D. Card (eds), *Handbook of Labor Economics*, vol 3C, New York: Elsevier.

Nickerson, C., Schwarz, N., Diener, E. and Kahneman, D. (2003), "Zeroing in on the dark side of the American dream: A closer look at the negative consequences of the goal for financial success," *Psychological Science*, 14, 531–36.

Nordhaus, W. and Tobin, J. (1973), "Is growth obsolete?," in M. Moss (ed), *The Measurement of Economic and Social Performance*, New York: National Bureau of Economic Research.

Nozick, R. (1974), *Anarchy, State and Utopia*, New York: Basic Books.

Nussbaum, M. (2000), *Women and Human Development: The Capabilities Approach*, Cambridge: Cambridge University Press.

O'Connor, T., Caspi, A., DeFries, J. and Plomin, R. (2000), "Are associations between parental divorce and children's adjustment genetically mediated? An adoption study," *Developmental Psychology*, 36, 429–37.

Office of National Statistics, UK (ONS) (2001), *Psychiatric Morbidity Among Adults Living in Private Households, 2000*, London: Her Majesty's Stationery Office.

O'Guinn, T. and Shrum, L. (1997), "The role of television in the construction of consumer reality," *Journal of Consumer Research*, 23, 278–94.

O'Neill, O. (2002), *A Question of Trust*, Cambridge: Cambridge University Press.

Orford, J., Sproston, K., Erens, B., White, C. and Mitchell, L. (2003), *Gambling and Problem Gambling in the British*, London: Bonner–Routledge.

Parekh, B. (1974), "Bentham's justification of the principle of utility," in B. Parekh (ed), *Jeremy Bentham: Ten Critical Essays*, London: Frank Cass.

Peters, M. (1998), *The Elder Pitt*, London and New York: Longman.

Phillip, Z. (1990), *A Skeptic's Guide to the 12 Steps*, Center City, MN: Hazelden.

Phillips, D. (1983), "The impact of mass media violence on US homicides," *American Sociological Review*, 48, 560–68.

Pinker, S. (2002), *The Blank State: The Modern Denial of Human Nature*, London: Penguin.

Plomin, R., DeFries, J., McClearn, G. and McGuffin, P. (2001), *Behavioral Genetics*, New York: Worth Publishers.

Popenoe, D. (1996), *Life Without Father*, Cambridge, MA: Harvard University Press.

Post, F. (1994), "Creativity and psychopathology: A study of 291 world-famous men," *British Journal of Psychiatry*, 165, 22–34.

Postlethwaite, A., Cole, H. and Mailath, G. (1998), "Class systems and the enforcement of social norms," *Journal of Public Economics* 70, 5–35.

Potter, L. et al. (2001), "The influence of geographical mobility on nearly lethal suicide attempts," *Suicide and Life-Threatening Behaviour*, 32 (special supplement), 42–48.

Putnam, R. (2000), *Bowling Alone: The Collapse and Revival of American Community*, New York: Simon and Schuster.

Rabin, M. (1998), "Psychology and economics," *Journal of Economic Literature*, 36, 11–46.

———. (2000), "Diminishing marginal utility of wealth cannot explain risk aversion," in Kahneman and Tversky (2000).

Rainwater, L. (1990), "Poverty and equivalence as social constructions," Luxembourg Income Study Working Paper 55.

Rawls, J. (1971), *A Theory of Justice*, Cambridge, MA: Harvard University Press.

Rayo, L. and Becker, G. (2004), "Evolutionary efficiency and mean reversion in happiness," University of Chicago, mimeo.

Redelmeier, D. and Singh, S. (2001), "Survival in Academy Award—winning actors and actresses," *Annals of Internal Medicine* 134, 955–62.

Regier, D., Narrow, W., Rae, D., Manderscheid, R., Locke, B. and Goodwin, F. (1993), "The de facto US mental and addictive disorders service system," *Archives of General Psychiatry*, 50, 85–94.

Rice, T. and Feldman, J. (1997), "Civic culture and democracy from Europe to America," *Journal of Politics*, 59, 1143–72.

Richards, R., Kinney, D., Lunde, I., Bennett, M. and Merzel, A. (1988), "Creativity in manic-depressives, cyclothymes, their normal relatives and control subjects," *Journal of Abnormal Psychology*, 97, 281–88.

Ridley, M. (1996), *The Origins of Virtue*, London: Viking.

Riis, J., Loewenstein, G., Baron, J., Jepson, C., Fagarlin, A. and Ubel, P. (2002), "Ignorance of hedonic adaptation to hemo-dialysis," University of Michigan, mimeo.

Rilling, J., Gutman, D., Zeh, T., Pagnoni, G., Berns, G. and Kilts, C. (2002), "A neural basis for social cooperation," *Neuron*, 35, 395–405.

Robbins, L. (1932), *An Essay on the Nature and Significance of Economic Science*, London: Macmillan.

Robinson, P. and Darley, J. (1997), "The utility of desert," *Northwestern University Law Review*, 91, 453–99.

Robinson, R. and Downhill, J. (1995), "Lateralization of psychopathology in response to focal brain injury," in R. Davidson and K. Hugdahl (eds), *Brain Asymmetry*, Cambridge, MA: MIT Press.

Romano, J. and Turner, J. (1985), "Chronic pain and depression: Does the evidence support a relationship?," *Psychological Bulletin*, 97, 18–34.

Rosenkranz, M., Jackson, D., Dalton, K., Dolski, I., Ryff, C., Singer, B., Muller, D., Kalin, N. and Davidson, R. (2003), "Affective style and in vivo immune response: Neurobehavioral mechanisms," *Proceedings of the National Academy of Sciences*, 100, 11148–52.

Roth, A. and Fonagy, P. (eds) (1996), *What Works for Whom?*, New York: Guilford Press.

Runciman, W. (1966), *Relative Deprivation and Social Justice*, London: Routledge and Kegan Paul.

Russell, B. (1930), *The Conquest of Happiness*, London: George Allen and Unwin.

Russell, J. and Carroll, J. (1999a), "On the bipolarity of positive and negative affect," *Psychological Bulletin*, 125, 3–30.

——. (1999b), "The Phoenix of bipolarity: Response to Watson and Tellegen," *Psychological Bulletin*, 125, 611–17.

Rutter, M. (2001), "Intergenerational continuities and discontinuities in psychological problems," Institute of Psychiatry, London.

Rutter, M. and Smith, D. J. (eds) (1995), *Psychosocial Disorders in Young People: Time Trends and Their Causes*, Chichester, UK: John Wiley.

Ryff, C. and Singer, B. (2003), "The role of emotion on pathways to positive health," in R. Davidson, K. Scherer, and H. Goldsmith (eds), *Handbook of Affective Science*, New York: Oxford University Press.

Sahlins, M. (1972), *Stone-Age Economics*, Chicago: Aldine-Atherton.

Sampson, R. and Groves, W. (1989), "Community structure and crime: Testing social-disorganization theory," *American Journal of Sociology*, 94, 774–802.

Sampson, R., Raudenbush, S. and Earls, F. (1997), "Neighborhoods and violent crime: A multilevel study of collective efficacy," *Science*, 277, 918–24.

Samuelson, P. (1948), *Foundations of Economic Analysis*, Cambridge, MA: Harvard University Press.

Sanderson, K., Andrews, G., Corry, J. and Lapsley, H. (2003), "Reducing the burden of affective disorders: Is evidence-based health care affordable?," *Journal of Affective Disorders*, 77, 109–25.

Schmidtke, A. and Häfner, H. (1988), "The Werther effect after television films: New evidence for an old hypothesis," *Psychological Medicine*, 18, 665–76.

Schor, J. (1999), *The Overspent American: Upscaling, Downshifting and the New Consumer*, New York: HarperCollins.

Schou, M. (1979), "Artistic productivity and lithium prophylaxis in manic-depressive illness," *British Journal of Psychiatry*, 135, 97–103.

Schreiner, O. (1911), *Woman and Labour*, London and Leipzig: T. Fisher Unwin.

Schudson, M. (1984), *Advertising, the Uneasy Persuasion: Its Dubious Impact on American Society*, London: Routledge.

Schwartz, B., Ward, A., Lyubomirsky, S., Monterosso, J., White, K. and Lehman, D. (2002), "Maximizing versus satisficing: Happiness is a matter of choice," *Journal of Personality and Social Psychology*, 83, 1178–97.

Schwartz, S. (1970), "Elicitation of moral obligation and self-sacrificing behaviour: An experimental study of volunteering to be a bone marrow donor," *Journal of Personality and Social Psychology*, 15, 283–93.

Scitovsky, T. (1976), *The Joyless Economy. An Inquiry Into Human Satisfaction and Consumer Dissatisfaction*, New York: Oxford University Press.

Scott-Clark, C. and Levy, A. (2003), "Fast forward into trouble," *The Guardian Weekend*, June 14.

Seligman, M. (1994), *What You Can Change and What You Can't*, New York: Knopf.

——. (2002), *Authentic Happiness*, New York: Free Press.

Sen, A. (1970), *Collective Choice and Social Welfare*, San Francisco: Holden-Day.

——. (1992), *Inequality Re-examined*, Oxford: Oxford University Press.

——. (1999), *Development as Freedom*, Oxford: Oxford University Press.

Sen, A. and Williams, B. (1982), *Utilitarianism and Beyond*, New York: Cambridge University Press.

Senik, C. (2003), "What can we learn from subjective data? The case of income and well-being," Working Paper 2003-06, CNRS and DELTA-Fédération Jourdan.

Sennett, R. (2003), *Respect*, London: Penguin Books.

Shao, L. (1993), "Multilanguage comparability of life satisfaction and happiness measures in mainland Chinese and American students," University of Illinois, mimeo.

Sherif, M. (1966), *Group Conflict and Cooperation: Their Social Psychology*, London: Routledge and Kegan Paul.

Shizgal, P. and Conover, K. (1996), "On the neural computation of utility," *Current Directions in Psychological Science*, 5, 37–43.

Sigle-Rushton, W. and McLanahan, S. (2002), "Father absence and child well-being: A critical review," CASE, London School of Economics.

Signorielli, N. and Morgan, M. (2001), "Television and the family: The cultivation perspective," in J. Bryant and J. A. Bryant (eds), *Television and the American Family*, Mahwah, NJ: Lawrence Erlbaum Associates.

Silbereisen, R., Robins, L. and Rutter, M. (1995), "Secular trends in substance use: Concepts and data on the impact of social change on alcohol and drug abuse," in Rutter and Smith (1995).

Singer, P. (1981), *The Expanding Circle: Ethics and Sociobiology*, Oxford: Oxford University Press.

Singer, T., Seymour, B., O'Doherty, J., Kaube, H., Dolan, R. and Frith, C. (2004), "Empathy for pain involves the affective but not sensory components of pain," *Science*, 303, 1157–62.

Skyrms, B. (1996), *Evolution of the Social Contract*, Cambridge: Cambridge University Press.

Smart, J. and Williams, B. (1973), *Utilitarianism For and Against*, Cambridge: Cambridge University Press.

Smith, A. (1759), *The Theory of Moral Sentiments*, 1976 edition, edited by D. Raphael and A. Macfie, Oxford: Oxford University Press.

——. (1776), *Wealth of Nations*, 1976 edition, Oxford: Clarendon Press.

Smith, D. (1995a), "Youth crime and conduct disorders: Trends, patterns and causal explanations," in Rutter and Smith (1995).

——. (1995b), "Living conditions in the twentieth century," in Rutter and Smith (1995).

Snyder, S. (1996), *Drugs and the Brain*, New York: Scientific American Library.

Solnick, S. and Hemenway, D. (1998), "Is more always better? A survey on positional concerns," *Journal of Economic Behaviour and Organisation*, 37, 373–83.

Solomon, A. (2001), *The Noonday Demon: An Atlas of Depression*, New York: Scribner.

Soroka, S., Helliwell, J. and Johnston, R. (2003), "Measuring and modelling trust," in F. Kay and R. Johnston (eds), *Diversity, Social Capital and the Welfare State*, Vancouver, BC: University of British Columbia Press.

Steedman, H. (2000), "Updating of skills audit data 1994–1998, report to the Department for Education and Employment," London School of Economics, Centre for Economic Performance, mimeo.

Stone, L. (1983), "Interpersonal violence in English society 1300–1980," *Past and Present*, 101, (Nov), 22–33.

Storr, A. (1972), *The Dynamics of Creation*, London: Secker and Warburg.

Stutzer, A. (2003), "The role of income aspirations in individual happiness," *Journal of Economic Behavior and Organization*, 54, 89–109.

Stutzer, A. and Frey, B. (2003), "Does marriage make people happy, or do happy people get married?," Working Paper, Institute of Empirical Research in Economics, University of Zurich.

Styron, W. (1991), *Darkness Visible: A Memoir of Madness*, London: Picador.

Suomi, S. (1997), "Long-term effects of different early rearing experiences on social, emotional, and physiological development in nonhuman primates," in M. Keshavan and R. Murray (eds), *Neurodevelopment and Adult Psychopathology*, Cambridge: Cambridge University Press.

Tarp, F. (ed) (2000), *Foreign Aid and Development: Lessons Learned and Directions for the Future*, London: Routledge.

Teicher, M. (2002), "Scars that won't heal: The neurobiology of child abuse," *Scientific American*, March, 68–75.

Thich Nhat Hanh (1975), *The Miracle of Mindfulness*, Boston: Beacon Books.

——. (2001), *Anger: Buddhist Wisdom for Cooling the Flames*, London: Rider.

Tienari, P., Wynne, L., Moring, J., Lahti, I., Naarala, M., Sorri, A., Wahlberg, K-E., Saarento, O., Seitamaa, M., Kaleva, M. and Läksy, K. (1994), "The Finnish adoptive family study of schizophrenia: Implications for family research," *British Journal of Psychiatry*, 164 (suppl. 23), 20–26.

Titmuss, R H. (1970), *The Gift Relationship*, London: Allen and Unwin.

Tomalin, C. (2002), *Samuel Pepys: The Unequalled Self*, London: Viking.

Turk, D. and Okifuji, A. (1994), "Detecting depression in chronic pain patients: Adequacy of self-reports," *Behaviour Research and Therapy*, 32, 9–16.

Turner, A. (2001), *Just Capital: The Liberal Economy*, London: Macmillan.

Van Praag, B. and Frijters, P. (1999) "The measurement of welfare and well-being: The Leyden approach," in Kahneman et al. (1999).

Veenhoven, R. (2000), "Freedom and happiness: A comparative study in 44 nations in the early 1990s," in Diener and Suh (2000).

Waite, L. (1995), "Does marriage matter?," *Demography*, 32, 483–507.

Waldfogel, J. (2002), "Childcare, women's employment and child outcomes," *Journal of Population Economics*, 15, 527–48.

Warnock, M. (1998), *An Intelligent Person's Guide to Ethics*, London: Duckworth.

Wells, E. and Horwood, J. (2004), "How accurate is recall of key symptoms of depression? A comparison of recall and longitudinal reports," *Psychological Medicine*, 34, 1–11.

WHO International Consortium in Psychiatric Epidemiology (2000), "Cross-national comparisons of the prevalences and correlates of mental disorders," *Bulletin of the World Health Organization*, 78, 413–26.

WHO World Mental Health Survey Consortium (2004), "Prevalence, severity and unmet need for treatment of mental disorders," *Journal of American Medical Association*, 291, 2581–89.

Wilkinson, R. (1996), *Unhealthy Societies: The Affliction of Inequality*, London: Routledge.

Williams, T. M. (ed) (1986), *A Natural Experiment in Three Communities*, New York: Academic Press, summarised in "The impact of television: A longitudinal Canadian Study," in B. Singer (ed), *Communications in Canadian Society* (1991), Scarborough, ON: Nelson Canada.

Wilson, J. Q. (1993), *The Moral Sense*, New York: Free Press.

Wilson, J. Q. and Herrnstein, R. (1985), *Crime and Human Nature*, New York: Simon and Schuster.

Winkelmann, L. and Winkelmann, R. (1998), "Why are the unemployed so unhappy? Evidence from panel data," *Economica*, 65, 1–15.

Wolpert, L. (1999), *Malignant Sadness*, New York: Free Press.

——. (2005), *To Believe Is Human: The Biology of Belief* (forthcoming).

Wolpin, K. (1979), "A time-series cross-section analysis of international variation in crime and punishment," *Review of Economics and Statistics*, 62, 417–23.

World Health Organization (2002), *Reducing risks, promoting healthy life*, The World Health Report.

Wright, R. (1994), *The Moral Animal*, New York: Pantheon.

——. (2000), *Nonzero: The Logic of Human Destiny*, New York: Pantheon.

Young, M. and Willmott, P. (1957), *Family and Kinship in East London*, London: Routledge and Kegan Paul.

Zahn-Wexler, C., Radke-Yarrow, M., Wagner, E. and Chapman, M. (1992), "Development of concern for others," *Developmental Psychology*, 28, 126–36.

Index

Some key page references are set in bold face.

INDEX

179, 187–202
advertising and, 160
changes in, 135, 138–41, 232
education and, 200, 201
ethical principles and, 5, 91, 110,
115–17
geographical mobility and, 145
money and, 140–41
personal, 63, 64, 71–73
spiritual, 90–93; *see also* religious belief
and traditions
teaching of, 200, 226, 228–29, 234
see also moral behaviour
Van Gogh, Vincent, 210, 220
Vidal, Gore, 151
Vietnam War, 144
violence:
television and, 78, 87–88
see also crime, criminal behaviour
voluntary exchange, 128–29, 131

wages, *see* income
war and peace, 69, 70, 106
Watson, John, 133
wealth:
television and, 87, 88–90
see also income
welfare, 168, 229
welfare-to-work approach, 172–75
widowhood, 64, 65
Williams, Bernard, 117–18
willingness-to-pay, 131, 132

women:
changing gender roles and, 82–85
happiness of, compared with men,
45, 62

Wodehouse, P. G., 11
work, 62–64, 67–68, **172–76**
career choice and, 116, 124
enjoyment of, 153
family-friendly policies at, 85, 178, 233
globalisation and, 169–70
hiring and firing practices, 174–75
income from, *see* income
mothers and, 82–84, 85
non-employment, 67
number of hours worked, 50–51,
134, 156
respect and, 156
reward systems at, 137, 140–41,
156–60, 227, 233
security in, 7, 170–71, 172–76, 232
skills needed in, 175–76
social relationships created by, 67, 225
stress involved in, 158
unemployment, *see* unemployment
work-life balance, 50–51, **151–56,** 230,
233
World Values Survey, 63–65, 68, 71
Wotton, Henry, 72

youth culture, 92, 201

zero-sum games, **95–96,** 98, 150–51, 228

Credits